The Legal Order of the European Union

The objective of European integration serves as an ideal of the legal order of the European Union and invites reconsideration of law's conceptual features. This book critically assesses the legal order of the European Union, focusing on the operative aspects of the Union constitution with particular reference to the institutional practices of the Court of Justice in expressing the values underlying this constitution.

Drawing together positivist and non-positivist accounts within an institutional understanding of law, Timothy Moorhead breaks new ground in applying a range of analytic jurisprudential perspectives to the Union legal order, and in employing the theoretical resources provided by the Union to model a revised conceptual viewpoint concerning legal order generally. In offering this conceptual approach, Moorhead emphasises the flexibility inherent in law's institutional character as the basis for a theoretical rationalisation of the Union legal order.

This book will be of great use and interest to scholars and students of European Union Law, Jurisprudence and European Constitutionalism.

Timothy Moorhead is an Assistant Lecturer at the University of Kent. His research interests include: Analytic Jurisprudence and European Union Law. His publications include: 'European Union Law as International Law' (2012) 5 *European Journal of Legal Studies*; and, 'The Values of the European Union Legal Order: Constitutional Perspectives' (2014), 16 *European Journal of Law Reform*.

Routledge Research in EU Law

Available titles in this series include:

Centralized Enforcement, Legitimacy and Good Governance in the EU
Melanie Smith

EU External Relations and Systems of Governance
The CFSP, Euro-Mediterranean Partnership and migration
Paul James Cardwell

The European Constitution, Welfare States and Democracy
The Four Freedoms vs. National Administrative Discretion
Christoffer C. Eriksen

EU External Relations Law and the European Neighbourhood Policy
A Paradigm for Coherence
Bart Van Vooren

The Evolving EU Counter-terrorism Legal Framework
Maria O'Neill

The Early Warning System for the Principle of Subsidiarity
Constitutional Theory and Empirical Reality
Philipp Kiiver

European Perspectives on Environmental Law and Governance
Suzanne Kingston

The Tangled Complexity of the EU Constitutional Process
The Frustrating Knot of Europe
Giuseppe Martinico

Criminal Law and Policy in the European Union
Samuli Miettinen

Local Government in Europe
The 'Fourth Level' in the EU Multi-Layered System of Governance
Carlo Panara and Michael R. Varney

The Legitimacy of the European Union through Legal Rationality
Free Movement of Third Country Nationals
Richard Ball

New Governance and the European Strategy for Employment
Samantha Velluti

Human Rights and Minority Rights in the European Union
Kirsten Shoraka

Turkey's Accession to the European Union
The Politics of Exclusion?
Edel Hughes

Forthcoming titles in this series include:

The Legal Order of the European Union
The Institutional Role of the European Court of Justice
Timothy Moorhead

Kadi on Trial
A Multifaceted Analysis of the Kadi Judgment
Matej Avbelj, Filippo Fontanelli and Giuseppe Martinico

The Governance of the European Union and the Internal-External Nexus
Paul James Cardwell

Towards a System of European Criminal Justice
The Problem of Admissibility of Evidence
Andrea Ryan

The Legal Order of the European Union

The Institutional Role of the Court of Justice

Timothy Moorhead

Routledge
Taylor & Francis Group
LONDON AND NEW YORK

First published 2014
by Routledge
2 Park Square, Milton Park, Abingdon, Oxon, OX14 4RN

and by Routledge
711 Third Avenue, New York, NY 10017

Routledge is an imprint of the Taylor & Francis Group, an informa business

First issued in paperback 2016

British Library Cataloguing in Publication Data
A catalogue record for this book is available from the British Library

Library of Congress Cataloging-in-Publication Data
A catalog record has been requested for this book

ISBN13: 978-0-415-52970-9 (hbk)
ISBN13: 978-1-138-68511-6 (pbk)

Typeset in 11/12 Garamond 3 LT Std by
Servis Filmsetting Ltd, Stockport, Cheshire

Dedicated to my wife, Sheila

Contents

1 Introductory chapter

Introduction

The theoretical component of this work can be summarised in the following proposition:

> The value of European integration, serves as a fundamental ideal of the legal order[1] of the European Union, inviting reconsideration of the conceptual features of law.

The practical component of this work can be summarised in the following statement.

> The Union Treaties as a constitution for the project of European integration provide a unique institutional context in which to consider the judicial role of the European Court of Justice.[2]

In exploring these propositions, I have drawn inspiration principally from the work of two writers, Neil MacCormick and Clarence Mann. MacCormick's institutional account of law captures the sense in which law as a positive, 'conventional' social practice is a result of an interpretation we give to this practice in light of the aims, functions or values we attribute to legal order. Law as 'institutional fact'[3] decries traditional analytic distinctions, affirming both

1 In this work, which concerns the practical operation of legal institutions viewed from a theoretical perspective, I employ the phrase legal order as opposed to legal system, following MacCormick's suggestion that '[a] legal system belongs to the real social world, as distinct from a pure world of ideas, to the extent that a corresponding legal order exists'. N MacCormick, *Rhetoric and the Rule of Law, a Theory of Legal Reasoning* (Oxford University Press, Oxford 2005) at 3, hereafter MacCormick, *Rhetoric and the Rule of Law*.

2 According to the first sentence of Article 19 TEU, '[t]he Court of Justice of the European Union shall include the Court of Justice, the General Court and specialised courts'. In this work, I shall be focusing on the judgments of the 'supreme' court in this hierarchy, the Court of Justice (previously the European Court of Justice).

3 N MacCormick, *Institutions of Law* (Oxford University Press, Oxford 2007).

non-positivist beliefs regarding the dynamic influence of underlying values of functions of legal order over legal outcomes, as well as positivist insights that recognise the necessity for legal demands to be identifiable by reference to (relatively) certain social conventions in order for the functions or values served by legal order to be realised in practice.[4] This is the only theoretical approach I have encountered that provides the analytic tools appropriate to understanding the Union legal order which, by contrast with statal orders, is based on the formation of a new political entity as an evolution of existing constitutional settlements.

MacCormick then has provided inspiration for the theoretical strand of this work. A second and related central theme concerns the institutional role of the European Court of Justice.[5] Here I owe a significant debt to Clarence Mann's seminal work, written in the early 1970s, *The Function of Judicial Decision in European Economic Integration*.[6] Mann's hugely impressive and insightful work is unique in its approach to understanding the judicial function in the European Union[7] setting. Mann offers a rationalisation of the Court's practices that directly engages with the fact that the Court is charged with giving legal effect to a unique instrument, the (then) European Economic Community (EEC) Treaty.[8] His insight was to appreciate that the judicial function in giving legal expression to the promotion and achievement of the various objectives contained in the Treaties is flexible enough to develop bespoke methods of reasoning that properly reflected these concerns.

In this regard, Mann's plausible analysis is that the Court's method of reasoning is thematic, focusing upon the achievement of the Treaty objectives centred on the creation of a single economic market amongst the Member States. Judicial articulation of these collective thematic concerns in the Court's judgments develops the project of European integration. In addition, the Court's presentation of the legal demands arising under the Treaties is contextualised and qualified by the wider institutional environment in which it operates, including the other Community institutions as well as the Member States. This institutional context means that the Court is perennially engaged in ensuring, in Mann's view, that its judgments exhibit practicality, purpose

4 Referring to 'legal order', MacCormick has noted that '[t]his presupposes a conception of law as in some degree systematic and orderly, a body of norms orderly and systematic in character'. MacCormick, *Rhetoric and the Rule of Law* at 2.

5 The first sentence of Article 19 TEU states that '[t]he Court of Justice of the European Union shall include the Court of Justice, the General Court and specialised courts'. In this work, I shall be focusing on the activities of the supreme court in this hierarchy, namely the Court of Justice, previously called the European Court of Justice

6 C Mann, *The Function of Judicial Decision in European Economic Integration* (Martinus Nijhoff, The Hague 1972), hereafter Mann, *The Function of Judicial Decision in European Economic Integration*.

7 The European Economic Community (EEC) at the time Mann was writing.

8 As well as, at that time, the European Coal and Steel Community (ECSC) Treaty. The EEC Treaty was amended then superseded by the EC/EU and then TEU and TFEU Treaties by the Single European Act (1980), Maastricht Treaty (1992), Amsterdam Treaty (1997), Nice Treaty (2001) and Lisbon Treaty (2007).

and authority. Mann's analysis forms the basis of my attempts in this work to describe the role of the Court as a supreme judicial institution charged with upholding in the Treaties a constitution for the European Union. This constitution directs the Court to the achievement of specified social and economic objectives, the thematic concerns of Mann's analysis, and ultimately towards European integration as an aspirational, uncertain and politically contested ideal.

Preliminary remarks

Generally, academic writing on the subject of law falls into two categories. The first concerns the organisational or systemic qualities of or between legal orders. Accounts of law in this category seek to clarify the meaning of legal governance as a form of political association arising in domestic, transnational or international settings.[9] Key issues are the locus of sovereign legal authority, how legal orders interrelate and the degree(s) of autonomy associated with sites of legal governance. Generally, accounts of legal order as a form of governance focus on the role of law in relation to particular political and/or cultural contexts.

The second category concerns the branch of legal philosophy known as analytical jurisprudence. Here inquiry[10] seeks to identify those conceptual features which are either necessary or sufficient to speak of the existence of law[11] as opposed to the contingent features of individual legal orders?[12] Law as the subject matter of analytical jurisprudence tends to produce insights

9 Typically asking whether constitutional (monist) or pluralist models are appropriate to understand the Union legal order and its relationship with Member States' legal orders and international law. For a variety of perspectives on these questions, see C de Burca and J H H Weiler (eds), *The Worlds of European Constitutionalism* (Cambridge University Press, Cambridge 2012) hereafter de Burca and Weiler (eds), *The Worlds of European Constitutionalism*.

10 The correct methodology of inquiry into law's conceptual features is also an important feature of analytic jurisprudential debates, and concerns whether inquiry into the nature of law, as opposed to resulting theoretical accounts, is itself essentially normative or descriptive. See generally, Dickson, *Evaluation and Legal Theory*, and V Villa 'Legal Theory and Value Judgments' (1997) 16 *Law and Philosophy* 447.

11 J Dickson, *Evaluation and Legal Theory* (Hart Publishing, Oxford 2001) at 23–24, hereafter Dickson, *Evaluation and Legal Theory*. Generally this will require identification of the internal and external characteristics of legal order. Internal features concern legal rules as an 'internalised' body of authoritative normative injunctions by citizens and legal officials, and external features concern the descriptive qualities of the institutional practices identified as legal in character. Clearly there are important connections between the two, concerning, for example, how the descriptively accessible institutional features of legal practices are capable of generating and upholding values and beliefs associated with legal forms of governance.

12 The characteristics of any given legal order system will be dependent on a number of 'locational' factors, expressive of the cultural and historical context in which they operate. In addition, the operational features of legal orders will be influenced by their relationship to other orders, a fact of increasing importance in light of the emergence in recent decades of a globalised legal culture. See generally, de Burca and Weiler (eds), *The Worlds of European Constitutionalism*.

that are abstract in the sense that they are not contingent upon cultural or historical factors but rather reflect upon innate features of human social existence.

Accounts of the legal order of the European Union tend to fall under the first of these two categories,[13] seeking to rationalise the operation of Union legal governance from a variety of perspectives of political theory. In this regard, as a jurisdictionally limited legal jurisdiction that privileges the aspiration of European integration and claims supreme hierarchical status within domestic legal settings, the Union challenges existing views concerning the operation of domestic legal orders based conclusively on a body of constitutional values of political morality. In addition, the mutual assertion of legal supremacy between the Union and Member States[14] has opened up an extensive literature on the subject of 'European constitutionalism'. This covers a range of topics relevant to the operation of legal orders generally; their origins,[15] the meaning of legal sovereignty,[16] the accommodation of mutually incompatible claims of legal jurisdiction[17] and the constitutionalisation of international law.[18]

In short, academic inquiry into the Union legal order has focused almost exclusively on developing or adapting received accounts of legal governance in order to explain the Union as opposed to the statal 'way of governance'.[19] Little attention has been given to how analytic accounts of law inform understanding of the Union legal order, or conversely whether existing analytic accounts of law may require modification if these are unable to fully account for the characteristics of this order. This second possibility might appear surprising, given that the task of analytic jurisprudence, the identification of universal features of law, would appear to militate against taking the features of a single legal order to uncover potentially new conceptual features of legal order generally. I would reject this intuition for the simple reason that there is no a priori reason why the conceptual properties we attribute to law as a

13 With limited exceptions, which have tended to apply a particular theoretical perspective to the Union legal order. See, for example, M L Jones, 'The Legal Nature of the European Community: A Jurisprudential Analysis Using H.L.A.Hart's Model of Law and a Legal System' (1984) 17 *Cornell International Law Journal* 1. I have not found any works that apply a reverse perspective, that is, exploring the implications of the Union order for how analytic jurisprudential models are themselves understood.

14 The Court has also affirmed the supremacy of the Union jurisdiction over that of international law following the *Kadi* judgment. Case C–402/05 *Kadi and Al Barakaat v Council and Commission*.

15 T Schilling, 'The Court of Justice's Revolution: Its Effects and the Conditions for its Consummation: What Europe Can Learn from Fiji' (2002) 27 *European Law Review* 445.

16 N MacCormick, *Questioning Sovereignty* (Oxford University Press, Oxford 1999), hereafter MacCormick, *Questioning Sovereignty*.

17 Ibid. See also Chapter 6 of this work.

18 G de Burca, 'The ECJ and the International Legal Order' in de Burca and Weiler (eds), *The Worlds of European Constitutionalism* at 131–138.

19 For one example amongst many, see J H H Weiler and M Wind (eds), *European Constitutionalism Beyond the State* (Cambridge University Press, Cambridge 2003).

social phenomenon should be limited by our current state of knowledge. As Julie Dickson has noted:

> Given that law is a complex and multi-faceted phenomenon however, we would seem to have no reason to believe that such properties will be few in number and indeed it is at least possible that there may be an indefinite number of such properties.[20]

One of the tasks of analytic jurisprudence is in my view to actively seek hitherto unconsidered conceptual features of law or legal order.[21] The legal order of the European Union, which undoubtedly offers new perspectives on legal governance, attested by a voluminous literature on the subject, would seem to be an appropriate candidate for inquiry.

Law's evaluative dimension

As an introduction to this task, consider the following working definition of the concept of law as:

> a formalised body of social practices comprising authoritative normative injunctions that serve to define, guide and enable all forms of social conduct in a manner that necessarily generates valued forms of social ordering.[22]

This definition has the virtue of identifying law's normative, formal and evaluative dimensions, each of which in fact possesses an evaluative significance as considered in Chapter 2. The predominant focus in this work however is upon the evaluative component of legal ordering in the sense of the underlying values that form the aims and functions of any given order. These functions concern broadly the justification of normative claims associated with practices

20 Dickson, *Evaluation and Legal Theory* at 20 (footnote omitted).

21 The opposite conclusion, that conclusive knowledge of these features has already been achieved, is highly counter-intuitive given that even in the natural as opposed to social sciences, no conclusively correct or comprehensive accounts of the physical world appear to exist. In this regard, *all* knowledge is based upon normative presuppositions illustrated by MacCormick's comment that:

> Our understanding of human understanding depends ultimately on our ability to grasp the human engagement in normative orders which being fundamental to the very concept of an admissible fact, is fundamental not only to legal knowledge but to all knowledge.
>
> (N MacCormick and O Weinberger, *An Institutional Theory of Law* (D Reidel Publishing Company, Dordrecht 1986) at 102)

22 Here I place law firmly within a social science tradition emphasising that law is first an observable social phenomenon albeit with links to a number of other disciplines, including philosophy, sociology, psychology and history. This definition is reconsidered in Chapter 2 to illustrate the senses in which different schools of analytic jurisprudence view the role of values in legal ordering.

of legal governance. How the justification of legal demands is linked to the concept of law is the subject of deep disagreement within existing analytic accounts. For non-positivists, the value(s) or functions on which we base such justification are correctly seen as inscribed within any conceptual account.[23] By contrast, for positivist writers, law is viewed as a descriptively accessible conventional social practice, 'valued' for its inherent (functional) capability to enhance human social existence.[24]

These two approaches to the concept are also linked to views concerning the role of values within legal practices. If we accept that upholding certain values or functions represents a conceptual feature of law, this suggests that values necessarily play a dynamic role within legal practices. Alternatively, if we affirm the conventional, 'constant' character of the social practices associated with law creation and application, then the values or functions of law will be an implicit or static feature of these practices. In short, different conceptual approaches reflect a variety of viewpoints concerning whether values, usually those of morality, may,[25] may not[26] or must[27] dynamically influence the form and substance of these practices.[28]

The precise role of values within a given legal order will depend on a variety of factors that concern the wider social, historical, political and cultural context in which legal demands operate as well as the overall objectives any given order is designed to achieve. In principle, as I shall argue, values

23 See, for example, S Perry, 'The Varieties of Legal Positivism' (1996) 9 *Canadian Journal of Law and Jurisprudence* 361, hereafter Perry, 'The Varieties of Legal Positivism'.

24 'Law just is the kind of thing that can realise some attractive ideals. That fact about law is not necessarily part of our concept of it.' J Coleman, *The Practice of Principle* (Oxford University Press, Oxford 2001) at 194. Raz has noted in a similar vein that:

> Even if a certain social fact entails certain moral consequences it can still be a source of law. It is a source of law as the social fact it is and not as a source of moral rights and obligations. It is a source of law under its naturalistic rather than under its moral description.
> (J Raz, *Ethics in the Public Domain: Essays in the Morality of Law and Politics* (Clarendon Press, Oxford 1994) at 235, hereafter Raz, *Ethics in the Public Domain*)

25 J Coleman, 'Negative and Positive Positivism' (1982) 11 *Journal of Legal Studies* 139.

26 S Shapiro, 'The Difference that Rules Make' in B Bix (ed.), *Analyzing Law: New Essays in Legal Theory* (Clarendon Press, Oxford 1998).

27 R Dworkin, *Law's Empire* (Hart Publishing, Oxford 1986).

28 A further question is whether concepts such as law and morality are relative to a given culture or can be formulated in a universal sense. Taking the former view, Raz has noted that:

> 'The concept of law is part of our culture and of our cultural traditions. It plays a role in the way in which ordinary people as well as the legal profession understand their own and other people's actions. It is part of the way they 'conceptualise' social reality.
> (Raz, *Ethics in the Public Domain* at 237)

For a view of law as embodying universal principles of practical morality that transcend the contingent features of individual societies/cultures, see E J Weinrib, 'Law as a Kantian Idea of Reason' (1987) 87 *Columbia Law Review* 472.

may feature as static/structural or dynamic features of any given legal order although in practice some degree of dynamic influence over legal outcomes is necessary for their effective expression. A rational account of legal order must therefore adequately convey the sense in which legal demands represent the values or functions law is intended to promote, as well as the need for relative certainty in the creation, application and interpretation of these demands to allow for the effective prosecution of these underlying functions.

The 'weak'[29] or 'post'[30] positivist institutional account of law by Weinberger and MacCormick fulfils these purposes, recognising both the 'social fact' and functional character of institutional practices of law creation and application. Their analysis therefore breaks down apparent divisions of positivist and non-positivist viewpoints, emphasising the conventional character of legal order while recognising the dynamic role of values as a driver of legal outcomes. An institutional perspective also, in my view, provides the analytic tools to achieve a full theoretical appreciation of the Union legal order.

The role of values in the legal order of the European Union: new directions

Domestic (statal) legal orders represent in principle an unlimited governmental jurisdiction constrained in practice by constitutional requirements endorsed by the relevant polity. By contrast, in the transnational setting, legal order is characterised by the attribution of defined legal competencies and hence by the positive exclusion of legal authority in areas not so identified. A further distinction lies in the fact that transnational legal orders may be based upon the promotion of particular political, social or economic objectives. Where, as in the Union Treaties, such objectives are stated in broad, aspirational terms and are linked to the emergence of a new governmental settlement, this raises important theoretical questions concerning the role of values underlying legal order.

The Union represents the exercise of legally conferred (by the Treaties) legislative, policy-making and regulatory powers, directed to the achievement of a politically momentous, and hence constitutionally significant objective (for the Member States), an integrated Europe.[31] The constitutional basis of

29 'My version of neo-institutionalism represents a weak positivism.' O Weinberger 'Institutionalist Theories of Law' in P Amselek and N MacCormick (eds), *Controversies About Law's Ontology* (Edinburgh University Press, Edinburgh 1991) at 50.

30 'The post-positivistic view of law presupposed for the purposes of this inquiry about legal arguments goes by the name of "the institutional theory of law".' MacCormick, *Rhetoric and the Rule of Law* at 2.

31 The Treaties are structured with a view to linking the various areas of Union regulatory competence to the overall objective of integration. For example, Article 174 TFEU states that '[i]n order to promote its overall harmonious development, the Union shall develop and pursue its actions leading to the strengthening of its economic, social and territorial cohesion'. According to Article 175 TFEU, '[Member] States shall conduct their economic policies and shall coordinate them in such a way as, in addition, to attain the objectives set out in Article 174'.

the Union legal order is the evolving political, social and economic objectives set out in the Treaties, crucially the creation and operation of the single market. These objectives operate as foundational legal values, alongside 'rule-of-law' concerns contained in Union general principles (which broadly reflect constitutional values of the Member States).[32] In sum, the staple concern of theoretical jurisprudential debates, the link between law/legal practices and morality, is challenged by the Union to explain the (further) sense in which political objectives may, in addition, serve as values underlying legal ordering.

The Union order also raises theoretical questions concerning the existence of mutual and conflicting claims of legal sovereignty relating to the jurisdiction conferred under the Treaties and affirmed by domestic constitutions respectively. These claims derive from competing rationales underlying the relationship between Union and domestic orders based upon the (Union law) supremacy doctrine and domestic constitutional supremacy affirmed by Union and domestic courts respectively.

Available theoretical models of law appear to lack the resources to account for these features of the Union legal order, particularly in relation to the constitutional role of the foundational values of the Treaties. The integrationist ambitions that form the overriding value concern of all Union law demands appear to be both limited and expanded by comparison with the functionalities associated with domestic legal orders. On the one hand, the judicial expression of Union legal demands is constrained by the reach of the powers conferred under the Treaties. On the other, the constitutional values of the Union order collectively represent the development of a grand political project with the potential to dramatically reconfigure Member States current constitutional settlements.

It is my contention that the European Union therefore highlights 'new' conceptual features of law relating to the role and scope of evaluative concerns underlying legal order generally. The Union legal order demonstrates that a political objective, European integration, operates as a foundational legal principle, informing the entirety of Union legal demands. Uniquely this principle offers the potential for a number of States to converge and ultimately merge their legal and political jurisdictions, providing an expanded conceptual appreciation of the possibilities inherent in legal ordering. The general conceptual feature of law highlighted by the legal order of the European Union then, concerns the fact that the evaluative propositions underlying all legal orders are not confined to 'universal' concerns of political morality however defined. They may also include specific political, social or economic objectives as constitutional and constituting values. The Union therefore

32 The European Community is however a Community based on the rule of law in which its institutions are subject to judicial review of the compatibility of their acts with the Treaty and with the general principles of law which include fundamental rights.

(Case C–50/00 *Union de Pequenos Agricultores v Council* [2002] ECR I–6677) at para 38.

provides subject matter relevant not only to accounts of legal governance, an area extensively commented upon, but also invites re-examination of questions of analytic legal philosophy relating to the role of values in legal ordering.

The Court of Justice and the Union Constitution

The role of the Court of Justice as the supreme legal authority within the Union institutional framework is central to understanding these possible conceptual developments. This work therefore combines inquiry into the analytic significance of the Union legal order with an examination of the institutional role played by the Court of Justice.

We may distinguish two senses in which the foundational values of the Union legal order govern the operation of Union laws within the Court's judgments. The first concerns the Court's recognition that the Treaty objectives[33] possess a constitutional status within a hierarchical system of Union and domestic laws. The second concerns the effects of all Union laws (primary and secondary) as a 'directly applicable' *body* of legal norms within Member States' legal orders that, according to the supremacy doctrine, possess constitutional status. The Union therefore represents a legal jurisdiction capable of advancing the project of European integration, affirming a body of legal regulation under the supremacy doctrine that operates to ensure the independence of this project.[34]

As supreme judicial authority of the European Union, the Court articulates the constitutional significance of the values underlying all Union legal demands, as well as the 'constitutionalising' effects of particular Union laws within Member States. The Court therefore faces the task of affirming the constitutional values of the Union project as influences over all Union law demands, while ensuring that these demands remain unqualified by domestic law. In this regard, the Court's judgments must be institutionally 'balanced', sustaining and (where possible) developing the principle of Union law supremacy in a manner consistent with Member States' constitutional requirements while advancing the project of European integration.

These roles reflect the variable character of judicial inputs to Union and Member State legal ordering by the Court of Justice. First, the Union is dedicated, in a foundational sense, to the achievement of European integration. This phrase is not formally defined within the Treaties nor is it helpful to identify a factual state of affairs the meeting of which at some future time would mean that a 'state of integration' had been reached. Any such attempt would be resisted by the Member States, as begging the highly contentious question of whether any proposed 'state of integration' was in fact the purpose of the Union. The Treaty preambles wisely pre-empt such a possibility by

33 Case 294/83 *Partie Ecologiste 'Les Verts' v European Parliament* [1986] ECR 1339.

34 The doctrine (of Union law supremacy) therefore represents both a political value relating to the promotion of European integration as well as a conflict of laws principle.

affirming the commitment of the signatory Member States to 'an ever closer Union'[35] thereby enabling a process of integration without prejudging what this might in fact entail. This 'core' objective of the Union project acts as an aspirational value or function, 'partially realised', yet always developing. As the Court noted in its Opinion 1/91, 'the objective of all the Community treaties is to contribute together to making concrete progress towards European unity'.[36]

A second characteristic of the Union legal order, expressed by the activities of the Court of Justice, is its evolutionary character. We may question however whether the evolutionary quality of the Treaties is *distinctive* by contrast with the operation of domestic constitutions, given the idea of an 'evolving' constitution is not uncommon in the context of States or federations. Michael Perry, for example, has commented in relation to the US constitution that:

> It is a communication to us (the present) from the ratifiers and framers (the past) *and*, in virtue of a role it has come to play in the life of our political community ... the Constitution is *also* a symbol of fundamental aspirations of the political tradition.[37]

I would suggest that the Union constitution is evolutionary in two ways that are distinctive by contrast with Perry's characterisation of the US constitution. First, the values that form the basis of the Union order do not, in the 'deep' sense envisaged by Perry in relation to the US constitution, symbolise the fundamental aspirations of Member States' polities.[38] At most, the objectives of European integration form a highly contested political ideal as one (amongst other more important) aspect(s) of these aspirations. Second, the evolutionary character of the Union constitution refers to both an 'open-ended' engagement with and transformation of Member States' constitu-

35 In the preamble to the Treaty on European Union.

36 Opinion 1/91 of 14 December 1991.

37 M Perry, *Morality, Politics, and Law* (Oxford University Press, Oxford 1988) at 133 (emphasis in original), hereafter Perry, *Morality, Politics, and Law*. See also Walker's comment in relation to the abandoned Constitutional Treaty project that:

> The written constitution is an important trace in that its very promulgation, or even its threshold consideration, is already a sign, however modest, of the commitment and common understanding it seeks to encode. And the written constitution is also a catalyst in so far as it provides a means by which and a context in which to stimulate the deepening of that commitment and common understanding.
>
> (N Walker 'The Place of European Law' in de Burca and Weiler (eds), *The Worlds of European Constitutionalism* at 104)

38 Although Walker has suggested that the Treaties may develop so as to reflect such affiliations in a partial sense that recognises both individual and Member States' ownership of the Union project. Ibid.

tional settlements by an independent institutional framework dedicated to the objective of European integration. This process is recognised by domestic constitutions only insofar as the Member States are voluntary partners in the Union project.

A final characteristic of the Union legal order relevant to the institutional role of the Court of Justice concerns the unique role played by law in relation to the development of the project of European integration. In this regard, the Court occupies a hugely influential position, defining the legal substance and status of the Union constitution as well as the relationship between Union constitutional values and the entire body of Union and domestic laws. A dedicated 'supranational' institution whose role is to express the process of European integration through the medium of law, the Court arguably possesses a limited mandate to qualify elements of Member States' incumbent constitutional requirements.[39] The Court's judgments therefore tend to result in activist interventions within domestic legal settings.[40] The Court's activities are also comparatively insulated from those of domestic institutional concerns which by contrast have been subject to profound developments as a result of these activities.

The ability to promote European integration through the medium of law that the Court's role arguably represents must nonetheless account for a complex array of institutional factors. These include the need to articulate Union legal demands in a manner viewed as legitimate by Union and Member State institutional actors as 'partners' in the European project. In this

39 Given that the commitments arising under the Treaties are based upon domestic constitutional recognition of the ongoing development of Union integration. The extent of that recognition is of course contested, both regarding the extent to which Union laws are permitted to encroach upon domestic constitutional demands, as well as in relation to the *Kompetenz Kompetenz* question: are Union or Member States' courts ultimately competent to determine the reach of their respective jurisdictions? These questions have been considered in a number of high profile legal judgments by Member States' constitutional courts, notably the German Federal Constitutional Court. See for an overview of these judgments, G Martinico and O Pollicino, 'Between Constitutional Tolerance and Judicial Activism: The Specificity of European Judicial Law' (2008) 10 *European Journal of Law Reform* 97.

40 For consideration of the Court's 'activist' tendencies, see Chapter 4. In this regard, the Court operates in a *relatively* closed institutional and political landscape by contrast with the separation of powers concerns of domestic courts, where a proper balance between the exercise of powers by the judicial, legislative and executive branches is vital to the system's continued stability and legitimacy. The Court also possesses a significant degree of institutional freedom in relation to other Union actors. For example, Pierson has noted that

> If the Council is prone to gridlock, the necessity of deciding cases inclines the ECJ to action. This inclination is strengthened by rules allowing simple majority decisions, and by a secrecy (neither actual votes nor dissenting views are made public) that shelters judges from member-state and popular pressures. ECJ judges also share a common professional background, legal cultures (at least on the continent) that seeks to effectively limit the influence of the member-states in judicial decision making.
>
> (P Pierson, 'Path to European Integration' in W Sandholtz and A S Sweet (eds), *European Integration and Supranational Governance* (Oxford University Press, New York 1998) at 36)

regard, the fact that the objectives of European integration relate ultimately to the emergence of a new transnational polity highlights the uniqueness of the institutional task faced by the Court. Polity formation is usually associated with a defining revolutionary or constitutional 'moment' which settles the ensuing political landscape for future time. The Union is by contrast a developmental project, largely reliant for its survival as such on sustaining an evolving legal and political consensus.

Conclusions

Analysis of the law of the European Union and institutional practices of the Court of Justice will allow me to develop theoretical approaches to legal order in two areas. First, I shall attempt to develop existing analytic models by reference to the unique body of values found within the Union 'constitution'. The resulting institutional model accounts for the possibility of contested, aspirational political social or economic objectives operating as foundational, 'directing' legal principles.[41] Second, the implications of these models for the institutional practices of the Court of Justice are explored by considering how the values set out in the preamble and opening Articles of the Treaties condition the judicial practices of the Court of Justice in law making, application and interpretation.

Chapter Outlines

These themes outlined above will be developed in the remaining chapters as follows. In Chapter 2 I consider various analytic approaches to law, focusing upon the relationship between legal rules, legal practices and the values underlying legal ordering. The objective here is to identify what features, if any, of different positivist and non-positivist models are of utility in accounting for the legal order of the European Union. My conclusion, as should by now be apparent, is that neither (non-positivist) accounts that necessarily implicate moral values in the articulation of legal demands nor (positivist) accounts that assert the primacy of the clear identification of legal as opposed to non-legal demands in order to guarantee their functional effectiveness can

41 'An adequate jurisprudence (there's no hope of constructing a full or complete one) offers accounts of the concepts of legality, authority and of those concepts that figure prominently in a theory of adjudication', J Coleman, 'Authority and Reason' in R P George (ed.), *The Autonomy of Law* (Oxford University Press, Oxford 1996) at 296. See also Dickson's comment that:

> it is important to note that a successful theory of this type must do more than feature *any* chosen sub-set of necessarily true propositions explaining those properties which something must possess in order to be law. This is due to the fact that some sub-sets will not fulfil the second criterion of a successful theory of this sort, namely that it must adequately explain what law is.
>
> (Dickson, *Evaluation and Legal Theory* at 23–24)

fully account for either the operation or substance of the foundational legal values of the Union legal order.

In Chapter 3 I set out the parameters of a conceptual model that allows for the possibility of legal order based upon the achievement of specific economic, social and political objectives within a limited jurisdictional sphere. These parameters are affirmed within an institutional account of legal order that recognises both the positive, institutional character of legal practices as well as the dynamic influence of the 'standing aims' or foundational values underlying legal order.[42]

In Chapter 4 I focus on the implications of the theoretical position defended in Chapter 3 for the institutional role and practices of the Court of Justice. Here, I identify the central concern of the Court to be the generation of legal demands allied to the objectives of Union integration. In this regard, and building on Mann's analysis of the Court's judgments,[43] I explore the implications for the Court's practices of the Treaty objectives, objectives that are transformative in a broad political sense yet operate as regulative ideals of the Union legal order.

In Chapter 5 I consider the legal effects of the constitutional values of the Union, namely the Treaty Articles and general principles, in light of selected judgments of the Court of Justice. I focus upon the techniques of legal reasoning employed by the Court in articulating the influence of these constitutional values/principles over the body of both Union and domestic legal demands. I also emphasise the importance of flexible and rhetorical, persuasive forms of legal reasoning by the Court that are sensitive to the political implications of its judgments within the Member States.

In Chapter 6, building on the analysis in Chapter 5, I consider the relationship between the Union and Member State legal orders, focusing upon the potential for and resolution of conflict between Union and domestic legal demands. These so-called *Kompetenz Kompetenz* questions concern the implications of Union legal demands for the constitutional ordering of Member States as well as the related issue of the influence of domestic constitutional norms over the Court's portrayal of Union legal demands. Examination of the *Kompetenz Kompetenz* perspectives of Union and Member States' courts within case judgments demonstrates that 'accommodating' judicial mechanisms serve to reconcile co-existing yet (potentially) conflicting Union and Member State (constitutional) demands. Such mechanisms are needed given the absence of any 'independent' incorporation of the ideals of European integration within

42 These standing aims within a Western cultural setting are minimally rule of law values relating to fundamental rights protection and due process in relation to activities of law creation, application and enforcement. There appears to be little dispute that these values in fact inform legal ordering properly understood yet a high measure of disagreement exists regarding their conceptual significance as well as the precise role they play in relation to individual legal demands. See MacCormick, *Rhetoric and the Rule of Law* at 252 and MacCormick, *Questioning Sovereignty*, Chapter 1.

43 Mann, *The Function of Judicial Decision in European Economic Integration* at 38.

domestic constitutions beyond the fact that the Treaties themselves have been incorporated. The take up of these ideals as a matter of law within domestic settings depends rather on the ability of the Court of Justice to formulate Union law demands in a manner that is acceptable to the Member States.

In Chapter 7 I address the question whether any difference exists between the account of the Union legal order I have presented and one based on the application of principles of international law simpliciter. In essence I contend there is not. However, I conclude that the Union represents an advanced form of international legal ordering that has been under-theorised, in common with the phenomenon of international law generally.

In the final chapter, I restate the book's central themes, namely the significance for analytic jurisprudence of the Union legal order as well as the judicial role in promoting the values underlying this order. I also consider a number of possible criticisms of my arguments including an implicit assumption that the ideal of European integration represents a 'value' as well as a constitutional legal principle. Finally I consider a possible future avenue of research raised by the claims defended in the book, namely whether the operation of the Union legal order may at some point give rise to a Union polity.

2 Theoretical perspectives on law and the law of the European Union

Introduction

In the following two chapters I attempt to meet the theoretical challenges posed by the legal order of the European Union. The aim in this chapter is to critically appraise positivist and non-positivist accounts of law and to contextualise the legal order of the Union within current strands of analytic thinking. In Chapter 3 I shall detail a theoretical approach that addresses identified shortcomings.

The chapter is set out as follows. In the first section I consider the idea of law as a pre-theoretical construct before linking debates in this area to the role played by values within positivist and non-positivist theoretical accounts. In the following section, I consider in overview the arguments of a number of individual positivist and non-positivist writers, assessing in each case their utility in providing a theoretical understanding of the Union order. The final section critically assesses the tendency of current theoretical accounts to equate the idea of law with the legal order(s) of States as well as the implications of this association for an adequate analytic account of the Union legal order.

Law's pre-theoretical features and associated theoretical accounts

As a general proposition, how a given area of inquiry is understood in a pre-theoretical sense will inform the methods of inquiry deemed appropriate and as a result the character of any subsequent theoretical model. In the natural sciences for example, observable and describable 'facts' about the physical world are taken to be the pre-theoretical information from which deductive or inductive propositions/principles/theories of the natural world are derived. As a result the scientific method consists in accessing and describing observable physical properties relevant to the phenomenon under inquiry. Where the subject matter is law however, the identification of the pre-theoretical subject matter and hence the 'correct' method of inquiry is less clear. The 'kind of thing' being enquired into and hence 'how we inquire' where law is concerned are matters over which one can identify profound disagreements, illustrated by current debates over the nature of legal philosophy itself.[1]

It would seem then that where law is concerned there may not even exist the possibility of meaningful disagreement between different theoretical approaches.[2] Positivists, who regard law in a pre-theoretical sense as a body of social facts albeit serving a normative function, advocate a social scientific method of inquiry based on identifying and describing the relevant social practices that give rise to law creation, application and interpretation. Non-positivists on the other hand advocate a pre-theoretical understanding of law as a normative imperative based on the (moral) need to ensure peaceable social co-existence. The method of inquiry here is therefore itself normative as opposed to descriptive.

Pre-theoretical and associated methodological uncertainty where law is concerned[3] is underlined by the fact that conceptual accounts of law are intertwined with our lived, 'political' experience of legal order. Concept and 'interpreted' experience are related in ways unknown to other areas of the humanities or the natural sciences. In this regard Phillip Allott has noted that:

> Political philosophy is a phenomenology, not a science. A phenomenon of the physical world, a phenomenon-for-science, is an event that is to be explained. The event is conceived as being something other than its explanation. But when the task is the task of explaining political behaviour, phenomena-for-philosophy of the social world, it is three times more problematic. In the first place, the thing to be explained is something that already contains ideas as an integral part of its functioning … And secondly, the political phenomenon we are studying is also being studied by those who participate in it as they act politically … Thirdly,

1 See generally, J Dickson, *Evaluation and Legal Theory* (Hart Publishing, Oxford 2001), hereafter Dickson, *Evaluation and Legal Theory*.

2 Bix has noted that '[i]t is not surprising that often the different participants in the conceptual debates in legal theory – debates about how the concepts are best defined – are often best understood as talking past one another'. B Bix, 'Conceptual Questions and Jurisprudence' (1995) 1 *Legal Theory* 465 at 474, hereafter Bix, 'Conceptual Questions and Jurisprudence'. See also Dworkin's comment that:

> Unfortunately the English word 'law' and parallel words in other languages are used in so many different ways, we have so many distinct concepts that we use those words to deploy, and the interrelationships among these concepts are so problematic and controversial, that different theories about the connections between law and practice are often answers to different kinds of questions.
>
> (R Dworkin, *Justice in Robes* (Harvard University Press, Cambridge, Massachusetts 2006) at 1)

3 See for a philosophical exploration of the pre-theoretical in relation to law, S Toddington, *Rationality, Social Action and Moral Judgment* (Edinburgh University Press, Edinburgh 1993), particularly Ch. 1 and R Dworkin, 'Objectivity and Truth, You'd Better Believe It' (1996) 25 *Philosophy & Public Affairs* 87.

> to philosophise is to act socially. To philosophise about political action is itself political action. We cannot avoid playing a part in the process we are studying.[4]

Despite these problematising factors around attempts to theorise the phenomenon of law, it is nonetheless far from clear, as well as counter-intuitive, that different theoretical schools represent wholly incompatible positions.[5] Indeed, a single working definition may illustrate a variety of theoretical positions. For example, in Chapter 1 I suggested a definition of law as:

> a formalised body of social practices comprising authoritative normative injunctions that serve to define, guide and enable all forms of social conduct in a manner that necessarily generates valued forms of social ordering.

Each component of this definition arguably represents a core claim of different jurisprudential schools that in turn shapes particular theoretical positions on the relationship between law and values. However, schools would agree to some extent with each one of these elements; it is the relative emphasis placed on one or other features that distinguishes positivist from non-positivist positions. If we add in the theoretical positions associated with each claim,

> law comprises a formal or structured body of social practices comprising authoritative normative injunctions (*positivism* and *non-positivism*) that serve to define, guide and enable all forms of social conduct (*positivism*) in a manner that necessarily generates valued forms of social ordering (*non-positivism*).

The importance given to one or other aspects coincides with viewpoints regarding law's pre-theoretical features, the 'kind of thing' law is held to be,

4 P Allott, 'The European Community Is Not the True European Community' (1990–1991) 100 *Yale Law Journal* 2485 at 2485 (footnote omitted). To these points can be added the historical and cultural contingency of legal theorising. In this regard, Dickson has noted that how we theorise about law will tend to reflect current historical concerns:

> For example the Hart–Fuller debate concerning the factors which bear upon the identification of valid law, and the normative consequences of law so identified, were prompted in part by events occurring during and after the Second World War and the Nuremberg trials.
> (J Dickson, 'Towards a Theory of European Union Legal Systems' in J Dickson and P Eleftheriadis (eds, *Philosophical Foundations of European Union Law* (Oxford University Press, Oxford 2012) at 27)

Allott's argument bears interesting comparison with the uncertainty principle in quantum mechanics, which asserts that as we attempt to specify with greater precision the location or energy state of an object our data becomes altered by the very process of measurement.

5 Weinberger has noted in relation to positivist and non-positivist theoretical approaches, '[i]n contemporary legal theory there is in fact a not insignificant tendency for the two theories to converge'. N MacCormick and O Weinberger, *An Institutional Theory of Law* (D Reidel Publishing Company, Dordrecht 1986) at 111, hereafter MacCormick and Weinberger, *An Institutional Theory of Law*.

as well as the 'correct' method of inquiry into the concept. Selected viewpoints will correspond to those adopted by other academic disciplines said to fall within the same category. Whether law is viewed as a manifestation of sociology, psychology, moral philosophy, discourse analysis or logic will be largely determinative of our pre-theoretical understanding, the method of theoretical inquiry applied and the resulting theoretical approach.[6] This gives rise to a variety of claims concerning arguably the central concern of analytic jurisprudence, the relationship between law and values.[7] These claims are considered in the next section.

Analytic theoretical perspectives

The identification of legal as opposed to non-legal norms or the features of legal as opposed to non-legal reasoning are typically understood in terms of the relationship between the values or functions law is said to express and the practices of legal institutions. As previously noted, the parameters of this relationship are disputed between positivist and non-positivist schools. The difference in approach, whose conceptual significance is arguably minimal, concerns whether the values or functions expressed within legal practices are dynamic drivers or implicit (static) features of those practices.

Non-positivists generally hold that moral values dynamically influence the substance and form of legal demands given that the underlying function of law is moral in character. Positivist thinkers, while accepting that law is an evaluative practice, argue that the values upheld by law are an ingrained feature of identifiable social practices of law creation and application.[8] Both sides agree that law is a functional and hence evaluative social activity.[9] The differences lie in how this functionality is rationalised.

6 Coleman, commenting on the debate between Dworkin and positivists has noted that:

> In relatively short order what was once an intervention in one debate turned into a broader dispute about the methodology of jurisprudence, that is whether an inquiry into the nature of law is a project in political philosophy, social science, conceptual analysis, or something else altogether.
>
> (J Coleman, 'Beyond Inclusive Positivism' (2009) 22 *Ratio Juris* 359 at 360)

7 For example, positivist accounts affirm both a descriptive model of law and legal practices as well as a 'social scientific' method of inquiry that seeks to identify and describe the social facts that constitute legal order. Non-positivist accounts by contrast privilege law's normative character and hence a method of inquiry that involves normative and hence moral judgements.

8 So positivists may reject a 'broad' version of the separability thesis which holds that no necessary connection exists between legal order as a form of governance (as opposed to the character of individual legal rules and morality). See J Coleman, 'Beyond the Separability Thesis: Moral Semantics and the Methodology of Jurisprudence' (2007) 27 *Oxford Journal of Legal Studies* 581 at 583, hereafter Coleman, 'Beyond the Separability Thesis'.

9 A Marmor, *Positive Law and Objective Values* (Clarendon Press, Oxford 2001) at 154, hereafter Marmor, *Positive Law and Objective Values*; S Perry, 'The Varieties of Legal Positivism' (1996) 9 *Canadian Journal of Law and Jurisprudence* 361, hereafter Perry, 'The Varieties of Legal Positivism'.

Positivism

For legal positivists, the clear demarcation of the legal from the non-legal realm is affirmed as a conceptual or necessary feature.[10] This implies the identification of legal demands according to descriptively accessible and hence certain social-fact criteria that as such do not engage moral or other (inherently uncertain) evaluative judgements.[11] Positivist analytic approaches fall broadly into two camps, exclusive and inclusive positivism.

Exclusive positivism

Exclusive or 'hard' positivists deny the possibility of evaluative standards ever acting as criteria of legal validity. Their central claim is that the term 'law' only applies to rules recognised exclusively on the basis of social-fact criteria (of legality).[12] This 'sources thesis'[13] entails the strict separation of

10 Most famously by Kelsen. See H Kelsen, *General Theory of Law and State* (Transaction Publishers, London 2008).

11 See for 'exclusive positivist' perspectives, J Raz, *Ethics in the Public Domain* (Clarendon Press, Oxford 1994), hereafter Raz, *Ethics in the Public Domain*; Marmor, *Positive Law and Objective Values*. For inclusive positivist accounts, see W J Waluchow, *Inclusive Legal Positivism* (Clarendon Press, Oxford 1994); Coleman, *The Practice of Principle* (Oxford University Press, Oxford 2001).

12 The assertion by exclusive positivists that law claims to be capable of possessing authority, and hence that the identification of legal standards must be based on identifiable social practices, is itself a normative conclusion concerning how law 'ought' to be conceived. On this point see F Schauer, 'Positivism through Thick and Thin' in B Bix (ed.), (1998) *Analyzing Law: New Essays in Legal Theory* (Clarendon Press, Oxford 1998) at 69–70. Raz, who defends the necessity of exclusively social-fact criteria of legal validity, appears to agree with Shauer's assertion in noting that the very fact that legal validity must be understood in this way may be a moral attribute of law. He states:

> In *Practical Reason and Norms* I argued (reformulating the point in a way I now find clearer and more accurate) that even if all the law's essential features can be stated without the use of moral concepts, it may be the case that, that it has those features entails that it has some moral merit.
> (J Raz, 'How Not to Reply to Legal Positivism' in G Pavlakos (ed.), *Law, Rights and Discourse: The Legal Philosophy of Robert Alexy* (Hart Publishing, Oxford 2007) at 20 (reference omitted))

Bix has noted in regard to the exclusive positivist claim that law is necessarily capable of possessing authority, that it, 'more assumes than sets out to elaborate the "necessity" argument'. B Bix, 'Patrolling the Boundaries: Inclusive Legal Positivism and the Nature of Jurisprudential Debate' (1999) 12 *Canadian Journal of Law and Jurisprudence* 17 at 28, footnote 60. According to Leiter, the claim that law necessarily claims authority is a culturally relative description. He notes, 'Raz does not argue from the service conception of authority on the ground that it is morally attractive or has morally good consequences: he argues that it is our concept. That is a descriptive claim.' B Leiter, 'Beyond the Hart/Dworkin Debate: The Methodology Problem in Jurisprudence' (2003) 48 *American Journal of Jurisprudence* 17 at 32. Perry also considers Raz's approach to be essentially normative in character, stating:

> Raz at points appears to accept methodological positivism ... but it can be argued that his argument for the sources thesis, based as it is on a moral conception of legitimate authority commits him to a more thorough-going normative methodology.
> (Perry, 'The Varieties of Legal Positivism' at 362, footnote 3 (references omitted))

legal from non-legal norms, a separation that ensures law's claim to be capable of possessing authority, a conceptual or necessary feature on this account. Accordingly, for Raz,

> The argument for the sources thesis is based on the conceptual point that, since the law demands compliance with its standards of conduct whether the subject thinks they are justified or not, those standards must be identifiable independently of justificatory considerations.[14]

The claim that legal standards cannot derive from evaluative (including moral) criteria of validity is a version of the separability thesis which denies the possibility of any association between criteria of legal validity and those of morality.[15] Together the sources thesis and (this form of) the separability thesis form the central tenets of exclusive positivism,[16] securing

> a basic underlying function of the law: to provide publicly ascertainable standards by which members of the society are held to be bound so that they cannot excuse conformity by challenging the justification of the standard.[17]

This underlying function, arises for Raz from the fact that '[i]t is a commonplace that social life requires and is facilitated by various patterns of forbearances, co-operation, and co-ordination between members of the society or some of them'.[18]

Coleman also suggests that Raz's jurisprudence is effectively normative in character, noting, '[I] think Raz's approach to law embeds his account within a substantive theory of legitimate authority.' Coleman, 'Beyond the Separability Thesis' at 598.

13 The sources thesis is defined by Marmor as follows: '[l]egal validity, according to this view which I will strive to defend here, is entirely dependent on the conventionally recognised sources of law'. Marmor, *Positive Law and Objective Values* at 50; Raz, *Ethics in the Public Domain* at 231–235.

14 Perry, 'The Varieties of Legal Positivism' at 366 (emphasis in original).

15 For consideration of various versions of the separability thesis (the claim that law and morality are distinct), see J Coleman, 'Beyond the Separability Thesis'.

16 Exclusive positivism advocates what Coleman calls an 'internal negation' formulation of the separability thesis, that is 'the claim that in all legal systems it is necessarily the case that the legality of a norm not depend on its morality or its substantive merits'. J Coleman, 'Second Thoughts and Other First Impressions' in B Bix (ed.), *Analyzing Law: New Essays in Legal Theory* (Clarendon Press, Oxford 1998) at 265, hereafter Coleman, 'Second Thoughts and Other First Impressions'. By contrast, inclusive positivists, including Coleman, advocate an external negation formulation, 'the claim that it is not necessarily the case that in any legal system the legality of a norm depend on its morality or its substantive merits'. Ibid. In an earlier article, Coleman offers a linked formulation of these two approaches as follows: '[t]he separability thesis is not the claim that law and morality are necessarily separated; rather, it is the claim that they are not necessarily connected'. J Coleman, 'Authority and Reason' in R P George (ed.), *The Autonomy of Law* (Oxford University Press, Oxford 1996) at 291, hereafter Coleman, 'Authority and Reason'.

17 J Raz, *The Authority of Law* (2nd edn, Clarendon Press, Oxford 2009) at 52, hereafter Raz, *The Authority of Law*.

18 Ibid. at 50.

Does, however, such a 'commonplace' of social life form the basis of the European Union legal order as well as the activities of the Court of Justice in expressing the constitutional legal demands underlying this order? In my view it does not for the following reasons.

For the Member States, the 'patterns of forbearance, co-operation and co-ordination' of human activity required for the purpose of social co-existence are matters fully addressed by their respective legal orders under the guidance of the written constitution. These are matters to which the Union legal order adds little in any necessary sense. From the time of the original European Communities, every Member State possessed and continues to possess legal orders that adequately serve the social functions identified by Raz as the basis of law's conceptual features. By contrast, the Union represents a transnational commitment to promote and realise through law qua revolutionary medium, the various objectives specified in the Treaties under the guiding rationale of European integration. The 'point' of the Union legal order is not simply, if at all, the guidance of conduct to enable social co-existence in any necessary sense, but rather the promotion of the Treaty objectives. A central justification for the sources thesis as presented by Raz is therefore not present within the Union setting, highlighting the inadequacy of exclusive positivism as an analytic approach to understanding the Union order.

A related tenet of exclusive positivism underlines an inability to account for the operation of the values represented by the Union Treaties. This concerns the contention that the values or functions served by legal order are 'embedded' within the conventional social practices creating or applying legal standards and cannot as such exert a dynamic influence over these practices without undermining their conventionality and hence constitutive function.[19] In this regard, for Marmor, the purpose of legal practices is to constitute a valued social domain and not to direct action according to moral (or other value based) reasons:

> There is no role constitutive conventions can play in determining that people should act according to moral reasons. Politics, morality, ethics, and similar considerations bear on our practical reasoning regardless of conventions. Constitutive conventions can make a difference only by determining specific ways in which such moral, political and other types of concerns become part of law, that is, part of a conventionally established social practice. And this is precisely what the conventions of recognition do: they constitute practices of making law, changing it, applying it to novel cases and the like.[20]

19 Shapiro has noted that: '[f]or the exclusive legal positivist, the conventionality of law is compromised whenever the rule of recognition conditions legal validity on the moral superiority or acceptability of a norm'. S Shapiro, 'The Difference that Rules Make' in B Bix (ed.), *Analyzing Law: New Essays in Legal Theory* (Clarendon Press, Oxford, 1998) at 57.

20 Marmor, *Positive Law and Objective Values* at 51 (footnote omitted).

Marmor's view that the constitutive function of conventional practices of law creation and application necessarily entails a static role for the values upheld by law can be challenged on two fronts. First because it fails to account for all possibilities of legal order or legal practices and second because values may in fact operate in a dynamic sense in relation to constitutive legal practices without undermining their conventional status and constitutive function. The second challenge, being based on an inclusive positivist claim, is considered below. In relation to the first challenge, some instances of legal order highlight the necessarily dynamic effect of underlying values, for example where, as in the Union, an evolutionary dynamic is a core feature of institutional design. In addition, in all instances of legal order circumstances may arise which require recognition of the dynamic effects of underlying values, for example in times of rapid social change.[21]

In relation to the Union, the underlying function of the legal order, to develop European integration *must* allow for the active engagement of this value in the institutional expression of legal demands. The Union represents a 'revolutionary' legal order[22] with the underlying values of the Treaties providing a dynamic influence over the substantive content of all legal outcomes as well as the hierarchical relationship between laws of Union and domestic origin. The Union represents an evolving constitution whose underlying values exert a decisive influence as qualifying factors of legal validity. Underlying values relating to European integration cannot operate as implicit features of Union legal practices in the manner suggested by Marmor, but form ideals that perennially generate development and change in the legal orders of both Union and Member States.

How then is Marmor's claim that '[t]here is no role constitutive conventions can play in determining that people should act according to moral reasons. Politics, morality, ethics, and similar considerations bear on our practical reasoning regardless of conventions'[23] to be understood in the context of the Union order? This argument appears to be irrelevant since clearly the value of European integration being a context specific political ideal has no bearing on our practical reasoning regardless of conventions. Marmor bases his view on a contextualisation of legal practices within the legal orders of States, orders that express in an inclusive sense the wider evaluative (political/moral/ethical) environment in which they operate. Within this context, there is therefore a

21 Absent this recognition, in times of rapid social change or indeed revolution, the values expressed through judicial practices will rapidly lose touch with the social, political or institutional environment in which they operate. Marmor accepts that '[a]ccounting for revolutionary changes of legal systems is a serious challenge for conventionalism, but I cannot hope to face it here'. Ibid. at footnote 4. The Union raises the possibility of legal order whose very nature is revolutionary in a weak sense and which therefore represents a challenge for conventionalist accounts of law in the form proposed by exclusive positivism.

22 T Schilling, 'The Court of Justice's Revolution: Its Effects and the Conditions for its Consummation: What Europe Can Learn from Fiji' (2002) 27 *European Law Review* 445.

23 Marmor, *Positive Law and Objective Values* at 51.

principled argument that distinguishes law from background value concerns of morality, ethics, politics.[24] Such a distinction is however largely irrelevant in relation to the values underlying the Union order and relating to European integration given these values are in an important sense acontextual and directed towards a *recontextualistion* of existing political settlements. Where the Union legal order is concerned, the dominant and only contextual and contextualising normative resource derives from the law itself.

Does then my contention that values operate as dynamic influences over legal outcomes in (for example) the Union setting mean that the conventional character of legal practices of law creation and application are fatally compromised as suggested by Marmor? This question is addressed by the other main school of positivist thinking, inclusive positivism.

Inclusive positivism

Jules Coleman, the most prominent exponent of inclusive positivism, has pointed out that all jurisprudential theories invoke some standard by which law is identified, a Rule of Recognition in Hart's terminology, and that '[i]f all that positivism meant by a rule of recognition were "the standard in every community by which a community's legal norms were made determinate," every theory of law would be reducible to one or another version of positivism'.[25]

24 Although I defend the opposing view that values play a qualified role in determining legal outcomes, by reference to the underlying value concerns of a given jurisdiction, without thereby disturbing the conventional character of legal practices.

25 J Coleman, 'Negative and Positive Positivism' (1982) 11 *Journal of Legal Studies* 139 at 139, hereafter Coleman, 'Negative and Positive Positivism'. Theoretical debates between inclusive and exclusive positivism have centred upon the question whether moral values can (inclusive positivism) or cannot (exclusive positivism) operate as criteria of legal validity in relation to existing law. Without wishing to diminish the philosophical insights generated by this question, it is in one sense a moot point. This is because it is assumed by all schools of positivism as well as by non-positivist thinkers that for any standard to count as legal in character, it must be recognised by the relevant institutions as such irrespective of the question whether this recognition necessarily embodies a moral element, although it may well do so. To illustrate this point, consider the evolution of a rule of recognition whereby it was universally accepted by officials and citizens that any morally correct determination also possessed legal authority. This evolution could only have resulted from the conventional practices of the relevant institutional branches – in our society, the governmental branches of the State – affirming such a view. It would still be institutional practices which would determine *what* is morally and hence legally required in any given situation. (See for a similar claim, Coleman, *The Practice of Principle* at 151). Irrespective of the question whether legal demands were *in fact* an expression of moral requirements, the norms of 'morality' that institutions of law purported to apply as criteria of legal validity in this example would remain distinctive as a result of their institutional expression. MacCormick recognises this point as follows:

> The institutional agencies that shape legal order ... construct norms or human conduct of a kind that differ critically from the moral norms and customs that would prevail in a wholly autonomous interaction of humans. They differ critically, just because they

However, positivism marks itself out from other jurisprudential approaches and in order to do so 'additional constraints must be placed on the rule of recognition'.[26] Coleman identifies these as follows:

> The first is the claim that the criteria of legality are social facts. Whether something counts as law or as legally valid depends on its social source. The second is the claim that the rule that sets forth the conditions of legal validity, the Rule of Recognition, is itself a social rule. [27]

For inclusive positivists, the second, but not the first, of these claims is viewed as an essential feature of legality so that:

> are interpersonally authoritative, relatively determinate, and equipped with agencies to enforce and interpret them, these agencies being in turn the creatures of institutional norms. That is the sense in which they are 'artificial', and give rise to an 'artificial' system of reasoning.
>
> (N MacCormick, *Rhetoric and the Rule of Law* at 47)

The association between law as a conventional institutional practice and morality would therefore in this example only exist in a rhetorical sense. This is because, without begging the question (and answer) of whether law is 'in fact' a moral form of governance, it is impossible to determine the form and substance of the institutional practices that give rise to this conclusion. Moreover, to the extent that an association between the criteria of legal validity and morality is accepted by officials and citizens, the moral authority of institutional practices relating to law's creation and application is arguably undermined. This is because any moral criticism of the law would then be an attack on the rule of law itself, facilitating destabilising political activism. As Weinberger has noted, '[m]orality is not a criterion for judging the validity of law. It is precisely the separation of the law from morality that makes possible moral judgments about the law.' O Weinberger, 'Institutionalist Theories of Law' in P Amselek and N MacCormick (eds), *Controversies About Law's Ontology* (Edinburgh University Press, Edinburgh 1991) at 50. This argument, however, has limited force because if a clear distinction is made between law and morality, then while moral criticism of the law is enabled, the possibility of addressing that criticism *as a matter of law* is diminished. If moral considerations external to the positive law are in principle excluded from judicial determinations then the reasoning capabilities of the courts in seeking to interpret and apply the law will arguably be restricted, potentially permitting legal demands that are irrational/immoral. Reasoned determinations by the courts when interpreting/applying the positive law must therefore include considerations that exist beyond the realm of the positive law. Mann has made the historical observation in this regard that:

> Since the turn of the century, important advances have been made in articulating the process of judicial decision. While not overcoming the scepticism toward an ascertainable system of natural law, they have demonstrated that a complete statement of the judicial process must encompass moral values lying outside the written law.
>
> (C Mann, *The Function of Judicial Decision in European Economic Integration* (Martinus Nijhoff, The Hague 1972) at 112)

26 Coleman, 'Negative and Positive Positivism' at 139.

27 Coleman, 'Second Thoughts and Other First Impressions' at 263. See also Coleman, 'Negative and Positive Positivism' at 140. Note that Coleman is referring here to the rule identifying the criteria of legality and not to the criteria themselves.

> The claim that law is a matter of social fact is the claim that in every community the criteria of validity are established by a social fact: a Rule of Recognition that is itself a social practice among relevant officials.[28]

The first claim, that the social practices comprising the Rule of Recognition can *only* represent or affirm social-fact criteria of legal validity (the sources thesis), is affirmed additionally by exclusive positivists but rejected by inclusive positivists. For inclusive positivists, the conventional social practices forming the Rule of Recognition may give rise to both social fact *and* evaluative/normative/substantive criteria of legal validity.[29] Coleman describes this 'positive' form of positivism as follows:

> The form of positive positivism that I want to characterize and defend has, as its point, not that law is largely uncontroversial – it need not be – but that law is ultimately conventional: that the authority of law is a matter of its acceptance by officials.[30]

In short, inclusive positivist approaches recognise the possibility of evaluative, in addition to social-fact criteria of legality, either (both) of which must be constituted by conventional official practices, that is by a 'social-fact' rule of recognition. I would reject, however, the possibility of legal order based exclusively on social-fact criteria of legality,[31] the *conceptual* position defended

28 Coleman, 'Second Thoughts and Other First Impressions' at 263.

29 Ibid. See also Coleman, 'Authority and Reason' at 306. Coleman describes a formulation of the sources thesis compatible with inclusive positivism as 'a constraint on the theory of authority, not on the theory of validity'. Ibid. at 308. By this Coleman means that the criteria of *identification* but not of the validity of laws subordinate to the Rule of Recognition may be subject to source based constraints in order to uphold law's claim to authority. Such source based constraints however place 'no constraint on the rule of recognition in its essential form, that is, as a validation rule'. Ibid. at 308. Raz, from an exclusive positivist perspective distinguishes between broad and narrow versions of the sources thesis:

> The narrow thesis concerns the truth conditions of pure legal statements only. Pure legal statements are those which state the content of the law, i.e. of legal rules, principles, doctrines etc. The wide thesis concerns the truth conditions of all legal statements, including applied ones. It claims that the truth or falsity of legal statements depends on social facts which can be established without resort to moral argument.
>
> (J Raz, *Ethics in the Public Domain*)

According to Raz, law's claim to authority 'supports the narrow sources thesis because it leads to a conception of law as playing a mediating role between ultimate reasons and people's decisions and actions'. Ibid.

30 Coleman, 'Negative and Positive Positivism' at 148.

31 The thesis of negative positivism. Coleman, 'Negative and Positive Positivism' at 140ff. Although it is possible to imagine a legal order in which values play such a static role, such an order could only exist in a notional state of complete political stability, a condition which is never in fact met. In the world as it is, all societies are sites of various, often conflicting political

by exclusive positivists. In my view the conventionally constituted rule of recognition *always* involves the positive recognition of underlying evaluative concerns, albeit that their impact over stated legal outcomes will be variable between legal orders. In this regard, the extent of value influences over the created, applied or interpreted law will depend upon the wider institutional context as well as the foundational objectives on which any given order is based.

Reconciling the conventionality of legal practices with the expression of foundational value concerns as dynamic operative features of legality is deemed possible by inclusive positivism but rejected by exclusive positivism. To defend the inclusive positivist position, with which I am in broad agreement, it is necessary to meet the exclusive positivist objection that values as operative features of legality would undermine the possibility of conventional legal practices,[32] capable of making good law's claim to authority (Raz) or ability to constitute a valued social domain (Marmor). I would meet this objection by stressing the weak dynamism of the interpretive effects of underlying value concerns over legal outcomes which do not as such undermine the conventional character of legal practices.[33] While values will generally not operate as independent criteria of legality nor provide directly enforceable legal requirements,[34] as the underlying functional concerns of any given order, they act as directing interpretive influences over all legal outcomes.

Legal outcomes are the result of (interpretive) reasoning by reference to a body of underlying value concerns. This understanding of the criteria of legality does not implicate ongoing shifts in the conventional practices of

currents and are therefore always in a relative sense unstable. Any adequate understanding of legal order must account for this aspect of human societies and therefore permit the dynamic and flexible expression of values said to be foundational to the legal order/society concerned.

32 Dworkin's objection to inclusive positivism that:

> there is no limit to how abstract a convention we may attribute to lawyers, we may use the strategy to count any legal practice as conventional no matter how much it seems to defy positivism's traditional requirements' is, I would suggest incorrect insofar as it does not account for the fact that the legal effects taken by values are context sensitive and may vary in the extent to which they influence legal outcomes, as interpretive/legality review or directly enforceable rights/obligations.
>
> (R Dworkin, *Justice in Robes* (Harvard University Press, Cambridge, Massachusetts 2006) at 193)

33 These two elements, positive/conventional and evaluative, are both recognised in the institutional account of law I consider in Chapter 3 as adequate to the task of conceptualising the Union legal order. Institutional and inclusive positivist accounts of law are indeed closely related. As Coleman has noted, 'analytic jurisprudence generally and legal positivism in particular, aims to deepen our understanding of legal institutions. The subject of analytic jurisprudence is law, not "law".' Coleman, 'Second Thoughts and Other First Impressions' at 258.

34 In the Union setting, for example, the fact that a particular rule may promote European integration would not in any sense determine its status as a legal demand.

law creation and application but rather the living qualification of all legal outcomes by reference to the underlying functional concerns of any given order.[35] Exclusive positivist concerns that values cannot form operative features of legality are, in short, unfounded.

Non-positivism

Non-positivism also offers helpful insights into the dynamic sense in which values operate as foundational concerns of legal order. In general, non-positivism affirms law as a rational form of governance[36] that as such maintains necessary or conceptual affiliations with values of political morality.[37] My concern here is to consider briefly whether non-positivist accounts can assist in understanding the operative features of the 'directing' values underlying the Union order relating to European integration.

To this end, below I take a snapshot of the theoretical claims of three non-positivist writers, Mark Greenberg, Ronald Dworkin and Robert Alexy. These are in no way inclusive of the range of non-positivist approaches but do serve to illustrate the sense in which legal orders as functional social practices represent ideals of value as well as positive social facts. The issue for a theoretical model of the Union legal order is whether these ideals can also include aspirational political, social and economic objectives in addition to concerns of political morality.

For Greenberg, determining the law applicable to any given fact situation necessarily involves evaluative judgements external to existing legal

35 I would therefore reject Marmor's claim that while legal conventional practices are subject to constant interpretive pressure from value concerns external to the positive law, this causes gradual changes in the conventions themselves:

> 'From a historical perspective, constitutive conventions tend to be under constant interpretive pressure, which is partly due to external needs and values of a changing world, and partly due to novel interpretations of those same values which are inherent in the practice. But this is always a slow, gradual, almost invisible process that takes place over time, and it results in changes of the conventions themselves.
>
> (Marmor, *Positive Law and Objective Values* at 53 (footnote omitted). See also A Marmor, *Interpretation and Legal Theory* (Hart Publishing, Oxford 2005) at 35)

36 'Legal theorists generally take for granted some version of the claim that the relation between law practices and the content of the law is reason based.' M Greenberg, 'How Facts Make Law (I)' in S. Hershovitz (ed.), *Exploring Law's Empire: The Jurisprudence of Ronald Dworkin* (Oxford University Press, Oxford 2006), hereafter Greenberg, 'How Facts Make Law I'.

37 See, for example, R Dworkin, *Law's Empire* (Hart Publishing, Oxford 1986); R Alexy, 'On the Concept and Nature of Law' (2008) 21 *Ratio Juris* 281, hereafter Alexy, 'On the Concept and Nature of Law'; Perry, 'The Varieties of Legal Positivism'. A variation of this approach is that legal judgment is a form of rational discourse which as such necessarily involves moral considerations given a necessary link between morality and ideals of practical reason, of which legal reasoning is an example. See R Alexy, *A Theory of Legal Argumentation* (Oxford University Press, Oxford 1989).

practices (positive law). According to Dworkin, values of political morality external to the existing positive law provide interpretive authority in relation to the articulation of legal demands by the courts. For Alexy, law is an instance of practical reasoning directed (necessarily) towards moral social objectives. Each of these perspectives may, with some qualification, contribute to a theoretically informed account of the role played by values in the Union order.

Greenberg

For Greenberg, to determine the applicable law in any given situation, which he terms 'legal content', it is necessary for legal institutions to rely upon evaluative judgements that cannot derive from existing positive law/legal practices. To extract legal content, 'value-facts' are needed to identify and assign a relative importance to the set of possible legal outcomes drawn from existing legal sources. Greenberg therefore confronts the (exclusive positivist) sources thesis, according to which legal content can *only* be identified by reference to social-fact criteria of legality, the 'pre-ordained' positive law. Greenberg explains his position as follows:

> [I] have argued that law practices cannot themselves determine the content of the law because they cannot unilaterally determine their own contribution to the content of the law. There must be factors, independent of practices, that favour some models over others.[38]

Value facts form the basis of a 'rational relation' between existing legal practices and legal content, they do not in any way determine the content of these practices (the pre-existing positive law):

> This chapter's argument for the conclusion that value facts play a role in determining legal content is that value facts are needed in order to determine the relevance of law practices to the legal content. The argument therefore supports only that role for value facts. There might, of course, be different argument that shows, say, that morality or some other value supplants the law practices (though of course almost no contemporary legal theorist, least of all one of my positivist targets, thinks that there is such an argument).[39]

38 Greenberg, 'How Facts Make Law I' at 253. MacCormick makes the related point that the values that must be considered in any legal determination (in determining legal content in Greenberg's terms) are 'those which the branch of law in question makes relevant'. N MacCormick, *Rhetoric and the Rule of Law* (Oxford University Press, Oxford 2005) at 114. The values that the 'branch' of European law 'makes relevant' are in my view, those referred to in Arts 2–6 TEU.

39 Greenberg, 'How Facts Make Law I' at 262. See also Peczenik and Wroblewski's suggestion that in order to eliminate fuzziness from legal language '[a] non-deductive step may be needed to derive a conclusion about the content of a non-written legal norm from the legal

The importance of Greenberg's argument for present purposes is that the claimed rational relationship between legal practices (existing standards of legality) and applicable legal content is *not* confined to questions of the moral value of alternative possible legal outcomes. As he notes, '[i]t is not that the goodness of a candidate legal proposition counts in favour of its truth. Rather, the role of value is in helping to determine *how* practices contribute to the content of the law.'[40]

Greenberg's thesis is therefore relevant to understanding the role of values within the Union order, values which concern the objective of European integration. Here, the rational relation between the determinants of legal content and legal content is dependent on value judgements relating to the achievement of the Treaty objectives. The 'value' of European integration based on achieving the objectives set out in the opening Articles of the Treaties forms a substantive factor in determining the legal content applicable in any given case.[41]

Dworkin

According to Dworkin's account of law as integrity, 'the function of law is principled adjudication'.[42] Judicial practices in formulating legal demands comprise the best interpretation of existing (prior) legal practices in light of the requirements of political morality. By comparison with judicial activities in the Union setting, Dworkin privileges the role of politico-moral values in the judicial formulation of legal outcomes. For Dworkin, it is the *best* interpretation of existing law or legal practices in light of values of political morality that determines legal outcomes. For the Court of Justice by contrast, legal outcomes comprise an interpretation of positive legal sources that best promotes the Treaty aims subject to compatibility with requirements of political morality. This is more akin to a de minimis requirement respecting the extent to which values of political morality are relevant to legal outcomes as opposed to an active seeking of their maximum possible expression.

Dworkin's analysis illustrates my contention that the precise role played by values in any given legal order will vary according to context as well as substance of underlying functions. In common with positivist accounts considered above, Dworkin takes statal legal order as the object of his inquiry. The dynamic role played by values of political morality he describes is relative to statal legal governance for which the overriding functional concern is to

sources'. A Peczenik and J Wroblewski, 'Fuzziness and Transformation: Towards Explaining Legal Reasoning' (1985) 51 *Theoria* 24 at 36–37.

40 Ibid. at 264, emphasis added.

41 For the various 'positive' sources of European Union law, see J Bengoetxea, *The Legal Reasoning of the European Court of Justice* (Clarendon Press, Oxford 1993) at 66ff, hereafter Bengoetxea, *The Legal Reasoning of the European Court of Justice.*

42 Perry, 'The Varieties of Legal Positivism' at 374 citing R. Dworkin, *Taking Rights Seriously* (Duckworth, London 1978) at 346–349.

provide a moral form of political governance to the degree that the existing positive law permits of interpretive variation.

The Court's interpretive approach to the Treaty objectives based upon their substantive content, as well as the institutional context in which the Union operates, implies a stronger role for values relating to European integration in the determination of legal outcomes. The Treaty objectives influence the (existing) law of the European Union as 'directing' values and must therefore be applied by both Union and domestic courts when applying Union law in a way that fosters an evolutionary dynamic directed to European integration.

Alexy

Alexy's dual characterisation of the concept of law suggests that the distinction between positivist and non-positivist approaches is of little conceptual significance.[43] According to Alexy, law comprises formal and dynamic/evaluative elements, which he terms factual and ideal dimensions:

> The basis of non-positivism defended here is the thesis that the single most essential feature of law is its dual nature. The thesis of the dual nature of law presupposes that there exist necessary properties of law belonging to its factual or real dimension, as well as necessary properties belonging to its ideal or critical dimension. Coercion is an essential feature found on the factual side, whereas the claim to correctness is constitutive of the ideal dimension.[44]

The claim to correctness[45] also links both dimensions which Alexy describes as law's procedural and substantive aspects:

43 The view that there is little of conceptual significance between positivism and non-positivism has gained currency amongst legal theorists associated with these schools. For example, Perry, commenting on an article by Coleman has noted that

> Two of my strongest reactions to reading Coleman's article are, first, I am far less certain than I have been in the past as to what the differences are between positivist and non-positivist jurisprudential views, and second, that I am far from certain that attempting to state a precise distinction between these two types of views is a theoretically worthwhile enterprise.
>
> (S Perry, 'Beyond the Distinction between Positivism and Non-Positivism' (2009) 22 *Ratio Juris* 311 at 312 commenting on J Coleman, 'Beyond Inclusive Positivism' (2009) 22 *Ratio Juris* 359)

44 R Alexy, 'On the Concept and Nature of Law' at 292.

45 Which reflects Raz's view that law's claimed authority is also a necessary or conceptual feature of legal order. However, where Raz derives from this feature the sources thesis according to which the rule setting out the criteria of legality as well as the criteria themselves must be identifiable conventional social practices, Alexy derives from law's claim to correctness a necessary connection between law and morality.

> the correctness thesis, if true, plays a central role not only with respect to the ideal or critical dimension of law but also with respect to its factual or real dimension. The reason for this is that moral correctness comprises formal or procedural as well as substantive or material correctness.[46]

The link between law's real or formal institutional dimension as a coercive practice and the claim to correctness concerns the fact that the existence of law as a formal system of social organisation is rationally required to address the complex needs of human societies and prevent civil disorder. As Alexy notes, 'morality demands a resolution of these problems in order to avoid the moral costs of anarchy'.[47] The link between law's ideal aspect and its claim to correctness is demonstrated for Alexy by means of a performative contradiction that arises if law claims to be a non-moral enterprise:

> An example of a performative contradiction is the fictitious first article of a constitution that reads: 'X is a sovereign, federal, and unjust republic.' It is scarcely possible to deny that this article is somehow absurd. The idea underlying the method of performative contradiction is to explain the absurdity as stemming from a contradiction between what is implicitly claimed in framing a constitution, namely that it is just, and what is explicitly declared, namely that it is unjust.[48]

For Alexy, the claim that moral concerns are necessarily implicated as a feature of legal demands cannot be explained on the basis of the exclusive positivist attributed (or conferred) powers thesis.[49] However, Alexy's

46 Ibid. at 293.

47 Ibid.

48 Ibid. at 294. See for similar arguments, MacCormick and Weinberger, *An Institutional Theory of Law* at 141.

49 The idea that legal demands may express moral or other evaluative considerations only when institutional powers have been conferred on the decisions-maker by a legal source, identifiable by social-fact criteria, to create law on this basis. Alexy confronts this view as follows:

> Let us imagine a case in which the authoritative material allows for two different interpretations. A single additional argument is available, which is a moral argument that cannot either be reduced or traced back to a source. The moral argument speaks in favour of the first interpretation, rejecting, then, the second interpretation. I think that non-positivists are in agreement here with positivists ... That is, we ought to adopt the first interpretation, backed by the correct moral argument, and not the morally mistaken second interpretation. Still, positivists and non-positivists disagree sharply on how to understand or interpret this. Positivists say that we have to interpret what takes place as a law-making act that transforms moral considerations into law on the basis of legal empowerment and legal empowerment alone. If this thesis were true ... then, if the judge chose the morally mistaken interpretation, he would nevertheless be making a legally perfect decision ... My rejoinder is that this decision would not be a legally perfect decision in all aspects. Due to the fact that the claim to correctness necessarily raised by law necessarily comprises an ideal dimension ... a judge who chose a morally mistaken interpretation in a case in which the positive law allows as well

non-positivist analysis proceeds from a view of law's underlying function that is remarkably similar to that of Raz who argues from an exclusive positivist stance. Both Alexy and Raz contend that law's claim to possess moral authority (correctness) is its central conceptual feature.[50] The underlying function of law that gives rise to this conceptual claim for Alexy, namely 'to avoid the moral costs of anarchy'[51] is paralleled by Raz's claim that the need for legal order derives, as previously noted, from the 'commonplace that social life requires and is facilitated by various patterns of forbearances, co-operation, and co-ordination between members of society or some of them'.[52]

Neither analysis captures the sense in which the Union legal order is only indirectly and weakly relevant to these social functions said to underlie the need for legal order. The primary function of the Union constitution, European integration, is both too strong and too weak to serve as an underlying rationalisation of legal order in terms commensurate with the need to maintain social order. It is too weak in the sense that, as noted above, the underlying functions of legal order identified by Alexy and Raz are neither necessary nor rationally required in the Union setting, these functions being served by domestic (statal) legal orders. It is too strong in the sense that the value of integration arguably extends law's underlying functions beyond these necessities of social life, towards the purely aspirational. The values underlying the Union order remain the result of rational political judgement amongst the Member States concerning the desirability of pursuing identified economic, social and political objectives by ceding partial governmental responsibilities to an independent institutional framework.

Conclusions

This brief sketch of positivist and non-positivist approaches illustrates both a lack of significant differences providing an appropriately flexible understanding of legal order is employed, as well as the need to develop these approaches to provide adequate theoretical understanding of the Union order. The features of the Union order unaccounted for by existing jurisprudential approaches, relate in two senses to a substantive disconnect between the func-

> for a morally correct interpretation would not be making a legally perfect decision. In such cases, moral incorrectness implies legal incorrectness.
>
> (Alexy, 'On the Concept and Nature of Law' at 296)

50 While Raz focuses on the necessary features of legal practices in order to be capable of making this claim, Alexy focuses upon the necessary implications of this claim by reference to a belief in the possibility of legal decisions in fact possessing moral features. For examination of these moral claims as analytic features of law, see J Gardner, 'How Law Claims, What Law Claims' in M Klatt (ed.), *Institutionalized Reason: The Jurisprudence of Robert Alexy* (Oxford University Press, Oxford 2012).

51 Alexy, 'On the Concept and Nature of Law' at 293.

52 Raz, *The Authority of Law* at 50.

tions or values attributed to legal order (generally within States) and those underlying the Union order relating to European integration.

First, the Union introduces a substantive 'third dimension' into legal theorising, preoccupied with the relationship of necessary functionalities of legal order to legal practices in the state setting. This dimension concerns an underlying rationalisation of law based upon positive aspirational political objectives relating to integration that operate alongside similar, but in this context secondary, functionalities associated with the legal orders of States.

A second distinguishing feature of the Union order that escapes theoretical attention concerns the fact that the Union legal order is jurisdictionally non-inclusive. The focus of analytic jurisprudential accounts typically rests upon the jurisdictionally inclusive legal orders of States. This raises an important question. Is there any justification for restricting theoretical accounts of legal order to the jurisdictionally inclusive orders (of States), excluding in the result the Union legal order? This question is considered in the following section.

Legal order and statal legal orders

In this section, I consider the focus in existing theoretical approaches upon statal orders, identifying the rationale underlying this focus and questioning whether as a result the Union order constitutes appropriate subject matter for analytic jurisprudential inquiry. MacCormick clearly believed so in noting that:

> The community of legal theorists throughout Europe has until very recently, and with but a few honourable exceptions, shown an astonishing lack of interest in the development of European law, in the specific sense of the law of the European Community (EC). Here we have not merely a new legal system, but maybe even a new kind of legal system, unfolding in our faces and all about us. Yet we have largely contrived to ignore it. We have remained, as it were, bewitched with the paradigm of the state and its law. We have greeted this origin of a species with the comfortable complacency of juristic pre-darwinians. Yet the challenge is surely one that goes to the roots of an ontology of law. Can we be sure of our views about the existence and essence of law and legal system if we do not take fresh stock of this new addition to the stock of legal orders? Have we been too deeply schooled in the institutions of state law to welcome novel interlopers into our juridical consciousness?[53]

53 N MacCormick, 'Risking Constitutional Collision in Europe' (1998) 18 *Oxford Journal of Legal Studies* 517 at 517. See also N MacCormick, *Questioning Sovereignty* (Oxford University Press, Oxford 1999) at 105, hereafter MacCormick, *Questioning Sovereignty*.

MacCormick's comments, written in 1998, remain valid.[54] All the major analytic theoretical schools situate questions concerning law's existence and operational features within the setting of statal legal orders,[55] an approach which in MacCormick's view 'has had serious distorting effects for legal theory'.[56] Possible reasons for this association are the following. First, statal legal governance is 'inclusive' in two critical senses. On the one hand, the social concerns capable of being addressed, regulated, sanctioned and enforced by the State through the medium of law are unlimited. Legal regulation can in principle address through regulation any social need, broadly defined. On the other hand, State legal orders are inclusive in the sense that they (claim to) express and uphold a set of values that relate to the deep moral and political concerns of the society in question.[57] Legal order is understood to actualise a people's 'total' political and moral identity.[58]

Apart from this dualistic of inclusiveness, a further feature of State legal orders of central importance to analytic accounts concerns the direct relationship between legal rules and the institutional and behavioural effects that these create. The rights and obligations placed upon individuals and public bodies by legal rules are created, applied and enforced by an integrated institutional framework, that of the State. Legal order is understood in this sense as the institutional expression of a direct and inclusive relationship between individuals and the governmental framework to which they are subject.

Public international law (PIL) frameworks, by contrast with the legal orders of States, while increasingly subject to reclassification and alleged 'constitutionalisation',[59] arguably do not possess these characteristics. Created to achieve defined and limited objectives, they do not provide an inclusive governmental jurisdiction in the manner of statal orders. In addition PIL norms do not generally provide directly applicable legal authority within the domestic setting unless incorporated as such.[60] This suggests that the key

54 Notwithstanding increasing awareness of philosophical issues raised by European Union law, the implications for 'pure' analytic jurisprudence have been largely ignored. See for a welcome development in this regard, J Dickson and P Eleftheriadis (eds), *Philosophical Foundations of European Union Law* (Oxford University Press, Oxford 2012).

55 See, for example, H Hart, *The Concept of Law* (2nd edn, Oxford University Press, Oxford 1994) at 17.

56 MacCormick, *Questioning Sovereignty* at 9.

57 So the public sphere represents a 'complete' identification of law and the individual.

58 I am not claiming here that in order to qualify as 'law' this actualisation must necessarily occur. For example, the values expressed in the constitution may on the one hand be forward-looking aspirations that have little chance of realisation in the near future or, as critical theorists have pointed out, law 'in action' may subvert those ideals to inequalities of economic, political and social power.

59 See C de Burca and J H H Weiler (eds), *The Worlds of European Constitutionalism* (Cambridge University Press, Cambridge 2012).

60 Either by a general clause within the constitution recognising all international legal instruments to which the State is a party (a monist approach), or in virtue of legislative acts recognising the domestic legal authority of individual public international law Treaties (a dualist approach).

features of legal order taken as the focus of analytic jurisprudential inquiry are only partially represented, if at all, in the international law setting.[61]

What then of the Union legal order? Clearly the Union is not inclusive either in terms of its regulatory jurisdiction, or in relation to the 'corresponding' jurisdiction of the Union constitution, the Treaty Articles and general principles. However, and notwithstanding that these questions are ultimately matters of degree, the Union constitutes an independent regulatory regime, directly upheld and enforced by the public institutional activities of the Member States. The overriding concern of legal theory, to explain the relationship between law, individuals and the public sphere, therefore implicates the Union legal order as a subject for analysis.[62] Existing positivist and non-positivist analytic jurisprudential models are premised, as noted, on the identification of legal order with an inclusive jurisdiction directly regulating communal social existence. The challenge posed by the Union order then is to account for a non-inclusive yet directly applicable legal order,[63] whose limited jurisdiction is linked to the promotion of specific (economic social or political) objectives as constitutional values/functions.[64]

Conclusions

An overview of existing positivist and non-positivist analytic jurisprudential accounts highlights their inability to account for jurisdictionally limited legal orders that, while possessing directly applicable governmental authority, are based on the achievement of specific social, economic or political objectives.[65]

61 In Chapter 7 I explore the possibility of understanding the Union as a developed form of international legal order, illustrating that the distinctions I have drawn here are relative, not absolute.

62 For example, Lamont's definition would clearly include the Union legal order:

> Law itself may be defined as 'A system of juridical rules, constituting norms of behaviour for the persons who have directly or indirectly participated in their creation, and directing action or forbearance for the promotion and protection of private and public conceptions of the good'.
>
> (W D Lamont, *The Value Judgement* (Philosophical Library Inc., New York 1955) at 305)

63 Whose legal claims are superimposed over the existing legal frameworks of the Member States.

64 A limited legal jurisdiction may also be 'neutral', for example within a federal division of powers. Here the constitution remains the exclusive preserve of the federal level of governance while delegated powers of legal regulation to the constituent States relate to technical areas that remain subordinate to the values affirmed by the constitution. By contrast, the limited powers conferred under the Union Treaties relate to a project positively directed towards European integration. The directed character of the Union legal order is linked in an obvious sense to its 'conferred' and hence limited legal jurisdiction. In a less obvious sense, the values underlying the Union order are themselves a positive constitutional expression of the project of integration.

65 In practice, this commitment may vary depending on institutional design and assigned jurisdictional authority as well as the ability of the objectives in question to dynamically influence legal demands.

The Union legal order highlights a need to go beyond existing theoretical paradigms while retaining insights from both positivist and non-positivist schools. The aim, a theoretical model able to account for the range of possibilities afforded by legal order, clearly addresses a need where individual orders, the European Union being the outstanding example, possess features as yet under or un-theorised within existing approaches. This does not imply a complete break with existing models but rather their qualified development, a task undertaken in the next chapter.

3 Institutional perspectives on the legal order of the European Union

Introduction

The previous chapter focused on how different analytic jurisprudential approaches may inform understanding of the distinctive features of the law and legal practices of the European Union. I highlighted two key features of the Union order that cannot be adequately understood within the context of existing theoretical models. The first concerned the fact that the Union Treaties represent an object-specific constitution insofar as they extend beyond generalised concerns of political morality and relate instead to the political 'project' of European integration within a limited jurisdictional sphere designed for that purpose. The second related feature concerns the flexible, dynamic role played by the foundational values of the Treaties within the practices of the Court of Justice in determining Union law demands.

To meet these challenges for analytic inquiry posed by the Union legal order, in this chapter I build upon arguments in the previous chapter relating to the context-specific and variable role of values underlying all legal orders. To do so, I draw upon an institutional theoretical approach capable of rationalising the wider possibilities of legal order implicit in this account, an approach defended by MacCormick and Weinberger.[1] Drawing upon positivist and non-positivist insights, this model emphasises both the dynamic and flexible institutional expression of values as underlying features of all legal orders while allowing for the possibility of particular social, economic or political objectives as the core functional concerns underlying a given order, for example European integration in the Union setting.

The chapter is set out as follows. In the first section, I consider the key claims of institutionalist theoretical approaches to law. I then apply this understanding to the Union legal order, drawing on the notion of a fuzzy rule of recognition developed by Peczenik and Wroblewski to rationalise the creation and application of Union legal demands in light of the Treaty objectives.

1 N MacCormick and O Weinberger, *An Institutional Theory of Law* (D Reidel Publishing Company, Dordrecht 1986), hereafter MacCormick and Weinberger, *An Institutional Theory of Law*.

In the final sections I consider the implications of the preceding analysis for understanding the authority of Union legal demands within Member States.

Institutional Theoretical Approaches

In the last chapter, I observed that although the relationship of law and values is the subject of a number of apparently irreconcilable theoretical claims, all accounts recognise certain features of legal order. These concern law as a directing social activity that involves the public creation, application and interpretation of public normative standards according to conventionally constituted institutional practices. For institutional theorists such as MacCormick and Weinberger, 'law as institutional fact' is a key theoretical claim. However, 'institutional' practices, in the sense of those social activities to which we attribute legal properties, are also necessary features of positivist and non-positivist theoretical accounts of law and therefore reconcile positivist and non-positivist insights. What then are the defining features of institutionalist accounts?

Within all stable, effectively functioning, modern societies, the creation, interpretation and application of legal standards relies on the ability of institutions to provide a framework for action within which regulative ideals of political morality can be authoritatively expressed. In this regard, institutional practices represent both the factual (formal) basis of legal practices as well as their interpretive character in light of a body of values or functions. MacCormick explains 'institutional' by contrast with 'brute' facts as follows:

> 'Institutional facts' are ... those facts that depend not only on some physical events and occurrences which are supposed to have taken place, but also on an interpretation of these (and/or other) events or occurrences in terms of some stable set of norms (either institutional or conventional norms) of conduct or of discourse.[2]

Uncovering these dual features where law is concerned is the aim of analytic jurisprudence which MacCormick describes as follows:

> The rational reconstruction of the legal system ... [which] must be developed so as to reveal the complex structures which are necessary for understanding the existence of positive legal principles and the teleological underpinning of the legal system.[3]

2 N MacCormick, *Rhetoric and the Rule of Law, a Theory of Legal Reasoning* (Oxford University Press, Oxford 2005) at 65, hereafter MacCormick, *Rhetoric and the Rule of Law*.

3 MacCormick and Weinberger, *An Institutional Theory of Law* at 119. Weinberger and MacCormick describe their positions as 'weak positivism' and 'post-positivism' respectively. O Weinberger, 'Institutionalist Theories of Law' in P Amselek and N MacCormick (eds), *Controversies About Law's Ontology* (Edinburgh University Press, Edinburgh 1991), hereafter Weinberger, 'Institutionalist Theories of Law' at 50; MacCormick, *Rhetoric and the Rule of Law* at 2.

Law as institutional fact then comprises a positive social practice that expresses underlying normative concerns. For Weinberger, this normative core is a directing idea which stands at the heart of all institutional forms:

> It is a main thesis of institutionalism that the basis of institutions is an *idée directrice*, that is, an idea with a 'task of realisation'. This idea ... is the nucleus around which the institutions crystallise ... The *idée directrice* evokes human action and cooperation in institutions. The idea with its 'task of realisation' is also the intellectual centre which facilitates the identification of people with the institution.[4]

Where statal legal orders are concerned, the 'directing idea' will generally refer to concerns of political morality contained in the written constitution as an ideal expression of a society's moral, political and social convictions. These foundational value concerns will necessarily inform all legal outcomes given that, as noted by MacCormick,

> too much is at stake when laws are being applied in real life to make acceptable any flatly formalistic approach to law-application. Regard must always be had to consequentialist considerations, and to overarching moral concerns.[5]

My contention in this work is that the overarching value concerns of political morality typically found within domestic constitutions, while both necessary (and sufficient) to form the basis of legal order, do not restrict the possibilities in this regard. 'Constitutional' values may additionally include directing ideals in the form of specific political, social or economic objectives, subject to their compatibility with general concerns of political morality.

At the heart of institutional theoretical approaches is the recognition that law comprises positive, conventional social practices, expressive of underlying value concerns.[6] Emphasising the underlying normative concerns of legal order, institutionalist approaches recognise the link between the values

4 Weinberger, 'Institututionalist Theories of Law' at 44.

5 MacCormick, *Rhetoric and the Rule of Law* at 252. Weinberger defends a normative or neo-institutional, as opposed to classical institutional, perspective, noting that:

> Any cooperation, any collectivity of humans, is possible only on the basis of rules of competence and rules of conduct. That is why anti-normativism and the belief of classical institutionalism that institutions exist by themselves and independently of norms are not acceptable. Practical information (and especially norms) are not epiphenomena of institutions, but on the contrary, constitutive elements of each institution.
>
> (Ibid. at 46)

6 So for Weinberger, '[n]eo-institutionalism is an analytical theory of law with a normativist basis. This means that it conceptualises law as a dynamic system of norms'. Weinberger, 'Institutionalist Theories of Law' at 49.

underlying legal order,[7] the wider (non-legal) social concerns they serve and the active expression of these values through legal practices, a point expressed by MacCormick as follows, '[n]ow, however, it seems to me that the whole enterprise of explicating and expounding criteria and forms of good legal reasoning has to be in the context of fundamental values that we impute to legal order'.[8]

Institutionalist theoretical approaches therefore raise the possibility of incorporating and reconciling a range of positivist and non-positivist theoretical insights in relation to the institutional expression of underlying values that form the normative core of legal order. How do these observations assist in theorising the Union legal order?

An institutional account of the Union legal order

An institutionalist understanding of legal order suggests that the functional 'political' tasks assigned under the Treaties may operate as foundational values and hence directing influences over all Union legal demands. These objectives, relating to the achievement of the single market and associated social rights, represent the core functional concerns of the Union under the overarching ideal of European integration.[9]

The relevance and explanatory merit of an institutional theoretical account of the Union order lies in the ability to explain how underlying value concerns of legal order operate *contextually*, that is, in a relatively static or dynamic manner in relation to practices of law creation, application and interpretation. This allows theoretical purchase on those under-theorised features of the Union order identified in the last chapter which, to recap, were the Union's non-inclusive jurisdiction and the achievement of specific political, economic and social objectives as foundational value concerns of this jurisdiction. An institutional approach is therefore able to account for the fact that the foundational values of the Union order relate collectively to an ideal of European integration as weak constitutional aspirations deriving from the existing constitutional settlements of the Member States. This weakness derives from the fact that a failure to realise 'integration' in any given legal outcome would not provoke constitutional crisis or the breakdown of legal order. In a positive sense, the ideal of integration operates as a foundational legal principle, and contested political objective, giving rise to weak, yet politically and constitutionally significant, interpretive legal effects, as opposed to directly enforceable rights or obligations.

An institutional account is capable of accounting for these features of the Union order, contextualising Union law and legal practices within the

7 Usually expressed within a written constitution.

8 MacCormick, *Rhetoric and the Rule of Law* at 1.

9 Article 5 TFEU.

political, legal, economic, cultural environment in which they occur.[10] This environment includes crucially the Member States governmental branches as well as the terms of the Treaties themselves as a constitutional document.[11] This distinctive combination of factors, a challenging institutional context and an underlying function based on the achievement of specific, politically controversial objectives, suggests a degree of uncertainty in the identification of Union legal demands not present in statal settings. The possibility of uncertain criteria of legal validity expressed in the rule of recognition is considered by Peczenik and Wroblewski in their analysis of 'fuzziness' in law. Their analysis provides a useful framework from which to consider the rule of recognition in the Union setting.[12]

Fuzzy rules of recognition

Peczenik and Wroblewski contend that language in general can be hard, soft or fuzzy.[13] Classification of the type of language used in any given instance relates to the question whether

> some element of reality belongs to the linguistic class of references of a name or description (x belongs to A) to its negation, (x does not belong to A). [para] In a hard language, for every x one accepts the thesis that either x belongs to A or it is false that x belongs to A. (1) [para] In a soft language, the thesis (1) is negated, i.e. for every x it is not true that either x belongs to A or it is false that x belongs to A. (2) [para] In a fuzzy language, for some x the thesis (1) is true, and for some x the thesis (2) is true.[14]

They then apply the notion of fuzziness of language to ideas of legal system and legal validity, linking different conceptions of legal system with corresponding (hard, soft or fuzzy) criteria of legal validity (rules of recognition).[15]

Peczenik and Wroblewski identify the various conceptions of legal system as follows:

10 Such a broad range of contextual factors is implicated by the revolutionary objective of an integrated Europe.

11 Paragraph 21 of the Court's Opinion 1/91 on the Draft Agreement between the (then) Community and countries of the European Free Trade Association (EFTA) to create a European Economic Area (EEA).

12 A Peczenik and J Wroblewski, 'Fuzziness and Transformation: Towards Explaining Legal Reasoning' (1985) 51 *Theoria* 24, hereafter Peczenik and J Wroblewski, 'Fuzziness and Transformation'.

13 Ibid. at 25.

14 Ibid. I have stated the mathematical formulation in written English instead of reproducing the mathematical notations used in the original text. I have also omitted the mathematical formulations in the second part of the paragraph which simply reproduce the written points.

15 'There are several conceptions of a legal system, linked with corresponding conceptions of validity.' Ibid. at 27.

> Firstly. A legal system consists of enacted rules (LSLE) ... The enacted rules are identified by proper procedures ... Secondly, a legal system includes inferred formal consequences of enacted rules (LSFC) ... thirdly, a legal system contains not only formal consequences but also interpretive consequences of enacted rules i.e. rules constructed by legal interpretation (LSIC) ... fourthly, a legal system includes also the so-called individual legal norms, i.e. decisions of concrete cases, forming operative law (LSOL) ... Fifthly, there are theories according to which a legal system includes 'principles, policies and other standards', referred to in general legal rules, used in legal decisions, or derived via creative moral reasoning from 'legislative history' together with 'the sense of appropriateness (LSPP)'.[16]

These different conceptions of 'legal system' are not mutually incompatible forms of legal ordering; any given legal order may include various manifestations of legal system and hence associated criteria of legal validity. Each conception of legal validity gives rise to 'hard', 'soft' or 'fuzzy' rules of recognition, or a combination thereof. Peczenik and Wroblewski consider that a fuzzy rule of recognition exists in relation to the LSIC and LSPP conceptions of legal validity which relate to the interpretive consequences of enacted rules and the legal influences of principles or policies.[17] In relation to the identification of legal requirements deriving from fuzzy rules of recognition generally, an active interpretive exercise in light of some other relevant value(s) or principle(s) is required to identify the applicable law.

Interpretive intervention by the decision maker, which Peczenik and Wroblewski describe as 'non-deductive steps', operates to transform the 'fuzzy' law, relating to both the criteria of validity (rules of recognition)

16 Ibid.

17 Peczenik and Wroblewski consider the LSOL conception ('individual legal norms, i.e. decisions of concrete cases forming operative law,' ibid. at 27), corresponding to a soft rule of recognition, to be irrelevant as

> Soft rules of recognition do not determine criteria of validity, leaving them for concrete decisions of decision-makers using the norms. This is an extreme case which can only be accepted in some forms of the decisionism closely connected with the extreme Legal Realism mentioned above ...
>
> (Ibid. at 30)

They characterise the LSFC, which is formally deductively inferred consequences of duly enacted rules, as 'by definition based on hard criteria determined by the applied formal logic'. Ibid. at 30. In relation to the conception of a legal system as a body of duly enacted norms (LSLE), they note while this 'is based, in principle, on a hard rule of recognition because the enactment, derogation and logical consistency are defined in a hard manner. There is however an exception concerning inconsistencies and collision norms.' Ibid at 30. In addition, they acknowledge that where fuzziness of language exists in relation to individual legal rules, '[t]he decision maker uses directives of interpretation as instruments to eliminate the fuzziness of legal language'. Ibid. at 33.

and individual legal rules, into legal outcomes in any given instance of law application:

> To eliminate the indecidability, resulting from fuzziness of legal validity and legal rules, one must change the (fuzzy) valid law, not merely deductively infer its formal consequences. Had logical deduction been sufficient to eliminate 'indecidability' due to 'fuzziness' then both the 'indecidability' and the 'fuzziness' would by definition be apparent only, not real.[18]

The changes to 'fuzzy' law that Peczenik and Wroblewski describe will occur within legal reasoning by reference to some other values or principles to justify the actual decision reached. The question for our purposes is: how does the idea of fuzzy rules of recognition and the associated role of values in relation to legal outcomes play out in the Union setting?

Fuzziness as a feature of legal validity in the Union legal order

As noted, the existence of a fuzzy rule of recognition will require that the existing (uncertain) law is altered to produce applicable (certain) legal outcomes. In this regard, Peczenik and Wroblewski note in relation to legal orders generally that:

> The fuzziness of the law and the precise role of evaluation in legal interpretation cause the fact that modern legal systems contain an unusually large number of transformations ... Legal reasoning contains many transformations because the law is fuzzy. Many linguistic and social factors cause the fuzziness. Both the fuzziness and the transformations are adapted to the role of evaluations in the law.[19]

The contention that '[l]egal reasoning contains many transformations because the law is fuzzy' parallels my claim that all legal orders possess foundational functional or evaluative concerns that dynamically influence the entirety of stated legal demands. Clearly such a conception of legal validity is fuzzy in character with clear links to the two conceptions of legal system Peczenik and Wroblewski describe as giving rise to a fuzzy rule of recognition, namely the interpreted consequences of formally enacted rules and the legal influences of principles and practices. Moreover, the linguistic and social factors that Peczenik and Wroblewski affirm broadly reflect my contention that the scale and force of the dynamic effects of underlying value concerns will vary depending on contextual institutional factors as well as the substance of these concerns.

The context and substance of the values underlying the Union legal order suggest a rule of recognition whose degree of fuzziness is significantly higher than those found in statal legal settings. While the Union undoubtedly

18 Ibid. at 35.
19 Ibid. at 38.

provides 'hard' criteria of legal validity in relation, for example, to the conditions for legislative enactment,[20] the dominant conceptions of validity relate to the need to secure the Treaty objectives as well as the institutional acceptability of Union demands to Member States. These conceptions of legal validity, deriving from the institutional location of all Union legal demands as well as the nature of the Treaties as a governing legal instrument, represent a strong dynamic element within the Court's legal reasoning that extends beyond that typically associated with statal legal orders.

Conclusions: the role of the Court of Justice

The fuzziness of the rule of recognition employed by the Court of Justice is implicated *whenever* Union legal determinations impact upon Member State legal orders. The dynamic character of the Treaties has enabled the development of 'evolutionary' as opposed to merely uncertain criteria of legal validity in relation to all Union legal requirements expressive of the supremacy and direct effect doctrines.[21] Even where the 'pedigree' of binding rules of Union law is unimpeachable, doubts as to legal effects will always be present in light of their status as hierarchically supreme rules that may also give rise to directly enforceable rights within domestic settings.

As noted, several factors have contributed to the high degree of fuzziness of the criteria of legal validity relating to Union legal demands. First, an activist interpretive approach is implicit in the framework of the Treaties. Second, the Court must exhibit sensitivity to the institutional relationship between the Union and Member State orders in light of the constitutional implications of its judgments deriving from the operation of the supremacy doctrine. Finally, uncertainty regarding the precise scope of 'conferred' areas of Union competence creates corresponding legal uncertainty in the relationship between Union and Member State orders.[22] Taking these factors as a whole, the following comment by Mann is instructive:

> The judicial function … cannot be fully explained or properly distinguished in terms of determinate norms or reasoned principles. The purely formal criteria of those theories offer no insight into *either* the creative process of legal development through judicial decision *or* the responsible limits of that process. And yet, where the question in dispute goes to the very heart of a constitutional order, precisely these two matters are of vital importance.[23]

20 Article 294 TFEU.

21 For an account of the evolutionary character of Union legal demands from a systems-theoretical perspective, see M Amstutz, 'Marleasing and the Emergence of Interlegality in Legal Reasoning' (2005) 11 *European Law Journal* 766.

22 This issue is considered in Chapter 4.

23 C Mann, *The Function of Judicial Decision in European Economic Integration* (Martinus Nijhoff, The Hague 1972) at 168.

Every decision by the Court of Justice represents a reasoned expression of Union law demands stated in light of the supremacy doctrine and so 'goes to the heart of' the constitutional relationship between Union and Member State orders. Similar considerations apply regarding the doctrine of direct effect; all directly effective rights are assured under the supremacy requirement and will override any conflicting domestic legal demands, including those contained within the constitution.

The high degree of fuzziness of the Union rule of recognition reflects the Court's institutional role, to advance the project of European Union while affirming a European identity-through-law.[24] This raises a question concerning the authority or legitimacy of Union legal demands as a form of 'directly applicable' public institutional control by Member States. The lack of a direct democratic mandate for Union legal authority would appear to militate in principle against a rule of recognition possessing a high degree of fuzziness given the constitutional implications for Member States this entails. Indeed, legal practices associated with a high degree of fuzziness would intuitively relate to a polity in which a high degree of consensus was also present in relation to the political and constitutional shifts that such a rule might entail. Given the clear absence of such consensus within the wider institutional and socio-cultural environment of the Union jurisdiction – Union law developments are perennially contested in the legal and political arenas of most Member States – on what basis can we understand the authority of the Union legal order? This question is considered in the final section of the chapter.

The authority of Union law

The Union is not a natural evolution of existing cultural, social or political affiliations amongst the Member States but rather a creation of their governmental branches. In addition, processes of Treaty amendment or the creation of new Treaties, as well as the exercise of Union law-making powers are subject to ongoing concerns regarding an alleged democratic deficit. In this regard, Allott has commented that:

> At the heart of the system remains the fantasy of the Diplomatic General Will, the idea that the controllers of the public realms of the Member States are able to represent the totality of the national interests of the participating peoples, and hence that the public interest of the EU – which is expressed in the law of the EU – is nothing more than the aggregate of the public interests of the Member States, mediated through the collective willing of the public-realm controllers. The underlying supposition is that the infinitely complex and intense social phenomenon known as *politics*, which is at the heart of the process of will-formation in

24 J Přibáň, 'The Juridification of European Identity, its Limitations and the Search of EU Democratic Politics' (2009) 16 *Constellations* 44.

> a democracy, can be transmuted and subsumed in a bargaining process among the controllers of the respective public realms, spuriously legitimated by mobilising the ante hoc or post hoc consent of this or that institution within the Member States.[25]

Given this relative lack of democratic legitimation, either in the creation of the original communities or subsequent Treaty developments, or in relation to Union law-making powers, how can the authority or legitimacy of Union laws be understood? This question is in a sense self-answering: in an important sense this authority is based upon the *fact* that Union laws are followed by public and private actors within the Member States as operative features of their respective public realms. By this I mean that the authority of Union law is most adequately understood in terms of its successful incorporation within and affiliation to existing institutional settlements, namely those of the Member States.[26]

In light of the above, an Austinian perspective linking the authority of legal rules to the fact of obedience by those subject to legal demands offers an appropriate rationalisation of the authority of Union law.[27] Coleman has recently defended Austin's thesis, arguing that the fact of obedience constitutes a convergent social practice which as such is authority conferring.[28]

Coleman explains the authority-conferring quality of convergent practices as follows:

> Acceptance from an internal point of view is expressed through the behaviour of appealing to the rule as a grounds of criticism and justification. This amounts to the view that what makes a norm reason-giving is the fact that the majority of individuals treat it as such. In other words, the rule itself does not create a reason for acting: rather, the fact that the majority of the population treats it as reason-giving makes it so.[29]

25 P Allott, 'The Crisis of European Constitutionalism: Reflections on the Revolution in Europe' (1997) 34 *Common Market Law Review* 439 at 477, hereafter Allott, 'The Crisis of European Constitutionalism'.

26 I am assuming here that Member States' legal orders in fact possess authority; my intention is not to address the wider question of the authority of law but rather to consider the most adequate understanding of the authority of Union law.

27 J Austin, *The Province of Jurisprudence Determined* and *The Uses of the Study of Jurisprudence* (Hackett Publishing Company Inc., Indianapolis 1998).

28 J Coleman, 'Authority and Reason' in R P George (ed.), *The Autonomy of Law* (Oxford University Press, Oxford 1996) 287. Hereafter Coleman, 'Authority and Reason'. Coleman challenges Hart's argument that it is the internal attitudes of officials or citizens that transform what would otherwise be a convergent social practice into one that is authority conferring, noting, '[e]ither convergent practices can be reason-giving or they cannot be. If they can be, there is no need to introduce the internal point of view. If they cannot be, then the internal point of view cannot help matters.' Ibid. at 299; H Hart, *The Concept of Law* (2nd edn, Oxford University Press, Oxford 1994), Chapter 5.

29 Ibid. (erroneous spelling of 'grounds' in original).

Coleman offers two arguments to support the conclusion that a convergent practice of obedience amongst social actors should make a rule reason giving. First, using the example of the traffic law that (in most countries) everyone must drive on the right hand side of the road, he notes that:

> On the assumption that I am self-interested, the fact that everyone drives on the right side of the road gives me a reason for doing the same thing. In general, my interests often require me to coordinate my behaviour with others, and when they do, I can have a reason to do what others do simply because they do what they do.[30]

Coleman also offers a moral justification for the reason giving or authoritative quality of convergent practices:

> Suppose that I am motivated to do the right thing, but am uncertain about what morality requires of me. If I believe that others are similarly motivated, then I have a reason to do what they are doing. It is not because in doing so I coordinate with others; rather, given certain natural assumptions, in following their lead, I am more likely to be doing what I ought to do, that is, the right thing.[31]

Coleman's remarks demonstrate that the fact of compliance with Union demands by the majority of public and private (Union and Member State) actors as incorporated aspects of domestic public spheres underlies their authoritative character.[32]

In short, Union legal demands arguably generate obedience and hence derive authority as a result of their successful expression within domestic institutional frameworks, frameworks that express the 'constitutional psyche' of the Member States.[33] The lack of a corresponding constitutional allegiance

30 Ibid. at 301.

31 Ibid. This argument breaks down in the case of wholly corrupted States such as Nazi Germany where a significant proportion of the populace have been induced to act in an immoral fashion by State coercion or as a result of ideological indoctrination.

32 Ernst-Joachim Mestmäcker, 'On the Legitimacy of European Law' (1994) 58 *Rabels Zeitschrift für ausländisches und internationales Privatrecht* 615.

33 A phrase borrowed from Allott, 'The Crisis of European Constitutionalism' at 475. Allott is highly critical of the claim of European States to be the bearer of the European peoples' constitutional authority and voice, posing and replying to the following rhetorical question:

> How is it that European mind has produced the European Union that we know, a misbegotten and anachronistic product of interstatal Europe, of one uncharacteristic phase of European history, standing in the way of a true European re-unifying, of another self-surpassing achievement of the great and ancient tradition of Europe's unity-in-diversity? What we find is that the European Union is a product of a particular developmental process in the most dynamic European societies, a process which enabled the *State* (in its internal sense) to acquire an ideal, real and legal hegemony over the other totalizing complexes of society (especially *society* and *nation* and *economy*) and to acquire an external hegemony over

to 'Europe' by the Member States' citizenry, however, suggests a form of legal authority existentially derived from the ability of law to parasitise existing constitutional allegiances.

Conclusions

In this chapter I have defended a normative institutional perspective to explain the Union legal order, emphasising the dynamic role of underlying value concerns within positive institutional practices relating to law creation, application and interpretation.[34] I have suggested that values may exert varying degrees of influence over the formulation of legal outcomes depending on a number of factors, including their substantive content as well as the wider institutional context in which a given legal order operates.[35] The ideal of European integration underlain by 'hard' legal rights in the economic freedoms and other areas of Union legislative competence forms the central directing idea or *idée directrice* of the Court's institutional practices. The Court's legal reasoning in seeking to promote the Treaty aims is also subject to a requirement of compatibility with 'rule of law' (human fundamental rights and due process) requirements in the general principles.[36]

The form of institutionalism defended emphasises a flexible view of legal order as a creative political force, whose underlying value concerns need not relate to an incumbent polity or prior cultural or political association. In the Union, historical links between a number of States have sufficed to produce a legal order whose underlying function is to foster a transnational

> all other transnational phenomena (the internal *State* externalized to become the *State* of all so-called international relations and international law).
>
> (Ibid. at 475)

See also P Allott, 'The European Community Is Not the True European Community' (1990–1991) 100 *Yale Law Journal* 2485.

34 In this respect I have assimilated the character of principles and values, drawing support from Alexy's suggestion that '[a]part from the fact that one operates in the deontological field (the realm of the ought) and the other in the axiological field (the realm of the Good), principles and values have basically the same conceptual structure'. R Alexy, *A Theory of Constitutional Rights* (Oxford University Press, Oxford 2002) at 93.

35 The values underlying legal order may include 'rule of law' concerns (typically found within domestic constitutions), broad political aspirations or specific economic or social objectives. The Union legal order provides examples of each of these possibilities. The Treaties affirm: (1) the political ideal of European integration, (2) rule of law values as general principles and (3) the practical objectives of achieving a single economic market supported by associated social rights and necessary economic regulatory harmonisation.

36 Union fundamental rights also derive from the Charter of Fundamental Rights recognised as having the same legal status as the Treaties under Article 6(1) TEU. The constitutional role of the general principles can be contrasted with that of constitutional standards in the domestic setting both in relation to their jurisdictional reach which is limited to those matters covered by the Treaties, and their relatively weak symbolic role in relation to the self-identification of a European polity. These issues are considered in more detail in Chapter 5.

constitutional polity. In this regard, Weinberger's comment that '[j]urists ought to understand their activity as a political duty, a job of political engineering'[37] is relevant. The Union legal order as a project in European integration is an example of political engineering par excellence, superimposed over existing political and legal settlements. In the following chapter I consider how the project is expressed within the practices of the Court of Justice.

37 Weinberger, 'Institutionalist Theories of Law' at 50.

4 The Court of Justice

Introduction

In this chapter I consider the institutional role of the Court of Justice. The Court is the authoritative voice of a legal jurisdiction, limited in scope according to the terms of the Treaties yet based on the achievement of a specific political vision. Union legal demands, directed towards European integration, are incorporated within Member States orders as independent sources of legal authority claiming supreme status[1] over all laws of domestic origin.[2]

1 I have adopted a 'supremacy' as opposed to 'primacy' reading of the relationship between Union and domestic law, notwithstanding that for several writers, the term supremacy inaccurately portrays that relationship given the inability of Union laws to deny all legal effect to incompatible rules of domestic law as well as to challenge the legal validity of domestic constitutional norms. Joined Cases C-10–22/97 *Ministero delle Finanze v I.N.C.O.G.E'90* [1998] ECR I-630. The primacy reading has also been defended on the basis that it does not represent an expression of the foundational relationship between orders but only describes outcomes when a substantive conflict arises between Union and domestic law requirements. See for a UK judicial pronouncement to this effect, *Thoburn v Sunderland City Council* [2002] EWHC 195 at paragraph 69 of the judgment. For defence of the primacy reading, see M Avbelj, 'Supremacy or Primacy of EU Law – (Why) Does It Matter?' (2011) 17 *European Law Journal* 744; O Spiermann, 'The Other Side of the Story: An Unpopular Essay on the Making of the European Community Legal Order' (1999) 10 *European Journal of International Law* 763; K Lenaerts and T Corthaut, 'Of Birds and Hedges: The Role of Primacy in Invoking Norms of EU Law' (2006) 31 *European Law Review* 287; B de Witte 'The European Union as an International Legal Experiment' in C de Burca and J H H Weiler (eds), *The Worlds of European Constitutionalism* (Cambridge University Press, Cambridge 2012). In this work I have used the term supremacy as oppose to primacy to indicate that implicit in the primacy reading is the possibility that this relationship, read in light of the overall objectives of the Treaties, will evolve into a fully hierarchical relationship reminiscent of that between domestic constitutions and lower order domestic laws. The primacy reading, while perhaps accurately describing how the relationship between Union and domestic laws presently operates, fails to account for the evolution of this relationship since the time of the original Communities, as well as possible future developments.

2 For these reasons, the Union order is difficult to classify within existing paradigms of law. Those who focus on the alleged wide ranging scope and supreme character of Union legal governance consider this represents an emerging system of federal law. See, K Lenaerts, 'Constitutionalism and the Many Faces of Federalism' (1990) 38 *American Journal of Comparative Law* 205. For others, the limited authority conferred under Treaties represents a purely intergovernmental

The Court's role in expressing these unique features of the Union jurisdiction forms the subject matter of this chapter.

The Court of Justice was originally part of the institutional framework created to administer the European Coal and Steel Community, the forerunner to the European Economic Community, later renamed the European Community and subsequently the European Union.[3] Shapiro has highlighted that the Court's role was originally expected to be minor, adjudicating disputes between the (then) European Coal and Steel Community and the Member States. In fact the Court has evolved into a constitutional court for the European Union, overseeing a legal order that arguably rivals in scope and complexity those of the Member States. A number of features, attributed by the Treaties, have contributed to the Court's evolution as a major institutional player, described by Shapiro as follows:

> In choosing to adopt an institutional form with a long culturally determined repertoire, one must take the bitter with the sweet. The very attributed characteristics of legality, neutrality and independence, the very institutional strengths of low visibility, incremental, esoteric, epistemically defended, and precedent-driven decision-making that led to the instituting of a judicial conflict resolver for the ECSC entailed a potential for path-dependent consequences. That is, once created, the Court would be required to make new law and would be institutionally strong enough to do it.[4]

This institutional feature of the Court's role identified by Shapiro, that is the ability to create path dependent consequences relating, as I shall argue, to the

arrangement between sovereign States as 'directing' authorities. See references in P Pierson, 'Path to European Integration' in W Sandholtz and A S Sweet (eds), *European Integration and Supranational Governance* (Oxford University Press, New York 1998) at 33. For still others, the European Union represents a complex form of international legal order distinguished by its evolutionary character, a view defended in Chapter 8 of this work.

3 The European Coal and Steel Community (ECSC) was created by the Paris Treaty (signed on 18 April 1951 and entered into force on 23 July 1952 and expired on 23 July 2002). The European Atomic Authority and European Economic Community were added in 1957 by the Treaty of Rome (signed on 25 March 1957, entered into force 1 January 1958). The three Communities adopted the same institutional framework following the 1966 Merger Treaty. The European Economic Community (EEC) was renamed the European Community (EC) by the Maastricht Treaty (signed on 7 February 1992, entered into force on 1 November 1993), which also created the European Union (EU) and provided for separate, mainly intergovernmental procedures within the Community institutional framework for co-operation between Member States in areas outside the remit of EC law. Following amendments made by the Amsterdam (signed 2 October 1997, entered into force on 1 May 1999) and Nice (signed on 26 February 2001, entered into force on 1 February 2003). Treaties, the Lisbon Treaty (signed on 13 December 2007, entered into force 1 December 2009) collapsed the 'three pillar' system created by the Maastricht Treaty into a single European Union and European Union legal order.

4 M Shapiro, 'The European Court of Justice' in P Craig and G de Burca (eds), *The Evolution of EU Law* (Oxford University Press, Oxford 1999) at 328.

promotion of European integration, form the subject matter of this chapter. The chapter is set out as follows. In the first section, I consider the institutional role of courts within State legal jurisdictions before contrasting this role with that of the Court of Justice in giving effect to the Treaties. In the second section, I consider whether the features of the Court's role identified justify claims of undue activism.

Judicial institutional roles

To understand the institutional roles of domestic and Union courts respectively, it is helpful to reiterate the underlying value concerns of statal legal orders and the Union, as set out in domestic constitutions and the Union Treaties respectively.

(Member) State constitutions

In general, constitutional values or principles, as operative features of institutional practices of law creation, interpretation and application within States, serve as guiding political and moral ideals in relation to the governed social environment.[5] The constitution expresses the ultimate functions served by legal order, as well as society's self-understanding of these functions. I stressed in Chapter 2 that legal governance occurs within States, in a jurisdictionally inclusive sense; the constitution representing a set of regulative ideals that govern the overall functioning of the society concerned.

The Union Treaties

By contrast with the concern of domestic constitutions to ensure beneficial forms of social order in this inclusive sense, the Union Treaties are based on regulative ideals relating to the ideal of European integration. In the Union setting, it is the Treaty objectives and not generalised concerns of political morality found within domestic constitutions that comprise a foundational and programmatic source of legal authority in the sense highlighted by Barak: '[t]hese are the purposes that every legal text in the system must achieve, the

5 Here, Bengoetxea has noted that:

> As was pointed out above, no theory of law can ignore the role played by evaluative choices in the application and interpretation of the law, as well as in law making. The requirement of axiological acceptability can thus be incorporated into our model of operative validity.
>
> (J Bengoetxea, *The Legal Reasoning of the European Court of Justice* (Clarendon Press, Oxford 1993) at 56, hereafter, Bengoetxea, *The Legal Reasoning of the European Court of Justice*)

Bengoextea relates this requirement to how we understand legal order (legal system in his terminology): '[i]n my opinion the notion of "legal system" operates as a regulative ideal in the different stages of law: law creation, law interpretation, legal doctrine, application'. Ibid. at 57.

fundamental values – or the proper balance between them when they clash – that every text must express'.[6] Although Barak's comment is intended to apply to legal orders in the inclusive sense I have described in relation to States, he accurately conveys the sense in which the foundational objectives of the Union Treaties inform every legal demand presented by the Court. Turning then to the institutional roles of domestic courts and then the Court of Justice.

Domestic judicial practices

'Rule of law' legal order within States is generally characterised by institutional practices offering (procedural) certainty in the creation and application of legal standards, relative certainty in relation to the substance of legal demands and the maintenance of minimum fundamental rights protections. Underlying these requirements is the principle of separated governmental powers between the legislative, executive and judicial branches. The legislative arm addresses ongoing social and economic regulatory needs through legal enactments, while the executive 'executes' (puts into effect), using the resources of the State, regulatory schemes so enacted. Both legislative and executive practices will generally be subject to superior principles of law found in the constitution, governing the procedures and (in a largely negative sense) substance of legislative enactments.[7] The judicial branch provides authoritative determinations on the meaning and effects of all legal standards, including those found in the constitution. In this regard, supreme courts are engaged in reasoned value judgements expressive of the 'constituted' legal environment, and linked to the wider value concerns of the governed society.[8]

6 A Barak, *Purposive Interpretation in Law* (Princetown University Press, Princetown 2005) at 149 (footnote omitted), hereafter Barak, *Purposive Interpretation in Law*.

7 In relation to positive legislative duties imposed by the constitution, see S Bandes, 'The Negative Constitution: A Critique' (1989–1990) 88 *Michigan Law Review* 2271; D P Currie, 'Positive and Negative Constitutional Rights' (1986) 53 *University of Chicago Law Review* 864; M J Gerhardt, 'The Ripple Effects of *Slaughter-House*: A Critique of a Negative Rights View of the Constitution' (1990) 43 *Vanderbilt Law Review* 409.

8 Here, 'reasonableness' is not simply equated with deductive logic leading from applicable legal standard to legal outcome by means of a legal syllogism. As Barak notes, '[r]easonableness is a process of assessment. It is not a process of description. It is not a concept defined only by deductive logic. It is not purely rational.' A Barak, *The Judge in a Democracy* (Princeton University Press, Princeton 2006) at 68 citing N MacCormick, 'On Reasonableness' in C Perelman and R V Elst (eds), *Les Notions à contenu variable en droit* (Bruylant, Brussels 1985) at 131 and 136. See also Weinberger's comment that 'it is possible to argue rationally, even *de lege ferenda* but only relatively to particular axiological presuppositions'. O Weinberger, 'Institutionalist Theories of Law' in P Amselek and N MacCormick (eds), *Controversies About Law's Ontology* (Edinburgh University Press, Edinburgh 1991) at 50, hereafter, Weinberger, 'Institutionalist Theories of Law'.

Union judicial practices

While domestic judicial practices are generally a relatively benign expression of the values/principles set out in the constitution,[9] those of the Court of Justice, or domestic courts when applying laws with a Union connection, remain inherently contested, both symbolically and politically. This suggests that the Union's continued survival and development depend on the Court's ability to facilitate incorporation of the Treaty demands within Member States' legal orders.[10] A key institutional concern of the Court is therefore the acceptability of Union legal demands to domestic institutional actors. The Court's institutional role then expresses dual functions; to promote the overall objectives of the Union project while recognising the wider political and legal context within which Union laws take effect.[11] Considering each of these factors in turn.

The Court as promoter of the Treaty objectives

I argued in Chapters 2 and 3 that the foundational or constitutional values of legal order may include, in addition to rule of law concerns based on tenets of political morality, specific political, social or economic objectives.[12] Where the Union order is concerned, upholding rule of law principles is not the key functional concern, although compliance with due process and fundamental rights requirements is emphasized.[13] Instead, the single market and various social and economic policy objectives found in the Treaties form underlying aspirations relating to developing economic, social and political integration amongst the Member States.[14]

By contrast with domestic constitutions, the Treaty objectives represent both a limited and extended set of foundational value concerns. On the one hand, the limited jurisdiction of the Treaties lacks the quality of universality associated with domestic constitutions and is therefore incapable at present of

9 Although constitutional legal demands are rarely the subject of a complete consensus between the judiciary and the executive/legislative governmental branches. See in the UK context the *Belmarsh* judgment *A (FC) and Others (FC) (Appellants) v Secretary of State for the Home Department (Respondent)* [2004] UKHL 56.

10 And arguably less on the *existence* of conferred Union legislative or executive competencies in particular policy areas.

11 This conclusion is similar to that reached by Maduro when he says, '[t]he concrete interpretation to be given to legal rules is therefore a product of legal reasoning and of the institutional constraints and normative preferences that determine the role of courts in a given political community'. M P Maduro, 'Interpreting European Law: Judicial Adjudication in a Context of Constitutional Pluralism' (2007) 1 *European Journal of Legal Studies* 1 at 3.

12 Alongside other rule of law principles, for example, the requirement that institutions act within their allocated powers.

13 J Coppel and A O'Neil, 'The European Court of Justice: Taking Rights Seriously?' (1992) 12 *Legal Studies* 227.

14 Articles 1–3 TEU.

giving rise to an inclusive 'rule of law' legal order in the manner of domestic orders.[15] On the other, the Treaty objectives extend the concerns of political morality typically found within domestic constitutions, to include objectives relating to European integration. These objectives, set out in Articles 2 and 3 TEU,[16] constitute the 'normative core' of the Union order[17] and the Court, as the supreme judicial authority, seeks to maximise their expression through its legal judgments.

The Court as promoter of institutional stability between the Union and Member States

The Treaty objectives are based on a political vision that relates to no less than the supranational governance of the Member States as an 'integrated' Union. Developing this vision has relied upon the domestic 'constitutional' expression, under the supremacy doctrine, of Union regulatory inputs that would, as laws of domestic origin, be the subject of legislative intervention simpliciter. The Court has therefore required rhetorical expertise to ensure the incorporation of the Union's 'thin' yet significant constitutional mandate within the Member States in order to fulfil its institutional role to promote and develop the vision of the Treaties.

Lenaerts explains this feature of the Court's institutional role as follows:

> Knowing that the Community legal order and the national legal orders are closely intertwined and even interdependent in that the former can only function properly if the latter are willing to ensure the correct application of Community law, the Court of Justice and the CFI, when they are considering a particular case, will want to avoid 'going too far' and may therefore opt for a solution which is not necessarily the most ambitious, considered from the exclusive angle of Community law, but which has the advantage of being 'compatible' with the traditions of the Member States and of not hurting special sensitivities in certain Member States. The Community judge will thus try to establish 'the middle-line' which has the best chance of 'surviving' the relentless conflicts between the requirements of Community law and the interests of

15 This point is considered in Chapter 5.

16 The Court stated in an early judgment that Article 2 of the Treaty describes the task of the European Economic Community. The aims laid down in that provision are concerned with the existence and functioning of the Community; they are to be achieved through the establishment of the common market and the progressive approximation of the economic policies of Member States, which are also aims whose implementation is the essential object of the Treaty. Case 126/86 *Fernando Roberto Gimenez Zaera v Instituto Nacional de la Seguridad Social y Tesoreria General de la Seguridad Social* [1987] ECR 3697 at paragraph 10.

17 To recap, under the institutionalist account of legal order defended in Chapter 3, 'what is constitutive of any institution is practical information (norms, goals, values)'. Weinberger, 'Institutionalist Theories of Law' at 48. See also, N MacCormick, *Questioning Sovereignty* (Oxford University Press, Oxford 1999) at 128.

> national systems. In other words, he will seek a solution that does not risk encountering incomprehension or resistance in some Member States, which could undermine the effectiveness and the uniform application of Community law.[18]

In referring to the 'traditions' of the Member States, Lenaerts is indicating that the Court is primarily concerned to avoid disturbing domestic constitutional sensitivities as opposed to individual domestic regulatory demands except insofar as these have a bearing on issues of wider constitutional significance. The Court faces an ongoing potential for 'constitutional dissonance' between domestic institutional practices expressive of Union and domestic constitutional requirements respectively. This in turn underlies a need for a rhetorical, 'soft' style of legal reasoning within the Court's judgments, enabling the acceptance and development of Union legal demands, notwithstanding their political and constitutional significance within Member States.[19]

The legal reasoning of the Court

The Union under the constitution of the Treaties is dedicated to the achievement of a new social, economic and political settlement amongst the Member States. Driven by the medium of law, the Treaties represent an exercise in political engineering albeit one undertaken in a spirit of benevolence and firmly grounded in humanistic values. As a result, the Court's method of reasoning, according to an outstanding work written by Clarence Mann in the early 1970s, is focused upon the thematic concerns or topoi set out in the Treaties.[20] These concerns, for example non-discrimination in relation to the cross-border movement of economic goods, serve to orient the Court's reasoning towards achieving the underlying objectives of the Union. They may be understood as regulative objectives, directing the legal reasoning of the Court

18 K Lenaerts, 'Interlocking Legal Orders in the European Union and Comparative Law' (2003) 52 *International and Comparative Law Quarterly* 873 at 879–880, hereafter Lenaerts, 'Interlocking Legal Orders'.

19 C T Smith and T Fetzer, 'The Uncertain Limits of the European Court of Justice's Authority: Economic Freedom Versus Human Dignity' (2004) 10 *Columbia Journal of European Law* 445 at 470–471.

20 Mann draws parallels between his analysis of judicial reasoning and that of Alexander Bickel writing on the practices of the US Supreme Court. In *The Least Dangerous Branch*, Bickel stressed the counter-majoritan character of the legal authority of the Supreme Court which meant giving due regard to the (often) expedient decisions of the democratically elected executive and legislative branches. At the same time, decisions of the Court could not allow a total disregard within these branches of constitutional requirements. These principles had to be maintained as guiding standards for governmental practices. Bickel therefore regarded Supreme Court judgments as reasoned expressions of the Court's institutional role as the upholder of principle within governmental order that permits a wide discretionary authority to the democratically elected legislator. A Bickel, *The Least Dangerous Branch: The Supreme Court at the Bar of Politics* (The Bobbs-Merrill Company, Inc., Indianapolis, New York 1962).

towards a number of specified outcomes, notably the single market, each of which forms a building block of the project of European integration.[21]

Nowadays the range of topoi found with the Treaties are far more extensive than those present at the time of Mann's writing, a time when the European Coal and Steel Community and European Economic Community Treaties were in force. This does not alter the relevance of Mann's analysis, with the Court's judgments remaining rhetorically focused around a number of thematic or topical concerns, each contributing to the objective of European integration.

Both the key institutional concerns detailed above are addressed in practice by the Court's development of various categories of legal effect taken by Union laws over laws of domestic origin. The direct legality review and indirect (interpretive) effects of Union norms each represent differing degrees of intrusion within and over domestic legal orders. This has allowed the Court rhetorical license to adjudge and adjust the effects taken by Union laws in any given case, while progressively developing the reach of the Union's jurisdiction. For example, the doctrine of direct effect affirms the unqualified dominance of Union over domestic laws, representing an uncompromising assertion of Union legal authority. As a result, while clearly concerned to affirm and develop this doctrine as a key feature of Union legal demands, the Court has imposed strict conditions on when these effects may arise.[22] Legality review[23] and interpretive (indirect) effects,[24] of Union over domestic laws, owing to their softer, more discursive character, are presented as more expansively reasoned demands, allowing a greater degree of rhetorical

21 Mann comments in relation to the Court's interpretive approach towards the (now defunct) European Coal and Steel Treaty that:

> Such topoi as 'reasonableness,' 'common interest,' 'subvention,' and 'normal conditions of competition' became the rhetorical means for focussing judicial analysis in the ECSC on the problems of a common price system, orderly markets, special burdens and benefits to industry and a minimum degree of competition.
>
> (C Mann, *The Function of Judicial Decision in European Economic Integration* (Martinus Nijhoff, The Hague 1972) at 510, hereafter Mann, *The Function of Judicial Decision in European Economic Integration*)

Mann published his work in the early 1970s so his analysis is confined to the Court's judgments on the European Coal and Steel Community Treaty and the European Economic Community Treaty. His account nonetheless accurately identifies the Treaties and judicial interpretation thereof as oriented around a number of thematic concerns linked to the overall project of European integration, and remains highly relevant to the Court's practices today.

22 Although these have become less onerous over time. Compare Case 26/62 *Van Gend en Loos v Nederlandse Administratie der Belastingen* [1963] ECR 1 with Case 8/81 *Becker v Finanzamt Munster-Innenstadt* [1982] ECR 53.

23 Also called exclusionary or legality review effects. See P V F Regueiro, 'Invocability of Substitution and Invocability of Exclusion: Bringing Legal Realism to the Current Developments of the Case-Law of "Horizontal" Direct Effect of Directives' *Jean Monnet Working Paper* No. 7/02.

24 These various effects are considered in Chapter 5.

engagement with domestic institutions.[25] Reasoning around interpretive effects particularly appeals to a common judicial language, facilitating this engagement.

Subsidiarity and conferred competences principles

I have identified the potential for political tension between the Union and Member States if the Court presents Union legal demands in a way that does not reflect, to some degree, either Member States' constitutional propensities, or political attitudes towards resulting 'states of integration'. Aside from the Court's management of the relationship between Union and domestic orders according to the reasoning adopted in its judgments, the Treaties also seek to maintain the stability of this relationship in stating the conferred competences and subsidiarity principles.[26] The former principle restricts the permissible exercise of the Union's jurisdiction to those areas recognised by the Treaties while the latter requires all adopted Union legislation to be both necessary for the attainment of the Treaty objectives and relating to matters that can only be adequately addressed by Union as opposed to domestic action.[27] Both principles are designed to ensure the stable co-existence of the Union and its Member States, however they tend to express what Williams has termed a 'virtue of indeterminacy', reflecting as opposed to mitigating

25 The interpretive influences of Union laws have extended Union competence into areas previously regarded as incapable of giving rise to legal obligations. See for example, Case C–105/ 03 *Pupino* [2005] ECR I-5285 which affirmed the interpretive legal effects of measures taken under the old third pillar of the Maastricht Treaty (Police and Judicial Co-operation in Criminal Matters). For consideration of the constitutional implications of this judgment on the relationship between Union and domestic orders, see E Spaventa, 'Opening Pandora's Box: Some Reflections on the Constitutional Effects of the Decision in *Pupino*' (2007) 3 *European Constitutional Law Review* 5. See also M G G Ketvel, 'The Jurisdiction of the European Court of Justice in Respect of the Common Foreign and Security Policy' (2006) 55 *International and Comparative Law Quarterly* 77. Overall there has been a gradual blurring of the various types of legal effect created by Union laws, reflecting the singular rationale of the relationship between orders, that of Union law supremacy. For example, in the *Centrosteel* judgment, the interpretive effects of a Union provision resulted in the setting aside of an Italian law (albeit one whose incompatibility with Union law had already been recognised by the Italian Constitutional Court), thereby giving rise to individual rights recognised by a Union Directive, a result that could arguably be understood in terms of direct, indirect (interpretative) or exclusionary (legality review) effects. Case C-456/98 *Centrosteel Srl v Adipol GmbH* [2000] ECR I-6007. On the singular character of the supremacy doctrine which they describe as a 'basic conflict rule', see K Lenaerts and T Corthaut, 'Of Birds and Hedges: The Role of Primacy in Invoking Norms of EU Law' (2006) 31 *European Law Review* 287 at 289.

26 Article 5 TEU.

27 Article 5(1) TEU states that '[t]he limits of Union competences are governed by the principle of conferral. The use of Union competences is governed by the principles of subsidiarity and proportionality.' The Lisbon Treaty also introduced a limited form of review of draft Union legislation by domestic legislatures. See Protocol (No. 1) on the Role of National Parliaments in the European Union and Protocol (No. 2) on the Application of the Principles of Subsidiarity and Proportionality attached to the Treaties by the Lisbon Treaty.

the potential for conflict.[28] In any event, limited judicial pronouncements have demonstrated unwillingness by the Court to apply either principle as a legality review standard over Union legislation.[29]

Conclusions

Given that the Union relies for its survival on the political support of the various Member States, Union legal demands must be presented in a way that takes full account of the wider constitutional and institutional implications of any judgment within the Member States. The Court's legal determinations therefore involve an interpretive method of legal reasoning bespoke to the institutional environment created by the Treaties.[30] Given the Union's focus on political development through positive and directed legal activity, both the constitutional significance of the relationship between Union and

28 Williams states in this regard that:

> But of course what the Treaties are supposed to achieve remains subject to constant political negotiation. Conscious of this, the ECJ has displayed an approach of applying the best possible interpretation [of the Treaties] so as to avoid conflict and preserve the primacy of EU law as a means of ensuring the EU's continuing existence. I would suggest that one can go so far as to propose that EU law has been developed so as to make a virtue of indeterminacy through the adoption of a second order of principles such as those of subsidiarity, respect for diversity, flexibility and multi-level governance.
>
> (A Williams, 'Taking Values Seriously: Towards a Philosophy of EU Law' (2009) 29 *Oxford Journal of Legal Studies* 549 at 559)

In a related sense, Přibáň has commented, referring to Errera, on the inherent uncertainty in the subsidiarity and conferred competence principles:

> Vagueness, contradictory conclusions, and the opaque structure of current EU public law is illustrated by Roger Errera, an honorary member of the French Council of the State, who concluded that the very notion of divided sovereignty and competences and the principle of subsidiarity could not be 'a clear cut issue and had been painted in grey (and not black and white) as the main colour of the EU's public and constitutional law'.
>
> (J Přibáň, 'The Juridification of European Identity, its Limitations and the Search of EU Democratic Politics' (2009) 16 *Constellations* 44 at 47 (footnote omitted))

See also G Martinico and O Pollicino, 'Between Constitutional Tolerance and Judicial Activism: The Specificity of European Judicial Law' (2008) 10 *European Journal of Law Reform* at 119.

29 There is very limited case law on the subsidiarity or conferred competences principles with the Court showing more willingness to engage with questions of legal base, the requirement that all Union legislation must be referable to a specific Treaty Article, empowering the Union to legislate in that area. For a summary of the Court's judgments on subsidiarity, see N Burrows, C Carter and A Scott, *Subsidiarity and the Draft Treaty,* Discussion Paper, Brussels 27 April 2004 at 11–12.

30 One that, as noted by Mann, reaches beyond formal interpretative canons: '[t]here are no concrete rules … for ascertaining on specific questions when the creative task of interpretation has become a matter for legislative or administrative discretion rather than for judicial decision'. Mann, *The Function of Judicial Decision in European Economic Integration* at 168.

domestic laws as well as the project of integration itself represent dynamic evaluative concerns for the Court. Given variable degrees of political commitment amongst Member States to the pace as well as ultimate objectives of Union integration, the legal effects of the 'evolutionary' values set out in the Treaties must be applied flexibly by the Court. The dynamic integrationist objectives lying at the heart of all Union legal demands and consequent judicial activism implicit in the Court's institutional role have led to charges of undue activism; an illegitimate exercise of the powers assigned under the Treaties. These charges will now be considered.

Judicial activism by the Court?

The Court of Justice's institutional role in giving effect to the Treaty objectives has led to the charge by some commentators that it has engaged in unacceptable levels of judicial activism, a charge that will be considered in this section. Rasmussen, for example, has famously argued that the Court's practices have represented unacceptable intrusions upon the prerogative of other Union and domestic institutions.[31] Rasmussen premises the legitimacy of judicial activity generally on the ability of courts to respond to a range of 'policy inputs' from a range of relevant public and private actors, including the governmental branches of the Member States where the Union is concerned. In his view, the Court of Justice, by failing to account for the views of domestic institutional actors, has acted in an unduly activist manner, undermining both its legitimacy and ultimately that of the entire Union enterprise.

Rasmussen's argument suggests that the Court has not adequately performed one of the two key institutional roles I have stressed, namely to ensure the stability of the Union project. While Rasmussen is correct to point out that the viability of the Court's institutional practices undoubtedly depends upon their acceptability to (crucially) the Member States, at the same time, the Court's assigned role under Article 19 TEU to 'ensure that in the interpretation and application of the Treaties the law is observed',[32] arguably requires an active promotion of the Treaty requirements by reference to some notion of European integration. Rasmussen appears to confuse the viability of the Court's practices within the given institutional context with the acceptability of these practices to the Member States. The acceptability of Union law demands to the Member States has over the history of the Union often been lacking[33] but this is far from the conclusion that Union law demands have not

31 H Rasmussen, (1986) *On Law and Policy in the European Court of Justice: A Comparative Study in Judicial Policymaking* (Martinus Nijhoff Publishers, the Hague 1986), hereafter Rasmussen, *On Law and Policy in the European Court of Justice*. See also T C Hartley, 'The European Court, Judicial Objectivity and the Constitution of the European Union (1996) 112 *The Law Quarterly Review* 95.

32 Article 19 TEU.

33 The Member States are entitled to submit observations to the Court in Preliminary Reference proceedings and will often do so to voice opposition to legal outcomes that strengthen the authority of Union law and by implication diminish that of domestic law. For example, in

been institutionally viable. This viability is simply determined by the fact that the Court's legal demands are, and have been, followed by the majority of public and private actors within the Member States.[34] Clearly sustained opposition to Union demands falling short of outright non-compliance would eventually threaten the Union's viability but this has not occurred. It is the Court's ability to maintain a *sufficient* level of acceptability in relation to Union law demands within the Member States that is therefore crucial to the Union's survival and evolution, and which underlies the viability of its practices.

The viewpoint informing Rasmussen's arguments is that the rationale of European integration is a matter of pure politics which cannot as such legitimately influence Union legal demands, as articulated by the Court, without undue activism being present. This is an implausible position as it seeks to isolate Union regulatory demands from the rationale of the 'parent' legal order, thereby begging the question of their status as legal rules. By contrast, recognition that the value of European integration justifiably informs the Court's judgments on the basis of 'a cautious and balanced approach ... rather than a desire to promote integration at all costs'[35] forms a rational assessment of the Court's institutional acitivity, expressive of the legal framework set out in the Treaties.[36]

For others, the charge made against the Court is not that it is not entitled to adopt an activist approach in its legal judgments, but that it does so to an unjustified degree. De Waele, for example, has claimed that the Court, while entitled to a degree of activism given the wording of the Treaties, has in fact often engaged in *excessive* activism, ignoring express legislative injunctions set out in the Treaties. This in his view has undermined the authority and legitimacy of its rulings.[37] He states:

> Even if judges may roughly base a decision strengthening and expanding the European Union legal order on 'the system-at-large', it may be sincerely doubted whether it justifies those judgments in which the ECJ

Van Gend en Loos, a (then) majority of the Member States submitted arguments against the recognition of direct effect by the Court.

34 An argument considered in Chapter 9.

35 T Tridimas, 'The Court of Justice and Judicial Activism' (1996) 21 *European Law Review* 199 at 203, hereafter Tridimas, 'The Court of Justice and Judicial Activism'.

36 Cappelletti has criticised Rasmussen's argument as ignoring the legitimate role of constitutional courts generally and the Court of Justice in particular, which is to independently uphold the values of the rule of law, occasionally in the face of opposing views of other public and private actors. M Cappelletti, 'Is the Court of Justice "Running Wild?"' (1987) 12 *European Law Review* 3. Recent political and public opposition in the UK to the enfranchisement of prisoners, required under a European Court of Human Rights ruling, illustrates the legitimate opposition of legal demands to the views of other governmental actors. *Hirst v The United Kingdom (No. 2.)* [2005] ECHR 681. See also Tridimas, 'The Court of Justice and Judicial Activism' at 205.

37 H de Waele, 'The Role of the European Court of Justice in the Integration Process: A Contemporary and Normative Assessment' (2010) 6 *Hanse Law Review* 3, hereafter de Waele, 'The Role of the European Court of Justice in the Integration Process'.

> does not take small steps in the general direction, but leaps unexpectedly fast forward: cases like *Defrenne*, *Grzelczyk* and *Pupino* spring to mind here. In all then, perhaps the Court is supposed to act partisan to a certain extent, and rule in favour of the successful development of the supranational plane on most occasions. But again, there is no compelling reason why it should at any time provide for an extra impetus that exceeds the ordinary levels of toleration and knowingly accelerate and intensify the integration process.[38]

Again, these criticisms relate to the political (un)acceptability of the Court's judgments to Member States as opposed to an institutional derogation by the Court of its allocated functions under the Treaties, functions which mandate an activist institutional approach. Here, Dehousse's comments in relation to charges of judicial activism generally are relevant:

> Judicial activism is perceived as a dangerous phenomenon in all legal systems. Yet the arguments propounded to denounce it deal less often with pure institutional concerns than with the substance of judicial decisions: what is deplored is not so much the fact that judges arrogate excessive powers but rather that they put these powers in the service of a bad cause.[39]

The 'bad' causes in the Union setting, so far as the Member States are concerned, typically relate either to the project of Union integration itself, or disaffection with particular Union regulatory demands thought to intrude upon domestic constitutional prerogatives. Whether these political factors do or do not impact upon the legitimacy of the Court's institutional role is in a sense irrelevant. Ultimately, they cannot form the basis of a claim of undue activism because the crucial factor here is whether the court's legal demands have in fact been followed and are therefore sustainable within the Member States. It still remains worthwhile, however, to offer a positive justification of the degree of activism the Court is entitled to display in virtue of its allocated role under the Treaties.

Justifying the Court's institutional role

As I have repeatedly stressed, the objectives set out in the opening Articles of the Treaties, in conjunction with the general principles, represent the foundational values of the Union legal order, providing the underlying

38 De Waele suggests these concerns could be met by more careful drafting of its judgments, by passing more of its workload to lower Union courts and by improving democratic input to judicial appointments to the Court. De Waele, 'The Role of the European Court of Justice in the Integration Process' at 13.

39 R Dehousse, *The European Court of Justice: The Politics of Judicial Integration* (Macmillan Publishing Ltd, London 1998) at 121.

rationale for all Union law demands. The degree of activism linked to the Court's practices giving legal effect to these foundational concerns depends on a number of factors. These include their substantive scope and content, the allocated role of the Court under the Treaties and the wider political and legal context in which the Court operates. In domestic settings the activism of superior courts in relation to their ability to strike down or amend legislation that fails to conform with the constitution[40] is based upon the political intuition that the values expressed by the constitution are of singular importance to the stability and flourishing of the body politic.

On what basis, by comparison, do the values underlying the Treaties relating to European integration, combined with the institutional framework designed to put these into effect, mandate a greater degree of activism than that found within domestic settings? While the meaning of European integration is both uncertain and politically contested,[41] there is little doubt that the Treaties are directed to a process (of integration) if not to achieving an identifiable outcome conclusive of this objective. The Court of Justice therefore necessarily possesses a degree of flexibility regarding how it expresses this value of integration that is distinctive from the role of domestic courts in their treatment of the values underlying the domestic constitution. Here, the constitutional principles of political morality generally require positive recognition (normally implicit) in all legal outcomes. By contrast, the value of European integration allied to the Treaty objectives is definitionally less clear, aspirationally weaker and politically controversial.

Definitionally, the idea of European integration is notoriously difficult to quantify given its highly contested political character, not only as an 'end product', but also concerning the means employed to achieve this. As Tridimas has noted,

> the Treaty of Rome, was not and could not have been a politically neutral ideal. The dismantling of national frontiers and the free movement of the factors of production have perforce a subversive character. They contain the seeds of destruction of the State's monopoly on authority. The European Community is by its nature a dynamic entity.[42]

40 Though not in the UK, where primary (statutory) legislation is concerned. Here the courts are limited to disapplying (but not striking down) statutory requirements when these conflict with a requirement of European Union law. Where a conflict between a UK statute and a right arising under the European Convention on Human Rights (recognised by the Human Rights Act) arises, the Court of Appeal or Supreme Court can issue a declaration of incompatibility. While such a declaration will not affect the legal validity of the offending primary legislation, it will allow Parliament to make necessary amendments by means of an expedited procedure employing a statutory instrument as opposed to primary legislation. See Sections 4 and 10 of the UK Human Rights Act (1998).

41 For a systems analysis of the contested character of the Union project, see Z Bañkowski and E Christodoulidis, 'The European Union as an Essentially Contested Project' (1998) 4 *European Law Journal* 341.

42 Tridimas, 'The Court of Justice and Judicial Activism' at 205.

Simply recognising the value of integration within Union legal outcomes by the Court is therefore apt to invite charges of undue activism given the unsettling effect such recognition is likely to have upon domestic constitutional sensibilities. At the same time, the Court is not bound to represent the value of integration in all its judgments. The value has a weak aspirational character by contrast with domestic constitutional norms and (as such) may be qualified implicitly by reference to institutional (or fundamental rights) considerations.[43] Therefore, if the Court were to follow legislative injunctions that resulted in a negative effect on the integration process, its judgment would not as a result be called into account for failing to actively promote integration. When in fact it does do so, this appears more startling but does not however reveal undue activism but rather the political significance of the value that is being promoted.

These factors suggest that the Court's activities are far more likely to be viewed as activist, even unduly so, than their domestic counterparts, yet do not constitute undue judicial activism, political tensions deriving from its judgments notwithstanding. Rather the Court possesses a weak institutional mandate to promote and develop the highly politically controversial value of European integration through the various social and economic objectives set out in the Treaties.

Conclusions

In this chapter, I have highlighted the unique set of institutional factors to which the Court is subject, both under the terms of the Treaties and implicitly by virtue of the situated institutional context of the Union, that is, 'within' the Member States. In terms of the Court's judicial practices, I have identified two key institutional drivers, the need to promote the Treaty objectives and ensure the continued stability of the Union project. Both factors underlie the importance of rhetorical, interpretive forms of legal reasoning by the Court in setting out Union law demands. I have also considered charges of undue judicial activism against the Court, concluding that such charges are a misguided consequence of the 'politically subversive' institutional role the Court is called upon to perform and do not succeed in principle.

The Court's judicial practices have focused on fine tuning the constitutional innovations that Union legal demands represent within Member States, employing interpretive and rhetorical modes of legal reasoning. An interpretive form of legal judgment that addresses the contextual factors of Treaty content as well as the institutional setting of Union legal demands allows the Court of Justice to tailor judicial decisions to the current political and legal dynamic existing between Union and Member State orders. In this regard, the Court's skill and credibility as a legal actor lies in matching Union legal

43 Case C–112/ 00 *Schmidberger Internationale Transporte und Planzuge v Austria* [2003] ECR I-5659.

requirements to what is politically achievable,[44] without concern for possible short term negative feedback from Member States.

Judicial practices within the Union are not based upon 'rule of law' concerns alone, a fortiori given that the scope of application of the Union general principles is limited by the jurisdiction conferred under the Treaties.[45] The Court's institutional role is primarily to promote the Treaty objectives, thereby ensuring the continuing development, and viability, of the Union project.[46] The central role of the Court in the process of Union integration is paralleled by the importance of the institution of law itself in this regard. The incremental realisation of Union values relating to European integration as *legal* demands over the administrative and judicial practices of the Member States is a key strength of the Union project and a determining factor in its success. The Union is a creation of public international law and the legal demands articulated by the Court are the key to both its self-understanding as a political and legal entity, as well as the effective prosecution of the Union legal demands within the Member States.[47]

In the next chapter I develop the themes introduced in this chapter, focusing on how the twin elements of the Union constitution, the Treaty Articles and general principles, inform the legal reasoning of the Court of Justice.

44 The phrase 'Politics is the art of the possible' is attributed to Otto Von Bismark, the nineteenth century German politician.

45 Union legal demands have frequently been challenged in domestic courts on the basis that they undermine Member States' constitutional arrangements which represent an inclusive rule of law jurisdiction. Case 44/79 *Hauer v Land Rheinland* [1979] ECR 3727.

46 See generally M P Maduro, 'Interpreting European Law: Judicial Adjudication in a Context of Constitutional Pluralism' (2007) 1 *European Journal of Legal Studies* 1.

47 This importance is highlighted by a former judge of the Court as follows: '[t]he Community is only able to exist as a Community of law. It has no weapons or armies. It is held together by the authority of the law. The Court of Justice has to guarantee this authority.' U Everling, 'The *Maastricht* Judgment of the German Federal Constitutional Court and its Significance for the Development of the European Union' (1994) 14 *Yearbook of European Law* 1 at 18.

5 The values of the European Union legal order: constitutional perspectives

Introduction

In this chapter I shall examine the landscape of the European Union constitution,[1] offering a comparative and critical analysis of the values underlying this constitution by comparison with those of domestic legal orders. The chapter is set out as follows. First I consider the elements of the Union constitution, the Treaty Articles relating to European integration and rule of law principles, identified generally within the Treaties, and as general principles of law in the judgments of the Court of Justice. I then consider the relationship between the constitutional principles underlying legal orders generally and the core or deep values of the societies to which the constitution applies. Applying this analysis in the Union setting, I suggest that the Union legal order cannot, as a result of its limited jurisdiction and lack of historical longevity, be regarded as constitutive of Member States' societies (considered collectively) in the manner of domestic constitutions. Finally, I consider the

1 Following Esteban's formulation, I have adopted a 'material' reading of the Union constitution, treating those aspects of the Treaties that affirm the overall project of Union integration and fundamental rule of law values as the components of the constitution. At the same time, the supremacy doctrine clearly implies a constitutional significance for all Union legal demands arising under the Treaties, either directly or indirectly through secondary legislation, in terms of their operation within domestic settings. Esteban describes these two approaches as follows:

> Since the Court has stated that the treaties are a constitutional chart of a community of law, this would logically imply that *all* the elements of the constitutional chart are, by definition, constitutional; therefore all values and principles belonging to the founding treaties are constitutional. This *formal* definition of a value or principle as constitutional could be contrasted with a *material* definition, implying that only those values and principles which would traditionally be regarded as being of a constitutional character are constitutional values and principles.
>
> (M L F Esteban, 'Constitutional Values and Principles in the Community Legal Order' (1995) 2 *Maastricht Journal of European and Comparative Law* 129 at 132)

Of course the approach suggested requires a definition of the Union constitution primarily by reference to objectives (of integration) not generally recognised within domestic constitutions. I have defended this possibility in Chapters 2 and 3.

legal effects of the Union constitution, the Treaty objectives and general principles as overriding legal norms that condition all Union regulatory demands. In this regard, the interpretive effects of Union constitutional values are singled out as a method of legal judgment that promotes the broadest integrationist and rule of law objectives of the Union project by influencing the operation and development of domestic legal demands in areas of Union governance in an institutionally viable manner.

Domestic and Union legal orders: constitutional values

Subject to the following analysis, I understand constitutional values or principles as synonymous with a broad understanding of the rule of law. Accordingly, a rule of law constitution includes not only procedural requirements designed to ensure that public power is not exercised arbitrarily, but also the affirmation of substantive standards of right or justice, including fundamental rights, upheld by and through the exercise of public power. This is a view that has gained currency in recent years.[2]

The Union clearly adopts such a broad understanding of the procedural and substantive values on which it is based. Accordingly, Article 2 of the TEU (as amended) states that, 'The Union is founded on the values of respect

2 See MacCormick's opinion that:

> It is open to question whether such purely formal virtues and process-based values are sufficient to a proper conception either of the Rule of Law or of the *Rechtsstaat*. It can be argued that requirements of substance, such as observance of basic civil and political rights or even of various economic and social guarantees are also essential.
>
> (D N MacCormick, *Questioning Sovereignty* (Oxford University Press, Oxford 1999) 46)

See also that of Lord Bingham speaking in 2006 who, when considering the possibility of rule of law legal order based simply on the meeting of formal or procedural requirements, and which therefore allowed in principle for the enactment of morally repugnant laws, commented:

> On one view of the rule of law, this is enough: if clear laws, duly made and publicly promulgated, prescribe what is to be done or not done, and those rules are scrupulously observed, the rule of law is satisfied. On this view it does not matter how unfair or morally offensive the rules may be. They may, for instance, discriminate against an unpopular minority in an arbitrary and unjustifiable way, and yet – if the law is clear and unambiguous – be held to comply with the rule of law. This is not a view which commands very wide acceptance, and it is not one which I would endorse. While there is no universally accepted catalogue of rights and freedoms applicable in all countries at all times, and there is scope for local variations and development over time, there is nonetheless, I suggest, a broad measure of agreement in liberal democratic states on certain rights and freedoms regarded as fundamental to us all simply by virtue of our existence as human beings.
>
> (The Right Honourable Lord Bingham of Cornhill KG FKC Commemoration Oration 31 October 2007, 18.00, Great Hall, Strand Campus at 6)

See also F G Jacobs *The Sovereignty of Law: The European Way* (Cambridge, Cambridge University Press 2007).

for human dignity, freedom, democracy, equality, the rule of law and respect for human rights'.[3] Similar values are contained within Member States' constitutions which typically affirm not only formal or procedural rule of law requirements but also a range of civil and political rights, often combined with some recognition of social and economic rights, for example in relation to healthcare, housing and education.[4] This close correspondence between Union rule of law values and those found within Member States however belies clear differences in the operative features of the Union and domestic rule of law values.

Within Member States, the political and moral ideals contained within the constitution are generally regarded as synonymous with the 'deep' identity of the society, in which it (the constitution) forms the governing or supreme legal authority. In the Union setting by contrast, the legal authority conferred under the Treaties is directed to the achievement of specified objectives allied to deeper political, social and economic integration amongst the Member States. This ideal of integration, which itself may be regarded as a constitutional value, is however expressed within the limited or conferred domain of Union governance under the Treaties.[5] The Union constitution is therefore wholly distinctive by comparison with the comprehensive charter for rule of law governance found within domestic constitutions for the following reasons. First, as a result of the Union's status as an as yet 'unrealised' political project directed to the objective of integration, and second as a result of the limited powers conferred under the Treaties available to achieve this objective. These factors suggest the Union represents an opportunity to rethink received notions of the relationship between legal orders, and the values on which they are based understood as that between statal constitutions and the societies for which they provide an inclusive governmental institutional structure. This task is explored in the following section.

The relationship between the values of society and the constitution in domestic and Union settings

Member States

Within Member States a vital relationship exists between the interpreted constitution and the wider value concerns of their respective societies. Writing on the practices of the German Federal Constitutional Court, Komers describes this relationship as follows:

3 Article 2 TEU.

4 For analysis of the composition and normative underpinning of modern constitutions, see C Sunstein, *Designing Democracy* (Oxford University Press, Oxford 2001), hereafter Sunstein, *Designing Democracy*.

5 Article 5 TEU.

> An important interpretive canon postulates the interdependence of the constitutional order and the broader community. The nature of the community – i.e. the German people – defines and refines the constitutional order, just as the latter defines and refines the existential reality of the community.[6]

The importance of a wider normative context within which constitutional standards find expression and of which they are an expression, has also been highlighted by Barak, a former president of the Supreme Court of Israel:

> A constitution does not operate in a normative vacuum. Outside and around the constitution are values and principles that the constitution must actualise. These are not a judge's personal values but rather the national values of the country.[7]

MacCormick, makes a similar point, highlighting the interdependence of constitutional values and the wider social context in which they operate: '[l]aw has the function of regulating social coexistence in the service of certain aims and values that are independent of the activity of regulation'.[8] Value perspectives present within society act as an *interpretive guide* to constitutional meanings and thereby as constitutive elements of the fundamental values or purposes that the constitution expresses.

A direct link between the constitution and the constituted society?

These views all consider the constitution, as interpreted by the courts, to be a *direct* expression of the wider evaluative perspectives of the State or society to which it applies, notwithstanding the plurality of legal and cultural values present at any given time within most modern societies. The constitution remains a core and fundamental statement of the norms and values on which a society's identity and manner of government rests.[9] How then do these observations translate to the Union setting? To address this question we need to consider first the distinctive character of the Union constitution.

6 D P Kommers, 'Germany: Balancing Rights and Duties' in J Goldsworthy (ed.), *Interpreting Constitutions* (Oxford University Press, Oxford 2006) at 178.

7 A Barak, *Purposive Interpretation in Law* (Princetown University Press, Princetown 2007) at 237, hereafter Barak, *Purposive Interpretation in Law*.

8 D N MacCormick, *Rhetoric and the Rule of Law: A Theory of Legal Reasoning* (Oxford University Press, Oxford 2005) at 252 citing F Atria, *On Law and Legal Reasoning* (Hart Publishing, Oxford 2001) and R H S Tur, 'Defeasibilism' (2001) 21 *Oxford Journal of Legal Studies* 355.

9 'Fundamental values and conceptions surrounding the constitution constitute the objective purpose of the constitution itself. These are the nation's basic conceptions of its values and principles. They express society's basic positions about human rights, separation of powers and democracy.' Barak, *Purposive Interpretation in Law* at 153.

Union constitutional values: the general principles

The rule of law values affirmed as foundational to the Union legal order within the Treaties as general principles are similar to those found within domestic constitutions. A crucial distinction in their operation lies, as noted above, in the fact that the Union is an evolving political, legal and constitutional project whose limits are continuously developed, contested, denied and challenged by the Member States. By contrast, Member States' societies represent complex political and cultural associations with deep historical roots. This fact of itself does not mean that the Member States represent or even aspire to more 'ideal' forms of political association than the Union. However their historical and political roots run far deeper and as such represent more entrenched forms of social association. Such forms have attracted the emergence of inclusive constitutional charters for government, and Member States' constitutions therefore actualise a body of culturally and historically grounded values of political morality, to which their respective societies aspire.

In response to this, it might be said that any suggested view of constitutions as reflecting or giving effect to values of political morality expressive of the 'core' world views of the societies to which they apply is simply not realised in practice. Examples abound of constitutions that either impose narrow political ideologies upon the governed or, even worse, enable tyrannical forms of government that leave citizens open to arbitrary abuses of State authority. This historical observation where the Member States are concerned is not, of course, fatal to the argument that constitutions will *tend* to reproduce the broad sweep of rule of law values that promote beneficial and inclusive forms of social ordering.[10] We can also recognise that the present constitutions of the various Member States broadly express universal rule of law values whose legitimacy is not seriously disputed.[11] It may therefore be reasonably affirmed that Member States' constitutions in fact offer a justified and legitimate expression of the underlying value concerns of the societies to which they apply.[12]

This inclusive role is lacking, however, where the operation of Union general principles is concerned. The Union remains for the time being a limited project whose parameters of political and legal activity are defined by the Treaties. This means that the Union constitution cannot, even in a potential sense, express an inclusive body of politico-moral values in the manner of Member States' constitutions whose political authority to realise these values within the domestic constitution is assured. As a result, the rule of law

10 In this regard we may say that constitutions are chameleon like, expressing universal values that also represent a particular cultural identity.

11 Although the precise scope of constitutional rights is contested.

12 Subject of course to the social and political tensions which are endemic features of any society and which the constitution must allow for. This, according to Sunstein, is in fact a key role of the constitution – to enable an openness within civil society to disagreements of principle. Sunstein, *Designing Democracy*, particularly Chapter 4.

values set out in Article 2 TEU, whilst affirmed as 'foundational'[13] within the Treaties in the manner of domestic constitutions, are far from universal in application. They operate in fact to legitimise a limited programme for Union action whilst providing a 'declaratory' platform for further European integration.

This role appears in principle to be at odds with the 'constitutional' supremacy of Union laws within the domestic setting, and particularly regarding the foundational and inclusive requirements of political morality found within the (domestic) constitution. While the operation of domestic constitutional demands affirms a link between the supremacy of these demands with the universality, actual or potential, of the constitution's jurisdiction, this association is not available as a justification of Union law (supremacy). A principled distinction therefore exists between Union law supremacy, which operates to discharge Member States' Treaty obligations as a matter of international law, and the supremacy accorded to domestic constitutions based on their role as an inclusive charter for rule of law governance.

Union constitutional values: the Treaty objectives

The Court is faced with the task of ensuring the *positive* development of the Treaty objectives. Any other view would beg the question of what purpose the Union actually serves. Clearly this is not to address or resolve prior constitutional or political crises within the Member States given that no such elemental instabilities exist(ed) within these societies prior to the creation of the Union or during its existence.[14] Nor is this purpose to establish an *enhanced* order of rule of law governance by comparison with that already present within the Member States.[15] The aim of the Union project is rather the progressive development of European integration, an 'ever closer Union', as a desirable political objective.

The Court of Justice, when applying constitutional standards of Union law as Treaty objectives expresses, in common with domestic constitutional courts, what Barak has called 'purposive presumptions' in relation to the entire legal order. In his words,

13 Article 2 TEU.

14 Although the first Treaty creating the European Coal and Steel Community was undoubtedly a response to the upheaval caused by the Second World War aimed at preventing German re-armament by placing the administration of the coal and steel industries in the hands of a supranational institutional framework.

15 Although the requirement for a State to be a signatory to the European Convention on Human Rights as a precondition to accession to the Union may be may be noted in this regard. In addition, compatibility with fundamental rights/rule of law requirements is presented as a condition the meeting of which is necessary for *participation in* the Union project. Article 7 TEU. See for a critical analysis of this provision, A Williams, *The Ethos of Europe* (Cambridge University Press, Cambridge 2010) at 147ff.

> Presumptions of purpose reflect the fundamental values of the system. They are a mirror image of these values. They express the constitutional perspectives at the core of the legal system. I noted as much in a case before me: 'At the core of "presumptions of general applicability" are constitutional assumptions about the essence of the democratic regime, separation of powers, rule of law and human rights.'[16]

The fundamental values of the Union order include, in addition to the rule of law values Barak cites, the ideal of European integration. The interpretation of this 'constitutional value' is guided, in circular fashion, by the terms of the value itself as set out in the Treaties. In relation to this branch of the Union constitution we find as a result that the interpretative practices of the Court contrast with those of domestic constitutional courts who draw on the ethical and moral values of a particular society to guide constitutional interpretation. The Court adopts instead a purposive or teleological method of interpretation, directing legal meanings to the achievement of the Treaty objectives.[17] The Court's interpretation of Treaty requirements is *not* therefore based upon a historically grounded and inclusive resource of social values. The Treaties indeed do not purport to offer an authoritative expression of the values present within Member State societies except perhaps in the weak sense that the Treaty objectives are seen as politically desirable, in the sense of socially and economically beneficial, objectives by the governmental institutions of the Member States.[18]

This suggests that the underlying value basis of the Union constitution is in fact self-referential. Inquiry by the Court of Justice into the value basis of the Treaties is not, as with domestic constitutions, driven conclusively by the value concerns of Member State societies. Instead it is the Treaties themselves combined with the institutional practices of the Union in giving effect to their demands that form the 'final' evaluative backdrop to Treaty interpretation. The values underlying the Union project are finally located as a juridical expression of the Treaty objectives.

If the underlying rationale informing the Court's interpretation of the Union constitution is found within the Treaties themselves as opposed to deriving from a wider consensus of values within Member States' societies, this raises an important question: on what ultimate basis do the legal claims

16 Barak, *Purposive Interpretation in Law* at 172, citing the Israeli Supreme Court case, H.C. 953/87, *Poraz v Mayor of Tel-Aviv-Yafo*, 42 (2) P.D. 309 at 329 (Barak J).

17 J Bengoetxea, *The Legal Reasoning of the European Court of Justice* (Clarendon Press, Oxford 1993) at 233, hereafter Bengoetxea, *The Legal Reasoning of the European Court of Justice*.

18 The fact that the Union constitution is based on Treaties underlines the fact for Mueller that 'from its inception it has been a confederalist structure. Its institutions have been created through negotiations between representatives of the member governments'. D C Mueller, 'Federalism and the European Union: A Constitutional Perspective' (1997) 90 *Public Choice* 255 at 275 citing N Nugent, *The Government and Politics of the European Community* (Duke University Press, Durham 1991) at 42.

of the Union order rest? Generally, legal orders provide formalised methods of achieving and developing valuable social objectives, objectives that are both constituted by and consistent with the ethical and moral world views of the societies concerned.[19] Judicial articulation of constitutional standards therefore generally stands at a juncture of the 'deep' values endorsed by society at large and the expression of these values as a matter of law.

The direct link existing between domestic constitutions and the wider value concerns of the societies they address is not present where the Union legal order is concerned. The Treaties represent a positive commitment to the achievement of particular objectives and are not as such simply the assumption of a rule of law jurisdiction in these areas. This suggests at best a weak connection between the ethical/moral world views of Member State societies and the underlying values of the Union legal order.

Instead, the link between the Union and the body politic represented by the Member States is primarily a juridical construct expressing a relationship between legal jurisdictions governed by the supremacy doctrine. This 'systemic'[20] principle does not operate in the name of the values existentially present within the collectivity of Member State societies. Rather the doctrine is concerned with the maintenance and development of a hierarchical relationship of norms as between Union (superior) and domestic (inferior) legal rules. With these features of the Union constitution identified, we can now turn to consider how the Court of Justice expresses the legal effect of the general principles and Treaty objectives.

The legal effects of the Union constitution

Several of the Treaty Articles possess fundamental or foundational status. The opening Articles setting out the overall vision of the Union project, its commitment to fundamental rights and the establishment and functioning of the single market may be singled out as of particular significance, operating as governing principles that influence the entirety of Union legal demands. It is however the economic freedoms that are the central legal mechanism for developing the project of European integration. As Everling notes:

19 In the sense identified by Barak as follows,

> Judges should operate within society's established central framework, not the occasional temporary structures it may build. They need not give expression to the passing trends of a society that is not being true to itself. Judges should resist those trends and give expression to the social consensus that reflects the basic principles, 'deep' values and national credo of their society.
>
> (Barak, *Purposive Interpretation in Law* at 167)

These ideas can traced to John Locke's *The Second Treatise of Government* (first published 1689, Dover Publications, New York 2002) I.

20 T Tridimas, *The General Principles of EU Law* (2nd edn, Oxford University Press, Oxford 2006) at 4, hereafter Tridimas, *The General Principles of EU Law*.

The Common Market constitutes the starting point for the entire integration process and all attempts at more far-reaching economic and political progress stem from it. Running like a red thread through the whole of the Court's case law is the idea that this core of the Community must remain sacrosanct.[21]

21 U Everling, 'The Court of Justice as a Decision Making Authority' (1983–1984) 82 *Michigan Law Review* 1294 at 1305, hereafter, Everling, 'The Court of Justice as a Decision Making Authority'. The introduction of the later Treaties saw increasing policy and law-making powers conferred on the European Union in areas of more general social concern, for example in relation to consumer, environmental and employment rights. Christian Joerges has suggested that the Union project as a whole has been undermined by Treaty developments from the Single Market Act onwards. The 'constitutionalisation' of the economic objectives of the original Treaties, which Joerges terms the 'European Economic Constitution', was intended to achieve 'liberal', free market conditions across the Member States and promote social and political flourishing allied to European integration. The original Communities were founded on the ordo-liberal thesis that the maintenance of 'truly' free (liberal) market conditions has consequent social benefits and hence public regulatory intervention to rein in undesirable aspects of wholly unregulated market forces, for example by outlawing anti-competitive practices, is desirable. For Joerges, if the primary ordo-liberal regulatory function of the Union is to remain constitutionally legitimate, the Union must not gain additional redistributive policies unrelated to factors of economic rationality which are matters that should remain within the competence of the Member States:

> In the ordo-liberal account, the European polity has a twofold structure: at supranational level, it is committed to economic rationality and a system of undistorted competition. Redistributive (social) policies could – and should – be left to the Member States.
>
> (C Joerges, 'What Is Left of the European Economic Constitution? A Melancholic Eulogy' (2005) 30 *European Law Review* 461 at 461, hereafter .Joerges, 'What Is Left of the European Economic Constitution')

Joerges suggests however that this is exactly what has occurred, and since the time of Maastricht redistributive regulatory powers have increasingly transferred to the Union, thereby distorting and undermining the strong ordo-liberal premise of the Rome Treaty focused on the establishment of the common market. According to Joerges, the Union's increasing competencies in the regulation of social policy have undermined the liberalising effects of the Treaties in relation to economic practices. As he notes,

> How can one continue to assign a constitutive function to the 'system of undistorted competition', when the promotion of that system is only one among many other competing objectives and its relative weight has to be determined in political processes? ... The Maastricht Treaty was the end of the 'economic constitution'.
>
> (Ibid. at 474)

In addition, what he regards as unconstitutional, 'soft' methods of governance, for example, the open method of co-ordination have arisen in relation to Union social policy governance stating that:

> whereas ordo-liberalism sought to protect the ordo of the economy through a strong state which would rigorously enforce laws against restrictive business practices and abuse of private power, democratic experimentalism is relying on political processes, softer modes of co-ordination and the subtle power of transparency and exposure to public critique.
>
> (Ibid. at 483)

In other areas, competence is conferred on the Union to *develop* and enact regulatory policy, for example in relation to consumer rights or environmental protection.[22] Secondary legislation in these areas imposes Union regulatory controls irrespective of the existence of a cross-border element and arguably represents a more intrusive form of legal intervention within Member

He critiques these methods of governance as set out in the (now abandoned) Constitutional Treaty as follows:

> The commitments of the Constitutional Treaty to a 'social market economy', the new social rights and the turn to new modes of governance are not really trustworthy. Furthermore, they threaten the very idea of constitutionalism, namely, the idea of law mediated, and rule-of-law bound governance.
>
> (Ibid.)

I would challenge Joerges' suggestion that the European project has 'corrupted' an original (and constitutionally defensible) ordo-liberal vision that entails a strict exclusion of social regulation from Union competencies and which represents an exclusive focus on transnational economic rationalisation. The Treaties have never (and not simply from the time of Maastricht onwards) envisaged this 'pure' approach to Union governance based upon economic rationalisation at European level alone and with Member States retaining competences in areas of social redistribution (tax and spend). The original European Coal and Steel and Economic Communities were never conclusively intended to facilitate movement of economic factors alone. As the Preamble to the original European Coal and Steel Community States, the original contracting Member States were

> Resolved to substitute for age-old rivalries the merging of essential interests; to create, by establishing an economic community, the basis for a broader and deeper community among peoples long divided by bloody conflicts; and to lay the foundations for institutions which will give direction to a destiny henceforward shared.

While the objective of the original Treaties was clearly to establish an 'Economic Community', this was not to the exclusion of the potential assumption of competence in areas of social policy. The final paragraph of the ECSC Treaty preamble cited above clearly shows that the original Coal and Steel Community was viewed as the basis of a broader project of integration which has remained the underlying objective of all subsequent Treaties. Although the specific regulatory competencies assigned under the earlier Treaties were restricted to the establishment and maintenance of the common (later single) market, the underlying values of the Union have always included a mixture of economic, social, rule of law and political objectives. The relative importance of the economic freedoms for the Union project is by no means conclusive of what is understood by an integrated Europe, and is ultimately one (albeit highly important) factor in a broader project of integration. This fact does not however undermine the legal status of the fundamental economic freedoms, nor does it make them in some way subject to competing policy considerations in the manner suggested by Joerges. The economic Treaty rights remain the overriding functional concern of all Union laws and although an ever widening body of Union secondary legislation giving effect to a range of public policy concerns operates to qualify their operation, the Court continues to regard the economic freedoms as representing high constitutional principle and hence to be restricted to the narrowest degree possible. Finally, the lack of constitutional legitimacy of 'soft' methods of governance in areas of social policy by the Union claimed by Joerges is arguably a non sequitur. Coordinative approaches to policy at Union level will generally remain a political prerogative that does not give rise to binding legal demands.

22 Titles XV and XX TFEU.

States.[23] In relation to the legal effects taken by the Treaty Articles and general principles, these act as interpretive influences[24] and legality review standards[25] over secondary Union laws[26] and domestic laws connected with Union law.[27] They also act as interpretive influences over one another.[28] The Treaty Articles[29] and secondary Union legislative provisions also give rise to positive, freestanding rights, enforceable at the suit of individuals before domestic courts where the conditions for direct effect are met.[30]

In what follows I shall argue that the interpretive effects of superior Union laws are the key legal mechanism for developing the authority of the Union constitution within domestic jurisdictions.

The interpretive effects of the Treaty objectives and general principles

The Court has consistently adopted a teleological or purposive approach to the interpretation of all Union laws, aligning primary and secondary legislative meanings to the integrationist objectives found in Articles 1 and 3 TEU. This rationale is described in an early judgment as follows:

> Under Article 2 [Article 3 TEU] of the Treaty, which is placed at the *head* of the general principles which *govern* it, the Community has as its

23 In this regard, the Court in *Centrosteel* stated in relation to the effects taken by a Directive harmonising the requirements of commercial agency contracts that

> it must be noted that the Directive is intended to harmonise the laws of the Member States governing the legal relationship between the parties to a commercial agency contract, irrespective of any cross-border elements. Its scope is therefore *broader* than the fundamental freedoms laid down by the EC Treaty.
>
> (Case C–456/98 *Centrosteel Srl v Adipol GmbH* [2000] ECR I-6007 at paragraph 13 (emphasis added))

24 See Tridimas, *The General Principles of EU Law* at 3.

25 Ibid. at 36.

26 The legality review of the Treaty Articles (primary Union legislation) is not possible either by reference to other Treaty Articles or the general principles.

27 Tridimas, *The General Principles of EU Law* at 31.

28 Case C–112/00 *Schmidberger Internationale Transporte und Planzuge v Austria* [2003] ECR I-5659.

29 Case 26/62 *Van Gend en Loos v Nederlandse Administratie der Belastingen* [1963] ECR 1; Case 93/71 *Leonesio v Italian Ministry for Agriculture and Forestry* [1972] ECR 287 (Regulations); Case 41/71 *Van Duyn v Home Office* [1974] ECR 1337 (Directives); Case 9/70 *Grad v Finanzamt Traunstein* [1970] ECR 825 (Decisions).

30 Case 26/62 *Van Gend en Loos v Nederlandse Administratie der Belastingen* [1963] ECR 1 (Treaty Articles); Case 93/71 *Leonesio v Italian Ministry for Agriculture and Forestry* [1972] ECR 287 (Regulations); Case 41/71 *Van Duyn v Home Office* [1974] ECR 1337 (Directives); Case 9/70 *Grad v Finanzamt Traunstein* [1970] ECR 825 (Decisions). The general principles cannot operate as freestanding, directly effective rights and require instead a connection with Union law, or domestic laws with a Union law element, in order to give rise to interpretive or legality review effects.

> task to *promote* throughout the Community a harmonious development of economic activities by establishing a common market and progressively approximating the economic policies of Member States.[31]

The Court therefore exhibits a preference for a purposive and dynamic style of interpretation allied to the active promotion of the Treaty objectives, an approach which may modify otherwise clear meanings so that, according to Bengoetxea, 'even if the wording used seems to be clear, it is still necessary to refer to the spirit, general scheme and context of the provision; a fortiori if the wording is unclear'.[32] Crucially for present purposes the Court of Justice has presented the overall objective of European integration as an interpretive (indirect) influence over all Union and associated domestic legal demands. Everling, a former judge of the Court of Justice, explains the Court's approach as follows:

> It is common to refer to 'teleological' interpretation, and that presents relatively few problems if it is understood as meaning the purpose-oriented application of technical provisions. However, the word means more than this; the Greek term 'telos' in this context signifies

31 Case 167/73 *Commission v French Republic* [1974] ECR 359 at paragraph 18 (emphases added). See also the *Fernando Roberto* Case where the Court stated that:

> Article 2 of the Treaty describes the task of the European Economic Community. The aims laid down in that provision are concerned with the existence and functioning of the Community; they are to be achieved through the establishment of the common market and the progressive approximation of the economic policies of Member States, which are also aims whose implementation is the essential object of the Treaty.
>
> (Case 126/86 *Fernando Roberto Gimenez Zaera v Instituto Nacional de la Seguridad Social and Tesoreria General de la Seguridad Social* [1987] ECR-3697 at paragraph 10)

32 Bengoetxea, *The Legal Reasoning of the European Court of Justice* at 233 referring to D Vaughan (ed.), *Law of the European Communities, Vol. 1* (Butterworths, London 1986) Chapter 2, point 266. Bengoetxea divides these possibilities which he terms 'first order' criteria of interpretation into: '(i) semiotic or linguistic arguments, (ii) systemic and context-establishing arguments and (iii) teleological or consequentialist arguments'. Ibid. at 233. 'Semiotic or linguistic criteria ... draw arguments from semantic and syntactical features of legal language and from a comparison of the different language versions in which Community law is authentic.' Ibid. at 234. Systemic/contextual criteria provide that 'a legal provision (*materia*) is properly understood only when it is placed in a wider context (*sedes*)'. Ibid. at 240. Dynamic criteria concern 'functional, teleological and consequentialist arguments'. Ibid. at 251–252. What Bengeotxea terms a second level criterion privileges the teleological/contextual method of interpretation above semiotic or linguistic approaches. As a result,

> The second-level criteria for the use of first-level criteria are those of extensive interpretation: the Community Treaties, as the constitution of the Community are to be interpreted broadly using methods of constitutional interpretation ... Preference is usually given to systemic-functional criteria. There is a second-degree directive of preference in favour of systemic-cum-dynamic interpretation.
>
> (Ibid. at 233–234)

> the ultimate objective and the deeper purpose of the entire process of European integration.[33]

The Court affirmed this rationale in its *Continental Cans*[34] judgment which considered the interpretive effects of Article 3(f) EEC [Article 3(b) TEU][35] setting out the foundational Treaty objective of ensuring undistorted conditions of competition to be 'decisive' regarding the meanings of other Treaty rules relating to its implementation. The Court stated at paragraph 23 that:

> The applicant's argument that this provision merely contains a general programme devoid of legal effect, ignores the fact that Article 3 considers the pursuit of the objectives which it lays down to be indispensable for the achievement of the Community's tasks. As regards in particular the aim mentioned in 3(f), the Treaty in several provisions contains more detailed regulations for the interpretation of which this aim is decisive.[36]

This method of judgment is also affirmed in the Court's later ruling in *CILFIT* where it stated at paragraph 20 that:

> every provision of Community law must be placed in its context and interpreted in the light of the provisions of Community law as a whole, *regard being had to the objectives thereof* and to its state of evolution at the date on which the provision in question is to be applied.[37]

Crucially, the interpretive effects of the Treaty objectives and general principles are not conditional upon meeting justiciability requirements in the manner of direct effect. These standards are placed at the apex of a hierarchy of Union interpretive authority, enabling a discursive and rhetorical form of legal judgment[38] that allows the Court to effectively engage with

33 Everling, 'The Court of Justice as a Decision Making Authority' at 1305.

34 Case 6/72 *Europemballage and Continental Can v Commission* [1973] ECR 215.

35 Article 3(b) TFEU states that '[t]he Union shall have exclusive competence in the following areas … (b) the establishing of the competition rules necessary for the functioning of the internal market'. This provision needs to be read in conjunction with Article 3(3) TEU which states that '[t]he Union shall establish an internal market'.

36 At paragraph 23.

37 Case 283/81 *CILFIT (Srl) & Lanificio di Gavardo SpA v Ministry of Health* [1982] ECR 3415 at paragraph 20 of the judgment (emphasis added). See for comment on this paragraph, Bengoetxea, *The Legal Reasoning of the European Court of Justice* at 232. See also Case C-249/96 *Lisa Jacqueline Grant v South West Trains Ltd* [1998] ECR I-621 at paragraph 47.

38 Bengoetxea has noted that:

> The task of the Community is to achieve progressive integration (Article 2). This task amounts to a Community principle, and Article 164 [now Article 19 TEU] requires an

other institutional actors[39] while expressing legal demands relating to the broadest aspirations of the Treaties. In practice, dialogue between Union and domestic courts takes place through the use of the preliminary reference procedure, which allows domestic courts to refer questions on the interpretation and validity of Union legislation[40] to the Court of Justice.[41] The resulting ruling, which is binding on the question of Union law decided over all Member States' courts, allows the Court to place specific Union legal demands in the context of the wider objectives set out in the Treaties.

To explore this thesis further, it is helpful to consider two judgments in which the Court explicitly associates the interpretive effects of fundamental Treaty rights, the free movement of workers and general principles respectively, with an activist reconstruction of clearly stated Union legislative requirements. The ruling in *Hendrix*[42] illustrates the interpretive effects associated with the rights of free movement of workers, and in *Coote*,[43] deriving from the general principles of rights to equal treatment between the sexes in employment and to an effective judicial remedy.

Hendrix

In *Hendrix*, the Court was asked to rule on the compatibility with Union law of a residence condition attached to the receipt of a disability benefit under Dutch law. The Dutch claimant, Hendrix, was resident in another State but working in Holland at the relevant time. Two Union regulations governed the right in question. The first, Regulation 1408/71,[44] harmonised social

interpretation of Community law geared to the aims of the Treaty, requiring a dynamic and teleological interpretation.

(Bengoetxea, *The Legal Reasoning of the European Court of Justice* at 252 citing H Kutscher, 'Methods of Interpretation as Seen by a Judge at the Court of Justice' in *Judicial and Academic Conference* (Office for Official Publiations on the European Communities, Luxembourg 1976) Part 2, section 6(c) and R Lecourt, *L'Europe des Juges* (Bruylant, Brussels 1976) Part 3, section 2)

39 This is commonly seen in the Court's treatment of the legal effects of Directives which when not implemented by Member States act as a non-directly applicable form of Union law capable of creating constitutional type interpretive effects over domestic legislation. Case C-106/89 *Marleasing* [1990] ECR I-4135.

40 The Court is not however empowered to review the validity of the Treaty Articles but may rule on their interpretation.

41 Or to the General Court, previously the Court of First Instance, in limited circumstances.

42 Case C-287/05 *D.P. W. Hendrix v Raad van Bestuur van het Uitvoeringsinstituut Werknemersverzekeringen* [2007] ECR I-6909.

43 Case C-185/97 *Coote v Granada Hospitality Ltd* [1998] ECR I-5199.

44 Council Regulation 1408/71/EEC of 14 June 1971 on the application of social security schemes to employed persons and their families moving within the Community [1971] OJ L49/2. This Regulation has been largely repealed by Regulation 883/2004/EC of the European Parliament and of the Council of 29 April 2004 on the coordination of social security systems [2004] OJ L166/1 (as amended).

security rights for persons exercising their rights of free movement between Member States. The second, Regulation 1612/68, set out equal treatment rights, including certain social benefits, for Union workers exercising rights to free movement. The Court found that the benefit in question fell within the material scope of both Regulations with contradictory outcomes concerning Hendrix's right to its receipt. In relation to Regulation 1408/71, the Court found that the benefit in question was

> a special non-contributory benefit within the meaning of Article 4(2)(a) of Regulation 1408/71 with the result that only the coordinating provision of Article 10a of that regulation must be applied to persons who are in the situation of the applicant in the main proceedings and that payment of that benefit may validly be reserved to persons who reside in the territory of the Member State which provides the benefit.[45]

In relation to Regulation 1612/68, the Court found that the benefit in question was also a social advantage for the purposes of Article 7(2) and as such available on a non-discriminatory basis to all migrant workers. The Court noted as a result that 'a Member State may *not* make payment of a social advantage within the meaning of Article 7 of Regulation 1612/68 dependent on the condition that recipients are resident in the national territory of that Member State'.[46] However, under Article 42(2) of Regulation 1612/68, that Regulation did not affect co-ordinating provisions adopted under Article 42 EC of which Regulation 1408/71 was an example.[47] This appeared to militate conclusively in favour of the outcome dictated by Regulation 1408/71 which permitted the imposition of a residence condition on the receipt of the benefit by Member States. However, in relation to the legal effects of Regulation 1408/71, the Court concluded that:

> the provisions of Regulation No. 1408/71 enacted to give effect to Article 42 EC must be interpreted in light of the objective of that Article which is to contribute to the establishment of the greatest possible freedom of movement for migrant workers ... It follows that the condition of residence attached to receipt of the benefit under the Wajong can be put

45 Paragraph 38 of the judgment.

46 Paragraphs 48–50 of the judgment (emphasis added), referring to Case C–57/96 *Meints v Minister van Landbouw, Natuurbeheer en Visserij* [1997] ECR I-6689 paragraph 51 and Case C-337/97 *C.P.M. Meeusen v Hoofdirectie van de Informatie Beheer Groep* [1999] ECR I-3289 paragraph 21. If therefore Hendrix fell into the category of migrant workers, he would be entitled to receipt of the benefit in question under the terms of Regulation No. 1612/68. Hendrix, although employed throughout the material time in his home State (Holland), had changed to another Dutch employer after having moved to reside in Belgium. Given that Hendrix had changed employers while resident in another Member State, the Court found that he was a migrant worker, entitled under the terms of Article 7(2) of Regulation 1612/68 to receipt of the benefit on the same terms as his fellow nationals who were resident within their home State. See paragraph 48 of the judgment.

47 Paragraph 51 of the judgment.

> forward against a person in the situation of Mr Hendrix *only* if it is objectively justified and proportionate to the objective pursued.[48]

Affirming the fundamental Treaty objective of free movement of workers as interpretative authority that is determinative of the legal question to be decided, the Court qualifies the clear injunction of Article 4(2)(a) of Regulation 1408/71 as a stated exception to Article 7 of Regulation 1612/68, allowing Member States to make the benefit in question conditional upon home residence. Instead the imposition of such a condition is only possible when objectively justified and proportionate.[49]

In the result, the Court of Justice transforms a lawful Union authority, for Member States to make certain types of public welfare funding conditional upon residence, to one that is presumptively *unlawful* unless demonstrated (by Member States) as justified and proportionate to a legitimate aim as a matter of Union law.[50] The judgment rewrites clear Union and domestic regulatory requirements by reference to the interpretive effects of the fundamental Treaty objective, that of free movement of workers, thereby extending Union competence with a corresponding deficit in domestic legal competence.

Coote

In *Coote v Granada Hospitality Ltd*[51] we see a similar extension of Union competences by reference to the interpretive effects taken by the second 'arm' of the Union constitution, the general principles. The question referred to the Court,[52] again under the preliminary reference procedure, was whether the Equal Treatment Directive (hereafter the Directive)[53] provided for legal

48 Paragraphs 52–54 of the judgment (emphasis added).

49 Paragraph 54 of the judgment.

50 The Court found that the domestic measure was in fact justified and proportionate thereby in the result asserting Union competence in an area where it had been expressly excluded by Union legislation.

51 Case C-185/97 *Coote v Granada Hospitality Ltd* [1998] ECR I-5199.

52 From the UK Employment Appeals Tribunal.

53 Council Directive 76/207/EEC of 9 February 1976 on the implementation of the principle of equal treatment for men and woman as regards access to employment, vocational training and promotion and working conditions. As a result of the judgment in *Coote,* amendments were in fact made to the Equal Treatment Directive. Article 6 of Directive 2002/73/EC of the European Parliament and of the Council of 23 September 2002 amending Council Directive 76/207/EEC on the implementation of the principle of equal treatment for men and women as regards access to employment, vocational training and promotion, and working conditions [2002] OJ L269/15, states that:

> Article 7 [of Directive 76/207/EEC] shall be replaced by the following: . . . Member States shall introduce into their national legal systems such measures as are necessary to protect employees ... against dismissal *or other adverse treatment* by the employer as a reaction to a complaint within the undertaking or to any legal proceedings aimed at enforcing compliance with the principle of equal treatment.
>
> (emphasis added)

redress against the defendants, Granada Hospitality, previous employers of the claimant, Coote, who had refused her a job reference in retaliation for having instituted proceedings against the company under the terms of the Directive whilst she had been in their employ. Within the context of an ongoing employment relationship, it was clear that the implementing UK statute[54] prohibited any such retaliation. Would however a presumption of illegality in relation to retaliatory acts continue to operate when the employment relationship had ended? Under Article 7 of the Directive, only one form of retaliation by an employer against an employee who had previously alleged sex discrimination was prohibited, that of dismissal.

Advocate General Mischo considered that given the clear wording of the Directive, a retaliatory refusal to provide a reference for a prior employee, when not itself based upon the sex of the person concerned, would not be prohibited by the Directive, stating at paragraph 24 of his opinion that:

> It is clear from a reading of the provisions of the Directive that the Community legislature whilst perfectly aware that claims for sexual equality may irritate certain employers to the point of prompting them to engage in reprisals, intentionally took account of only one form of retaliation, the most serious but perhaps not the least common – dismissal.[55]

The Court disagreed, holding that the Directive implicitly outlawed any retaliatory action based on a previous complaint of discriminatory practices, irrespective of whether the employer/employee relationship was current. Article 7 therefore permitted, in the view of the Court, a right of redress in the instant circumstances. The Directive, according to the Court, provided a *non-exhaustive* set of criteria for redress aimed at achieving a result consistent with the general principles on which it was based, namely the right to an effective remedy and the right not to suffer discrimination.[56] However,

54 Section 4 of the Sex Discrimination Act (1975).

55 Paragraph 24.

56 The Court refers to the objectives of the Directive, in terms of the related general principles as follows:

> However, contrary to that Government's submissions, having regard to the objective of the Directive, which is to arrive at real equality of opportunity for men and women (Case C-271/91 *Marshall,* paragraph 24), and to the fundamental nature of the right to effective judicial protection, it is not, in the absence of a clear indication to the contrary, to be inferred from Article 7 of the Directive that the legislature's intention was to limit the protection of workers against retaliatory measures decided on by the employer solely to cases of dismissal, which, although an exceptionally serious measure, is not the only measure which may effectively deter a worker from making use of the right to judicial protection of 'real equality of opportunity for men and woman and to the fundamental nature of the right to effective judicial protection'.
>
> (Paragraph 27 of the judgment, referring to Case C-271/91 *Marshall v Southampton and South West Hampshire Area Health Authority* [1993] ECR I-4367, paragraph 24)

in so ruling the Court ignored the legislative intention to give effect to these general principles in defined circumstances, an intention reflected in the Advocate General's opinion.[57] Their interpretative effects resulted in the judicial creation of a new Union right in breach of the *contra legem* limitation generally placed upon such effects.[58]

In both these cases the Court employed a functional or teleological interpretive approach, not only as a method for 'filling in' the open texture of the Union legislation in question, but also as a vehicle for the development of the integrationist objectives of the Union. This method of reasoning by the Court has of course been the subject of extensive academic comment.[59] Less commonly considered is that this judicial approach incorporates value positions relating to the political aspirations of the Treaty as legal demands. A focus upon the interpretive authority of Union measures allows the Court to maximise the rhetorical force of these demands and hence develop and control the authority of superior Union norms in relation to the Member States. The language of interpretation forms as such a crucial aspect of a broader dialogue between Union and domestic courts underlying the Court's promotion of the overall process of European integration and awareness that it 'operates in a highly politicised milieu'.[60]

These judgments illustrate that the Court's privileging of the Treaty objectives as constitutional interpretive authority may be distinguished from the approach of domestic constitutional courts. Here judicial reasoning is also contextual or functional but in a contingent as opposed to a dynamic sense. Domestic courts will take into account changing social conditions in determining constitutional demands and may as a result adopt a strongly 'activist' approach towards the scope of these demands.[61] This activism, in the domestic

57 The Advocate General affirmed the need to respect the clearly expressed intention of the Union legislator in Article 7 of the Directive, stating at paragraph 27 of his opinion, in response to the argument that the Directive provided the protection sought, that

> It is not, however possible, by *any* legal reasoning constructed on the basis of such a view and of the regrets which may justifiably be felt as a result, to derive from the Directive obligations on the Member States which it does not contain.

58 Case C-334/92 *Wagner Miret v Fondo de Garantia Salarial* [1993] ECR I-6911; Case C-105/03 *Pupino* [2005] ECR I-5285.

59 Approaches divide into those who regard the Court's 'activist' approach to the interpretation of Union requirements as justified and those who do not. For examples of the former view, see T Tridimas, 'The Court of Justice and Judicial Activism' (1996) 21 *European Law Review* 199; M Cappelletti, 'Is the Court of Justice "Running Wild?"' (1987) 12 *European Law Review* 3, and of the latter, H Rasmussen, (1986) *On Law and Policy in the European Court of Justice: A Comparative Study in Judicial Policymaking* (Martinus Nijhoff Publishers, The Hague 1986). See also the analysis in Chapter 4 of this work.

60 Bengoetxea, *The Legal Reasoning of the European Court of Justice* at 50.

61 See in the UK context *Ghaidan v Godin-Mendoza* [2004] UKHL 30 where the House of Lords inserted a provision into a UK statute that extended rights of succession to a tenancy to the surviving partner of a homosexual couple where the legislative text in question clearly reserved

setting, is however parasitic upon the expression of 'freestanding' fundamental rights or due process requirements.[62] In the Union setting by contrast the Treaty objectives mandate in all cases an interpretive approach that expresses a positive dynamic relating to the advancement of European integration.[63] The values that comprise the Union constitution express a primary jurisprudential connection, not with features of State/society as from time to time are adjudicated upon for rights compliance but, instead, allegiance to a single political aspiration, that of European integration.

Conclusions

The values underlying the Union constitution are distinctive by comparison with those associated with domestic constitutions, whose effects concern all social activity in which the law, as an instrument of supreme governmental authority, claims an interest.[64] The uncontained character of domestic constitutional values stands in marked contrast to those asserted as foundational within the Union's legal jurisdiction according to the terms of the Treaties. The Treaties represent both supreme legal authority within the Union order, and the directed rationale underlying its very existence. As a result, the Union constitution, as a combination of specific aims relating to the project of European integration and rule of law principles that operate solely within the identified boundaries of this project, is wholly self-referential. It is the political vision of the Treaties themselves, as opposed to the background value concerns of Member State societies, that directly informs the expression of Union constitutional requirements by the Court of Justice.

the right for a surviving married spouse alone. See also the recent Data Protection ruling of the German Federal Constitutional Court which established a new 'fundamental right to confidentiality and integrity of information technology systems' 1 BvR 370/07 and 1 BvR 595/07, and for comment, G. Hornung, 'Ein neues Grundrecht' [2008] *Computer und Recht* 299.

62 The affirmation of a right in one area may indirectly boost a related right while on other occasions the strength of a given right will be in inverse proportion to that accorded to a conflicting right. For example, the right to religious freedom or to a private life (Articles 8 and 9 ECHR) may conflict with the right to freedom of expression (Article 10 ECHR).

63 From an institutional perspective, the interpretive techniques of the Court of Justice also represent a significant incursion into the role associated with domestic legislative and executive functions in the administration of social and economic policy. Within the Union setting it is a legal institution, the Court of Justice, that determines how the economic freedoms and associated social rights set out in the Treaties are to be given effect. In this regard, Carlos Ball has noted that '[t]he Treaty, as a transnational constitutional charter ... impose[s] *positive* obligations on Community institutions and Member States with the *functional* objective of establishing and maintaining a transnational capitalist society'. C Ball, 'The Making of a Transnational Capitalist Society: The Court of Justice, Social Policy, and Individual Rights under the European Community's Legal Order' (1996) 37 *Harvard International Law Journal* 307 at 308 (emphases in original).

64 J Locke, *The Second Treatise of Government* (first published 1689, Dover Publications, New York 2002).

Expressing the legal demands of a constitution which at its heart embodies an aspirational and contested political project has required the Court of Justice to develop methods of legal reasoning tailored to the unstable political and legal environment in which these demands will take effect. The Court has achieved an alignment of the two identified elements of the Union constitution within legal orders by focusing upon their interpretive effects. As techniques of legal judgment, these effects, over secondary Union laws and domestic laws, have provided the Court with opportunities for highly intrusive regulatory interventions within Member States relevant to the promotion of Union constitutional values. Judgments in cases such as *Hendrix* and *Coote* illustrate how the Court has allied the language of interpretation to a persuasive form of rhetoric, essential to the communication of a careful balancing of Union and Member State interests, while promoting the values of European integration.

6 Union or Member State *Kompetenz Kompetenz*: constitutional questions in the relationship between Union and domestic orders

Introduction

The Union and Member States form parallel sources of legal authority, each expressing jurisdictional independence, while recognising the jurisdiction of the 'other' order, the Union where Member States are concerned and domestic constitutions where the Union is concerned. Where jurisdictional claims by Union or domestic courts are uncertain, or have constitutional implications for the opposing order, competing claims of legal sovereignty may arise. In this regard, given the Treaties' temporally unlimited commitment to an array of social, economic and political objectives, domestic legal orders are variously co-opted, reconfigured and challenged by Union legislative and judicial practices. The Court of Justice must ensure these challenges do not lead to constitutional crises in either order, given the Union, as a derivative jurisdiction, remains dependent on the co-operation of domestic institutions. These themes, introduced in Chapters 3 and 4, are developed in this chapter, which examines the constitutional implications of co-existing yet independent, Union and Member State, legal jurisdictions.

As previously considered, the Court's role as supreme authority in the interpretation of Union legal demands reflects a complex mixture of concerns, including centrally the wider institutional, political and cultural context within which it operates. Everling therefore emphasises that '[f]rom the point of view of its role both as a constitutional court and as a court providing protection of individual rights, the essential factor is the Court's relationship with other Community institutions and with the Member States'.[1] In this regard, the Court's affirmation of Union law demands as supreme legal authority within the Member States clearly disturbs existing constitutional settlements a fortiori when they require (re)clarification of the boundaries between Union and domestic legal authority.

1 U Everling, 'The Court of Justice as a Decision Making Authority' (1983–1984) 82 *Michigan Law Review* 1294 at 1309, hereafter, Everling, 'The Court of Justice as a Decision Making Authority'.

Kompetenz Kompetenz (competence competence) questions concern the existence of (competing) legal claims on the part of Union or Member State courts regarding the scope or status of their respective legal jurisdictions. Parallel claims of legal competence in any given area have implications for the 'constituted' status of each order and hence for the relationship between orders.[2] For MacCormick, the question of 'which to respect' in the event of conflicting institutional normative claims is one of politics and not law.[3] However, given the constitutional implications of Union or domestic legal judgments making opposing jurisdictional claims, Union or domestic courts faced with such conflicts[4] must embrace political questions through legal conclusions regarding the 'constituted' legal authority of their respective jurisdictions. As considered in Chapters 4 and 5, any conclusion reached must be sensitive to the 'opposing' institutional perspective, a task complicated by the complex, shifting and contested boundaries between Union and Member State jurisdictions.

The chapter is set out as follows. In the first section, I consider the impact of potential and actual *Kompetenz Kompetenz* conflicts upon the institutional relationship of Union and Member State courts. In the following section, drawing on case judgments of both the Court of Justice and domestic courts, I argue that judicial approaches to different categories of legality review between Union and Member State orders represent a negotiated, discursive and flexible resolution of their respective *Kompetenz Kompetenz* claims. This analysis is developed finally by examining how the doctrine of Union law supremacy, as the dominant institutional factor in the relationship between

2 The fact that competences have been conferred upon the EU under the Treaties does not in itself determine this question given the possibilities for judicial interpretation of the Treaties by the Court of Justice. For example, by adopting a broad purposive interpretation of the Treaty Articles or general principles, or by recognising competencies not explicitly conferred but deemed necessary for the effective application of the overall Treaty objectives, the Court has been able to effect de facto enlargements to Union legal competencies. See, for example, Case C-185/97 *Coote v Granada Hospitality Ltd* [1998] ECR I-5199 (considered in Chapter 5 of this work), and Case C-70/88, *Parliament v Council (Chernobyl)* [1990] ECR I-2041. From a legislative perspective, the Union can enact measures under the catch-all legal basis of Article 352 TFEU which states that:

> If action by the Union should prove necessary, within the framework of the policies defined in the Treaties, to attain one of the objectives set out in the Treaties, and the Treaties have not provided the necessary powers, the Council, acting unanimously on a proposal from the Commission and after obtaining the consent of the European Parliament, shall adopt the appropriate measures …

3 '[I]nsofar as power-relations enter the question, the issue is, as I shall shortly try to show, one of politics.' N MacCormick, *Questioning Sovereignty* (Oxford University Press, Oxford 1999) at 9, hereafter MacCormick, *Questioning Sovereignty*.

4 Usually between domestic constitutional and Union regulatory requirements. Conflicts between Union and domestic regulatory requirements that do not implicate domestic constitutional principles are generally unproblematic, leading to the setting aside of the conflicting domestic legal requirement.

Union and Member State jurisdictions, has conditioned the respective judicial practices of Union and domestic courts.

Union and domestic legal orders: jurisdictional *Kompetenz Kompetenz*?

Introduction

The institutional authority conferred on the Union under the Treaties, and incorporated as an independent source of law within Member State legal orders, clearly raises *Kompetenz Kompetenz* issues of deep constitutional significance. In addition, the political project of European integration clearly threatens Member States' self-understanding as independent, self-contained legal jurisdictions.[5] The sharing of core constitutional values by 'independent' (Union and Member State) jurisdictions, as well as the directed character of the Union order (towards European integration), results in a need for co-operative legal strategies to mitigate the possibility of potentially damaging conflicts over whether Union or domestic legal requirements prevail in 'border' disputes.

Both Union and domestic courts claim final authority over the substance, scope and status of their respective jurisdictions[6] against similar and parallel claims of the Union where Member States are concerned, and Member States where the Union is concerned.[7] That is, Union and Member States' courts

5 See Chapter 5.

6 N MacCormick, *Questioning Sovereignty* (Oxford University Press, Oxford 1999) at 118.

7 Commentators have generally defended one or other of these positions. Schilling, for example, has argued that *Kompetenz Kompetenz* rests with domestic constitutional courts:

> It may well be that a legal order has a large degree of derivative autonomy, but the legal orders from which it stems have reserved power for their own institutions to interpret at least the constitutional rules of the otherwise autonomous legal order. Such an order would have derivative autonomy, but no interpretive autonomy.
>
> (T Schilling, 'The Autonomy of the Community Legal Order: An Analysis of Possible Legal Foundations' (1996) 37 *Harvard International Law Journal* 389 at 390, hereafter Schilling, 'The Autonomy of the Community Legal Order')

A similar argument is found in the judgment of Lord Justice Laws in the 'Metric Martyrs' case. Laws contended obiter that the constitutional foundations of the relationship between the EU and domestic legal orders were defined by domestic law while domestic (UK) law provided for the supremacy of Union over domestic laws in the event of any substantive conflict. *Thoburn v Sunderland City Council* [2002] EWHC 195. See also in support of this view from a German perspective, D Grimm, 'The European Court of Justice and National Courts: The German Constitutional Perspective after the Maastricht Decision' (1996–1997) 3 *Columbia Journal of European Law* 229. In defence of the existence of 'Union' *Kompetenz Kompetenz*, Everling has noted, referring to Member States' constitutional courts,

> if each of them decided about the application of Community law according to its own estimations, traditions and interests, the unity of the Community's legal order would be

present opposing positions concerning the institutional location of ultimate authority to determine the scope of the Union jurisdiction conferred by the Treaties, or, conversely, of domestic legal jurisdictions under the constitution, as qualified by Union demands. The rationalisation of these conflicting claims can be viewed from a perspective of the qualifying effect of the Union order over domestic constitutional settlements, or in terms of the qualification of Union legal demands by reference to domestic constitutions.

Clearly the legal consequences flowing from opposing *Kompetenz Kompetenz* perspectives cannot be understood simply in terms of traditional notions of legal hierarchy given opposing and concurrent hierarchical claims relating to the doctrines of Union and domestic constitutional supremacy. In addition, the fact that the Union is a significant governmental institutional framework created by Member States suggests these conflicting hierarchical perspectives have practical effects on the constituted legal environment of the Union and Member States, and do not simply exist in the abstract. In light of these factors, the manner in which *Kompetenz Kompetenz* authority is expressed by Union and domestic courts itself represents a distinctive, bespoke and accommodating institutional mechanism designed to ensure the existence of opposing jurisdictional and hence constitutional claims.

Kompetenz Kompetenz *and the Treaties*

The Treaties purport to govern the activities of both Union and domestic institutions, giving rise to a complex picture of legal governance within the Member States. The legal empowerment of the Union under the Treaties provides an undoubted challenge to Member State prerogatives to maintain incumbent forms of their respective constitutions. This challenge derives from

> threatened. The Treaty therefore confers on the Court of Justice the exclusive competence to decide about the validity and application of the legal acts of the Community in the territory of all Member States.
>
> (U Everling, 'The *Maastricht* Judgment of the German Federal Constitutional Court and its Significance for the Development of the European Union' (1994) 14 *Yearbook of European Law* 14 at 23)

Weiler advocates a more nuanced view of the relationship between domestic and Union legal orders according to which 'the jurisdictional line (or lines) should be a matter of constitutional conversation, not a constitutional *diktat*'. J H H Weiler and U R Haltern, 'The Autonomy of the Community Legal Order – Through the Looking Glass' (1996) 37 *Harvard International Law Journal* 411 at 447, hereafter Weiler and Haltern, 'Through the Looking Glass'. This is broadly the view I defend. More recently, writers have emphasised a 'soft', pluralist approach to the relationship between orders. This view emphasises the partial autonomy of Union and domestic orders and stresses the need for accommodation between conflicting views on the location of legal sovereignty. For different constitutionalist versus pluralist positions around the relation of Union to international and domestic legal orders, see M P Maduro, 'Interpreting European Law: Judicial Adjudication in a Context of Constitutional Pluralism' (2007) 1 *European Journal of Legal Studies*, hereafter, Maduro, 'Interpreting European Law'; G de Burca and J H H Weiler (eds), *The Worlds of European Constitutionalism* (Cambridge University Press, Cambridge 2012).

the scope and complexity of the Union order, its 'governmental' institutional configuration as well as the significant transfer of legal authority to the Union under the Treaties. In order to reconcile their respective institutional roles Union and domestic courts must therefore rationalise the limits and evaluative foundations of their respective jurisdictions in relation to concurrent (potentially opposing) jurisdictional claims.

As noted, judicial determinations regarding the respective competencies of Union and Member State legal orders address fundamental constitutional and hence politically significant issues.[8] For the Court of Justice, Union *Kompetenz Kompetenz* derives from the practical need to avoid the possibility of the legality review of Union measures by domestic courts thereby undermining the viability of the Union order as an independent source of legal authority.[9] From the perspective of domestic constitutional courts, *Kompetenz Kompetenz* expresses a belief in the final ability of the Member States to decide the limitations of State sovereignty ceded under the Union Treaties and hence the ultimate sovereign authority of the State. How are these respective claims reconciled?

A starting point is MacCormick's statement in relation to plural legal orders, cited above, which in full reads: '[t]he characteristic of an institutional normative order is that competent judgement in it is conclusive within its own order, except to the extent there is *coordinated cross-recognition* of different orders'.[10] The highlighted phrase indicates that the stable co-existence of opposing *Kompetenz Kompetenz* claims may be possible in light of co-operative strategies of recognition between orders. In this regard, the Treaty principles

8 A role which in the context of international Treaties is typically reserved to the executive and legislative branches of contracting States. See J. F. McMahon, 'The Court of the European Communities: Judicial Interpretation and International Organisation' (1961) 37 *British Yearbook of International Law* 320 at 320.

9 Case 6/64 *Costa v ENEL* [1964] ECR 585 where the Court stated in its judgment that

> The executive force of community law cannot vary from one state to another in deference to subsequent domestic laws, without jeopardizing the attainment of the objectives of the Treaty set out in Article 5(2) and giving rise to the discrimination prohibited by Article 7.

10 MacCormick, *Questioning Sovereignty* at 8 (emphasis added). While MacCormick's analysis captures the counter-intuitive sense in which legal orders occupying the same juridical space are capable of de facto limitation in either jurisdiction or status as a consequence of co-operative practices between orders, it is also important to note that law qua institutional normative order may exhibit 'qualitative' variations. For example, under the institutional framework established by the Union Treaties, the measures adopted under the co-operative mechanisms of the Union Common Foreign and Security Policy (previously the second pillar) can be contrasted with the 'hard' legal demands arising under the ordinary legislative procedure (previously the co-decision procedure under the first pillar). Union competence in the former areas concerns critical areas of domestic sovereignty, areas in which public activity is executive dominated and subject to minimal judicial intrusion while institutional measures in these areas do not generally give rise to enforceable legal rights or obligations.

of conferred competencies, subsidiarity and proportionality[11] may be said to offer definitional clarity over the Union's assigned competencies, allay fears concerning loss of domestic constitutional protections and restrict possibilities for unacceptable, from Member States' perspectives, 'competence creep'.[12]

However, the picture of an effective reconciliation of Union and domestic order demands through the operation of stabilising mechanisms within the Treaties may be suspect. I highlighted in Chapter 4 arguments that the principles of conferred competencies, subsidiarity and proportionality, in fact reflect as opposed to mitigate uncertainties present in the relationship between orders, potentially giving rise to *Kompetenz Kompetenz* disputes. One might go further and suggest that the possibility of jurisdictional conflict is increased under the influence of these principles given the uncertainties in their operation.

Under the principle of conferred competencies, for example, the Union jurisdiction is defined by the wording of the Treaties, regarding which the Court of Justice is the ultimate interpretive authority. This suggests that it is the Union that possesses *Kompetenz Kompetenz*, at least in the narrow sense of being able to decide which legal powers have been conferred under the terms of the Treaties. On the other hand, the idea of *conferred* competencies is meaningless unless it is the Member States as subject 'conferrers' and not Union institutions as object 'conferees', which remain competent to determine the precise scope of powers actually conferred.[13] Similar considerations apply regarding the proportionality and subsidiarity principles. Given the Court's attributed role under Article 19 TEU as authoritative interpreter of the operative features of these principles, it is possible that *Kompetenz Kompetenz* disputes could arise concerning the operation of the very principles designed for their avoidance.[14]

Instabilities in relation to the jurisdictional boundaries between Union and domestic law are further underlined by the fact that these boundaries are not clearly identified within the Treaties themselves. As Weiler has noted, '[s]ince the jurisdictional limits laid out in the Treaties are notoriously difficult to identify with precision, the question of who gets to decide is of tremendous

11 Article 5 TEU.

12 Similar arguments have been made inter alia by Maduro, 'Interpreting European Law' and N Walker, 'The Place of European Union Law' in G de Burca and J H H Weiler (eds), *The Worlds of European Constitutionalism* (Cambridge University Press, Cambridge 2012).

13 This point loses some of its force if the possibility of transferring defined competencies to an independent institutional framework, charged with their interpretation, is admitted in principle.

14 I would suggest that the role of these principles has been rather political to reassure leaders in the bargaining process leading to Treaty revision and consequent Union expansion as well as generate a perception within the Member States that the political elites of the Member States are maintaining a tight rein on the scale and operation of the Union legal jurisdiction. Absent the subsidiarity or conferred competencies principles within the Treaties, it is unlikely that the Court would have attempted to seize greater jurisdictional authority for the Union than has otherwise occurred or would have positioned the Union jurisdiction in a way that was institutionally unsustainable within the Member States.

political importance for the relationship between the Community and the Member States'.[15] An approach to understanding the judicial practices of domestic and Union courts suggestive of a final location of boundary-setting authority in the manner suggested by Weiler is in my view impossible to realise. Instead I would emphasise the importance of the legal rhetoric of Union and Member States' constitutional courts as a communicative strategy to manage competing *Kompetenz Kompetenz* claims.

Rhetorically co-ordinated institutional frameworks

Schilling offers a helpful starting point to understand the implications of co-existing independent institutional frameworks in the Union and Member States in the following comment:

> The distinctiveness of the Community and Member State legal systems is not between on the one hand, the Community legal system in a narrow sense consisting exclusively of the rules found in the treaties and in secondary Community legislation, and, on the other hand, the Member State legal systems also in a narrow sense, consisting exclusively of the rules found in the Member State constitution[s] and in Member State legislation. The narrow systems clearly are not distinct, and Article 234 EC is the most obvious indication thereof. This distinctiveness is rather characterised by the very fact that both the Community and Member State legal systems are mutually incorporating the rules of the respective other one. It is between two incompatible constructions of the same legal material.[16]

Schilling here highlights the important point that different and potentially 'incompatible constructions of the same legal material', relating to the controversial political project of European integration, must somehow be recognised within the legal judgments of Union and domestic courts. How this recognition occurs in practice is illustrated by rhetorical approaches of Union and domestic courts to legality review claims which address questions of the jurisdictional boundaries between orders. Legality review judgments, which deal with the (in)compatibility and hierarchical positioning of laws, provide insights into how Union and Member States' courts rationalise the practical co-ordination of opposing jurisdictional claims.

In a doctrinal sense, legality review in the Union/Member State context refers to the ability of a conflict between a Union and domestic measure to result in the setting aside of the hierarchically inferior provision. However,

15 Weiler and Haltern, 'Through the Looking Glass' at 413 (footnote omitted).

16 T Schilling, 'The Court of Justice's Revolution: Its Effects and the Conditions for its Consummation: What Europe Can Learn from Fiji' (2002) 27 *European Law Review* 445 at 454, hereafter Schilling, 'The Court of Justice's Revolution'.

as Schilling illustrates, Union and Member State courts may be faced with 'incompatible constructions of the same legal material' corresponding to competing claims of supremacy in relation to the associated substantive claims. These conflicts cannot be resolved, as would normally be the case, by simply setting aside one or other of the respective 'constitutional' requirements of the Union and Member States. Instead, the rhetorical arguments made in legality review judgments illustrate how Union and domestic courts respond to conflicting, 'internalised' (Union and Member State) constitutional claims. These judgments enable a judicial constitutional discourse that has been instrumental in maintaining a viable legal and political relationship between the Union and Member States, and will be considered in the next section.

Cross-order legality review

In the Union/Member State setting, we may identify two general legality review categories. The first, 'cross-order' review, concerns the review of legal norms originating in one order by reference to those originating in the 'opposing' order. The second, internal-order review, concerns the review of legal measures originating in one order by reference to (superior) legal standards originating in the same order.[17] If we accept that no conclusive hierarchy exists between Union and domestic laws, then, in principle, four possibilities exist in relation to each category. Cross-order review by either the Court of Justice or domestic courts may be of Union rules by reference to domestic requirements, or of domestic rules by reference to Union requirements. Internal-order review by either the Court of Justice or domestic courts may be of Union measures in light of (superior) Union standards, or of domestic measures by reference to (superior) domestic standards.[18]

The possibility of internal-order reviews in relation to the internal hierarchies of the 'opposing' jurisdiction, for example the Court of Justice ruling on the legality of domestic laws by reference to the domestic constitution, can be discounted. Such review would require a complete mutual incorporation

17 This schematic, based on the institutional location of challenge and origins of the 'challenging'/'under challenge' legal measures, is complicated by the possibility of Member States (or individuals under limited circumstances) challenging the legality of Union secondary legislation before the Court of Justice under the terms of Article 263 TFEU. In addition, Member State courts may refer questions concerning the validity of Union measures to the Court of Justice under the Article 267 preliminary reference procedure. Furthermore, under Article 23 of Protocol (No. 3) on the Statute of the Court of Justice of the European Union, in Article 267 proceedings, 'the Member States … shall be entitled to submit statements of case or written observations to the Court'. These bilateral institutional mechanisms have clearly been of great importance as mechanisms for enabling a constitutional discourse between Union and domestic courts and thereby to advance the Union project while ensuring the institutional viability of Union legal demands.

18 In practice internal-order review by the 'opposing' court will not occur; this schematic is simply to illustrate the possibilities in principle given a degree of mutual incorporation of Union and domestic orders.

of Union and Member State constitutional jurisdictions, a situation that clearly does not exist. In addition, internal-order review by courts of the same jurisdiction, for example of Union laws by reference to Union laws undertaken by the Court of Justice, while clearly possible, is not directly relevant for the relationship between orders so will also not be considered here.[19] The following analysis will therefore focus on the four cross-order review possibilities. As I suggested above, the quality of review in all four types is not legality review *sensu stricto*, that is a conclusive ruling of the (in)validity of one law in light of a conflicting and superior legal rule. Instead, the judgments associated with each type of review illustrate rhetorically presented outcomes. These outcomes may variously be suggestive (as opposed to conclusive) of invalidity, or restrict the material scope of application of the conflicting rule, or finally, affirm (as yet) unrealised conditions in which invalidity would arise. Considering each of these possibilities in turn.

Cross-order review by the Court of Justice: of domestic law in light of Union standards

Under the Article 267 TFEU preliminary ruling procedure, following a written reference from a domestic court on a question of Union law, the Court of Justice is empowered to rule on the interpretation or validity of Union secondary laws and the interpretation (but not validity) of the Treaty Articles. This clearly authorises the Court to undertake an internal-order type review in relation to Union (secondary) laws said to be incompatible with superior Union laws (the Treaty Articles or general principles), but to preclude any authority to assess the validity of domestic institutional acts.[20] The Court has nonetheless frequently affirmed the (in)compatibility of domestic laws with Union legal requirements and hence implicitly taken a position upon their validity, at least insofar as they conflict with Union requirements.[21] Indeed the Court has consistently maintained that all domestic legal rules,

19 Article 263 TFEU and Article 267 TFEU.

20 A position the Court of Justice affirms in principle. See, for example, the statement in *Costa* which is representative,

> in the context of requests for preliminary rulings, the Court has no jurisdiction either to apply the Treaty to a specific case or to decide upon the validity of a provision of domestic law in relation to the Treaty ...
>
> (Case 6/64 *Costa v ENEL* [1964] ECR 585 at para. 1 of the summary)

21 For one example amongst many, see the judgment in *Tadao Maruko* where the Court stated in relation to a Directive's requirements that '[t]he combined provisions of Articles 1 and 2 of Directive 2000/78 *preclude* [domestic] legislation such as that at issue in the main proceedings'. Case C-67/06 *Tadao Maruko v Versorgungsanstalt der deutschen Buhnen* [2008] ECR I-1757 (emphasis added). See also G Martinico and O Pollicino, 'Between Constitutional Tolerance and Judicial Activism: The Specificity of European Judicial Law' (2008) 10 *European Journal of Law Reform* 109.

including the constitution, must not be applied where to do so would impair the effective application of Union demands.[22]

Limiting the consequences of incompatibility between Union and domestic law

The Court of Justice has sought to limit the consequences of a finding of incompatibility to requiring the non-application of the conflicting domestic measure,[23] as opposed to issuing a declaration of invalidity. This has allowed the supremacy of Union law to be maintained while restricting its intrusion upon the operation of domestic legal requirements to those matters addressed by Union legislation. A need to mitigate the intrusion of Union legal demands is also illustrated by the Court's preference towards the interpretive as opposed to legality review effects of Union laws in the event of conflict. This is illustrated by the judgment in *Mary Murphy v Bord Telecom Eireanne* where the question referred for preliminary ruling by the Court was whether the principle of equal pay for equal work contained in Article 119 EEC[24] and Directive 75/117 EEC[25] applied when a female employee was undertaking (dissimilar) work of higher value than a male colleague for less pay. The Court stated at paragraph 11 of its judgment that:

> In so far as it is established that the difference in wages in question is based on discrimination on grounds of sex, Article 119 of the EEC Treaty is directly applicable in the sense that the workers concerned may rely on it in legal proceedings in order to obtain equal pay within the meaning of the provision and in the sense that national courts or tribunals must take it into account as a constituent part of Community law. It is for the national court, within the limits of its discretion under national law, when interpreting and applying domestic law, to give to it, where possible, an interpretation which accords with the requirements of the

22 Case 11/70 *Internationale Haandelsgesellschaft mbH v Einfuhr- und Vorratsstelle fur Getreide und Futtermittel* [1970] ECR 1125 (*Solange I*), hereafter *Solange I*; Case 106/77 *Italian Finance Administration v Simmenthal* [1978] ECR 629. For analysis of the *Simmenthal* judgment, see K Lenaerts, 'Interlocking Legal Orders in the European Union and Comparative Law' (2003) 52 *International and Comparative Law Quarterly* 873 at 899–900, hereafter Lenaerts, 'Interlocking Legal Orders in the European Union'.

23 Joined Cases C-10/97 to C-22/97 *Ministero delle Finanze v I.N.C.O.G.E'90* [1998] ECR I-6307. Bieber and Salome have suggested that the outcome of norm conflict should be determined by the nature of Union competence in the area in question, noting that '[w]hile it appears acceptable that "indirect" collisions only render the national norm inapplicable, national legislation in areas of exclusive Community competence (and vice versa) should mean that the respective act is void'. B Bieber and I Salome, 'Hierarchy of Norms in European Law' (1996) 33 *Common Market Law Review* 909 at 914.

24 Now Article 157 TFEU following renumbering introduced by the Lisbon Treaty.

25 Article 1 of Council Directive 75/117 EEC of 10 February 1975 on the approximation of the laws of the Member States relating to the application of the principle of equal pay for men and women [1975] OJ L 45/19.

> applicable Community law and, to the extent that this is not possible, to hold such domestic law inapplicable.[26]

Domestic courts are here directed by the Court to actively seek an accommodation of Union requirements through the technique of compatible interpretation 'where possible' of existing domestic laws. This emphasises the Court's function in facilitating consensus between Union and domestic legal requirements.[27]

Cross-order review by the Court of Justice: of Union law in light of domestic standards

The Court of Justice has never recognised the possibility of the legality review of Union measures in light of domestic constitutional requirements, a fortiori in light of domestic law generally.[28] The Court will only permit internal-order review of Union laws, that is by reference to the requirements of Union law itself.[29] Where conflicts have arisen between Union and domestic constitutional laws, the Court has adopted a rhetorical strategy of de facto recognition of domestic constitutional requirements combined with their affirmation as sources of Union legal authority. This is illustrated by the Court's statement in *Nold*:

> As the Court has already stated, fundamental rights form an integral part of the general principles of law, the observance of which it ensures. In safeguarding these rights, the court is bound to draw inspiration from constitutional traditions common to the Member States, and it cannot therefore uphold measures which are incompatible with fundamental rights recognised and protected by the constitutions of those states. Similarly, international treaties for the protection of human rights on which the Member States have collaborated or of which they are signatories can supply guidelines which should be followed within the framework of Community law.[30]

26 Case 157/86 *Murphy v Bord Telecom Eireann* [1988] ECR 673 at para. 11 (emphasis added).

27 Whilst this may be seen as a natural outcome of the conflict between (superior and inferior) laws, there is an additional significance relating to the fact that the Union is keen to engage with and recognise the importance of domestic legal demands at all, an approach that arguably is not required as a matter of international law on which the Treaties are based. See in support of this argument O Spiermann, 'The Other Side of the Story: An Unpopular Essay on the Making of the European Community Legal Order' (1999) 10 *European Journal of International Law* 763, hereafter Spiermann, 'The Other Side of the Story'.

28 *Solange I*.

29 Articles 263 and 267 TFEU. The Treaty Articles and general principles as superior norms of Union law form the basis for the legality review of secondary legislation (regulations, directives and decisions).

30 Case 4/73 *Nold v Commission* [1974] ECR 491 at para. 13.

Lenaerts, a former judge of the Court, has noted that in this judgment

> the Court of Justice wanted to stress that the Community is embedded in the constitutional current of its Member States so that the protection given to the fundamental rights of the citizen in the different national constitutions constitutes not only a source of inspiration but even a binding guideline.[31]

Where Union legal demands conflict with domestic constitutional requirements, the Court has adopted a rhetorical form of 'anti' review. The Court's rhetoric affirms the superiority of all Union legal demands over all domestic legal demands, including the constitution, while vouchsafing the adoption/expression of key domestic constitutional requirements as a matter of Union law. In sum, domestic constitutional requirements have never formed the basis for the technical or doctrinal form of legality review of Union measures yet have nonetheless 'bound' the Court to recognise equivalent general principles of Union law. This approach, which originated in the Court's judgments, is now recognised within the Treaties.[32]

Cross-order legality review by Member State courts: of domestic law in light of Union standards

The Court of Justice has emphasised the ability of all levels of the domestic judicial hierarchy to immediately disapply domestic measures incompatible with Union legal requirements.[33] Over the life of the Union an ability of all binding Union demands[34] to render conflicting domestic regulatory requirements inapplicable (but not invalid), including in some instances those of constitutional standing, has increasingly been accepted by domestic courts over the life of the Union.[35] At the same time, the circumstances defined by the

31 Lenaerts, 'Interlocking Legal Orders in the European Union' at 87.

32 Article 6(3) TEU states that: '[f]undamental rights, as guaranteed by the European Convention for the Protection of Fundamental Rights and Fundamental Freedoms and as they result from the constitutional traditions common to the Member States shall constitute general principles of the Union's law'. The phrasing 'as general principles of the Union's law' emphasises the independence of the Union legal order and hence the Court of Justice's competence to decide whether a given principle is part of the common constitutional traditions of the Member States. As a result, the injunction provided by Article 6(3) TEU does not necessarily mean that Union demands will not be upheld by the Court in light of conflicting domestic constitutional demands, recognised as Union general principles. Some qualification of domestic constitutional requirements may instead be required, a possibility considered below.

33 And to set aside domestic procedural requirements that may prevent them from doing so, even if constitutionally inscribed. Case 35/76 *Simmenthal v Italian Minster for Finance* [1976] ECR 1871. *R v Secretary of State for Transport ex parte Factortame* [1989] 2 CMLR 353.

34 Treaty Articles, regulations and directives.

35 See in the UK context, the second House of Lords *Factortame* judgment in which the doctrine of parliamentary sovereignty was qualified by recognition of the ability of Union legal requirements to render conflicting statutory demands inapplicable.

Court in which a requirement to disapply arises have gradually broadened,[36] albeit subject to reservations where challenges to core features of the domestic constitution are concerned. These reservations concern the final review possibility of Union law(s) in light of domestic legal requirements by Member State courts.

Cross-order legality review by Member State courts: of Union law in light of domestic (constitutional) standards

In practice, no legality review claim against a Union legal rule by reference to domestic legal requirements has ever been conclusively upheld by a domestic court. However, the possibility of such review remains of key importance in the management by domestic and Union courts of opposing *Kompetenz Kompetenz* claims. Two types of claim involving the compatibility of the Union jurisdiction with aspects of the domestic constitution have been raised in legality review proceedings before domestic courts. The first concerns the constitutionality of substantive Union regulatory demands said to be incompatible with fundamental rights upheld by the domestic constitution. The second involves challenges to the constitutionality of Member States' 'incorporating acts' transferring (additional) powers to the Union as a result of Treaty amendment or acts of accession. In both areas, domestic constitutional courts have affirmed an ability to review the constitutionality of the Union jurisdiction, although the outcome has always been to qualify, as opposed to directly confront, the operation of this jurisdiction. Below each type of challenge is considered in turn.

Challenges to the (domestic) constitutionality of Union regulatory demands

This type of challenge concerns alleged breaches of substantive domestic constitutional requirements, generally concerning fundamental rights, by Union regulatory demands. Increasingly robust Treaty and judicial recognition of rule of law and fundamental rights requirements as Union general principles by the Court of Justice, as noted above, has contributed to a legal culture within Member States in which the compatibility of Union secondary legislation and domestic constitutional requirements is generally presumed.[37] Such a presumption is famously set out in the *Solange II* judgment of the German Federal Constitutional Court (FCC) as follows:

36 Particularly in the area of the legal effects created by directives. See the developments in Case C-129/94 *Criminal Proceedings against Rafael Ruiz Bernaldez* [1996] ECR I-1829; Case C-194/94 *CIA Security International SA v Signalson SA* [1996] ECR I-2201; Case C-72/95 *Kraaijeveld and others v Gedeputeerde Staten van Zuid-Holland* [1996] ECR I-5403.

37 Although lower domestic courts have been prepared occasionally to declare the unlawfulness of Union acts in light of constitutional requirements, such findings have never evolved into entrenched features of domestic legal orders. For an example of a subsequently overruled domestic judgment affirming the incompatibility (and hence invalidity) of a Union measure with the domestic constitution, see the German case of *Kloppenburg* 2 BvR 687/85.

> the Constitutional Court now adopted the position that so long as Community law and in particular the case law of the Court of Justice generally assured an effective protection of fundamental rights ... and which was substantially similar to the protection offered by the Federal Constitution, the Court would no longer exercise its powers of jurisdiction to decide on the applicability of secondary Community law or review such legislation by the standard of the fundamental rights contained in the Constitution. Accordingly, the claim ... that the EEC regulations and the interpretation given to them by the Court of Justice were incompatible with the Constitution, was inadmissible.[38]

The FCC's approach was reaffirmed in the *Bananas* judgment:

> constitutional complaints and references from courts alleging the infringement of fundamental rights enshrined in the Federal Constitution by secondary Community [Union] law, were inadmissible *ab initio* if their grounds failed to show that the development of European Law, and in particular the jurisprudence of the Court of Justice since the *Solange II* judgment of the Federal Constitutional Court, had fallen below the required standard of fundamental rights protection.[39]

By declaring claims regarding the unconstitutionality of Union laws by reference to the German Federal Constitution inadmissible *ab initio*, the Federal Constitutional Court bases the validity of all Union legal requirements on an assumption, largely unrelated to the specific claims of incompatibility raised, that the Union legal order as a whole maintains a sufficient level of fundamental rights protection. This assumption is linked to onerous conditions of rebuttal relating to the *admissibility* of any constitutional complaint alleging the incompatibility of Union demands with the domestic constitution. To have a complaint heard, a claimant must demonstrate a level (lack) of fundamental rights protection by the Union legal order as a whole that falls below minimum protections guaranteed under the constitution. This condition, in virtue of its generality, is so difficult to satisfy as to be practically meaningless. This does not mean that the Federal Constitutional Court's approach is one that sanctions 'law breaking' by the Union. However, the legal consequences for doing so would only be triggered by a failure in fundamental right protection on the part of the Union, so significant as to trigger political action, arguably rendering any legal response immaterial.

The *Solange II* and *Bananas* judgments eschew reasoned legal justification by the German FCC to resolve potential conflicts between Union regulatory and domestic constitutional demands. Instead, rhetoric is employed to

38 Case No. 2 BvR 197/83 *Wunsche Handelsgesellschaft (Solange II)*, Federal Republic of Germany, Federal Constitutional Court at para. 9 of the ratio, hereafter *Solange II*.

39 *Banana Organisation Constitutionality Case* 2 BvL 1/97 at para. 2 of the ratio.

convey a political message to the Union institutions concerning the importance of fundamental right protections upheld by the constitution. Domestic judgments in other Member State jurisdictions have accepted explicitly what is implicit in the *Solange II* and *Bananas* judgments, namely that a Union requirement may operate to qualify requirements of the constitution in some circumstances. This can be seen, for example, in the Belgian Conseil d'Etat ruling in *Orfinger v Belgian State (Minister for Civil Service)*.[40] The case involved an action for annulment of a Royal Decree, based upon a Treaty requirement, allowing other Member State nationals to obtain employment in the public services. The annulment claim was based upon Article 10(2) of the Belgian constitution which reserved employment in these areas to Belgian nationals. Article 34 of the constitution permitted the transfer of powers by the Belgian State to international originations. The Conseil d'Etat stated that

> The authority of the interpretation given to the EC Treaty by the Court of Justice was based on Article 34 of the Constitution even where it restricted the effect of Articles 8 and 10 of the Constitution. The application of the Treaty, in the interpretation given by the Court of Justice, was the consequence of the accession of Belgium to the Community. That application could always be brought to an end, at the initiative of the Belgium [*sic*] authorities, by the renunciation of that Membership or renegotiation of its conditions. In the absence of such an initiative, the principle of the rule of law required Community rules to be applied in full. Whilst it was desirable that the constitution should be adapted to the requirements of Community law, the application of Community law was not dependent upon such an amendment and was obligatory even in its absence.[41]

In the outcome, not only is the Union requirement upheld, but a conflicting, substantive aspect of the constitution is explicitly qualified (since held to be inapplicable). This indicates a flexible judicial approach to the constitution, allowing its qualification to comply with Union requirements.[42] Here, the result of a review claim by reference to the domestic constitution is the qualification *of* the domestic constitution by Union demands, illustrating the rhetorical (not doctrinal) approach of domestic courts seeking to reconcile conflicting Union and domestic constitutional demands.

40 Case No. 62.922, Belgian Conseil d'Etat (Sixth Chamber) (5 November 1996).

41 Paras 3 and 4 of the ratio. This judgment takes a similar approach to the legal obligations imposed by the Union on Member States defended by Spiermann in Spiermann, 'The Other Side of the Story'.

42 See in the Italian context *Spa Granital v Amministrazione Delle Finanze Dello Stato*, Italian Constitutional Court 8 June 1984, and in the UK context *R v Secretary of State for Transport ex parte Factortame* [1989] 2 CMLR 353.

Challenges to the constitutionality of the transfer of powers to the Union

The second type of challenge to Union measures in light of domestic (constitutional) demands before domestic courts is not directly concerned with Union activities as such. Instead, these claims focus on the legality of actions of domestic executive or legislative branches in authorising acts of Treaty accession or amendment that transfer (additional) powers to the Union. Member States' constitutional or supreme courts have always recognised the compatibility of such acts with the constitution, albeit with reservations.[43] The Danish Supreme Court judgment in *Carlsen and Others v Rasmussen*[44] is illustrative in this regard. In this case, amendments introduced within the EC Treaty by the Maastricht Treaty were challenged on the basis that Article 20 of the Danish constitution, which permits the transfer of powers to international organisations under special legislative procedures, had not been validly applied. Article 20(1) states that

> Powers vested in the authorities of the Realm under this Constitution Act may, to such extent as shall be provided by Statute, be delegated to international authorities set up by mutual agreement with other states for the promotion of international rules of law and co-operation.

In the Proceedings on the Merits before the Provincial Court, the applicants claimed, according to Oppenheimer,

> that Art 20(1) only gave authority for transfers of sovereignty 'to such an extent as shall be provided by statute' and that this condition had not been complied with. They referred in particular to the powers vested in the Council under Article 235 of the EC Treaty and to the 'judicial legislation' engaged in by the European Court of Justice. They also argued that the derogation of sovereignty was on such a scale and of such a nature as to be inconsistent with the Constitution's premise of a democratic form of government.[45]

The Eastern Provincial Court rejected this complaint and an appeal to the Supreme Court also failed. However the Supreme Court concluded that it

43 For a recent example, see the German Federal Constitutional Court ruling in *Gauweiler v Treaty of Lisbon* 2 BvE 2/08. For an overview of these cases, see G Martinico and O Pollicino, 'Between Constitutional Tolerance and Judicial Activism: The Specificity of European Judicial Law' (2008) 10 *European Journal of Law Reform* 109 at 111ff.

44 Case No. 272/1994 *Carlsen and Others v Rasmussen*, Danish Supreme Court (Admissibility), hereafter *Carlsen and Others v Rasmussen*.

45 A Oppenheimer (ed.), *The Relationship between European Community Law and National Law: The Cases Vol. 2* (Cambridge University Press, Cambridge 2003) at 176, hereafter Oppenheimer (ed.), *The Relationship between European Community Law and National Law: The Cases Vol. 2*. The claimant's arguments before the Supreme Court were similar.

retained in principle the right to review the legality of transfer of powers to the European Union, noting that

> The EC Treaty was based on a principle of conferred powers which implied a restriction on the powers of its institutions which complied with the requirement of Article 20 of the Constitution that only specified powers should be delegated.[46]

The Court developed this finding as follows:

> It was certainly true that, in adopting the Act of Accession to the EC Treaty, it had been recognised that the power to test the validity and legality of EC measures was vested exclusively in the European Court of Justice under the provisions of the Treaty. However, the requirement for specification contained in Article 20(1) of the Constitution, when taken in light of the power of Danish courts to review the constitutionality of acts, meant that national courts could not be deprived of their right to examine whether a particular EC measure exceeded the limits for the transfer of sovereignty brought about by the Act of Accession.[47]

The Supreme Court therefore expressly recognised the possibility of declaring Union measures ultra vires the powers conferred under the Treaties as a matter of Danish law. Moreover, the ability of the domestic constitutional court to review the legality of transfer of sovereign powers to an international organisation, including the Union, was effectively entrenched ('national courts *could not* be deprived of their right'), so could not be removed by an otherwise permitted transfer.

The Supreme Court also addressed the claimant's contention that the broad powers transferred to the Union under the Maastricht Treaty would undermine the democratic legitimacy of the Danish State as follows:

> According to Article 20 of the Constitution, powers could only be delegated to international bodies established by mutual agreement with other States for the promotion of international rules of cooperation. It was to be assumed that powers could not be transferred to such an extent that Denmark could no longer be considered an independent State. Whilst the determination of the limits of such a transfer had to rely almost exclusively

46 *Carlsen and Others v Rasmussen* at para. 2 of the ratio.

47 Ibid. at para. 5 of the ratio. See also the German Federal Constitutional Court judgment in *Kloppenburg* where the Federal Court stated that

> the Constitutional Court was competent to examine whether an international institution, within the meaning of Article 24(10), of the German constitution, had remained within or overstepped the boundaries of the sovereign rights assigned to it.
>
> (*Kloppenburg* 2 BvR 687/85)

> on considerations of a political nature, it was clear that sovereignty had not been transferred to the Community by the Act of Accession to such an extent as to violate the above-mentioned assumption.[48]

This response does not offer any legal justification for the conclusion that the transfer of powers to the Union under the Maastricht Treaty had not violated the stated assumption that powers could not be transferred to an extent that Denmark would no longer be an independent State. The Supreme Court curiously treats this assumption both as a purely political matter ('the determination of the limits of such a transfer had to rely almost exclusively on considerations of a political nature'), and one that it was entitled to offer an authoritative legal ruling upon ('it was clear that sovereignty had not been transferred to the Community by the Act of Accession to such an extent as to violate the above-mentioned assumption'). Again we see an avoidance of reasoned legal justification in favour of a rhetorical approach that represents a political signal affirming the integrity of the Member State on the one hand and the jurisdiction conferred upon the Union on the other.

Within the different categories of review outlined above, there are clearly a number of different rationalisations of the relationship between Union and domestic law. These correspond to a variety of rhetorical conclusions expressed within legal judgments concerning the claim that a (Union or domestic constitutional) law is invalid by virtue of its incompatibility with a superior (domestic constitutional or Union) law. Legal judgments regarding these claims by Union and domestic courts represent a complex, rhetorically constructed landscape comprising a number of institutional perspectives on the key constitutional themes in the relationship between the Union and its Member States. These are the supremacy of Union law, the sovereignty of the domestic constitution and, crucially, the impact of these two doctrines upon the legal demands of the opposing order. These judicial outputs are far removed from the expected conclusions of 'technical' legality review claims, namely that a particular law is valid without qualification, or that it is conclusively invalid and therefore no longer possesses any legal authority. The judgments considered all affirm the constitutional sovereignty of the jurisdiction in which judgment occurs, qualified in different ways by the jurisdictional demands of the opposing order.

Overall, the possibility of successful challenges to the applicability (if not validity)[49] of domestic laws by reference to Union requirements is far greater than those to the legality of Union measures by reference to domestic requirements. This is because it is the Union, as a created, evolutionary project of the Member States that is the driver of jurisdictional evolution between orders. The Court's rhetorical affirmation of the unqualified sovereignty of Union laws over domestic law as a sine qua non of the existence of the Union

48 *Carlsen and Others v Rasmussen* at para. 6 of the ratio.

49 Case 283/ 81 *CILFIT (Srl) & Lanificio di Gavardo SpA v Ministry of Health* [1982] ECR 3415.

project contrasts with the concern of domestic courts to secure the integrity (as opposed to existence) of the State qua political entity. Domestic courts have therefore sought to ring-fence the core constitutional concerns of the State, such as its democratic character and upholder of fundamental rights protection. However, it appears that it is only when these core concerns are threatened in a concerted and significant manner by acts of the Union institutions that domestic courts appear to countenance successful legality review challenges. The possibility of limited constitutional incursions is therefore conceded, with domestic judgments being more concerned to insist upon the political status of the Union as a rule of law jurisdiction, committed to fundamental rights protection.

Kompetenz Kompetenz, the supremacy doctrine and the legal rhetoric of the Court of Justice and domestic courts

The history of the relationship between the Union and Member States demonstrates a gradual strengthening of the supremacy doctrine as the governing rationale of the relationship between Union and domestic legal orders. As suggested in the last section, the evolution of the Union/domestic law relationship has not been a matter of legal exegesis *sensu stricto*. Instead this development suggests the unfolding of a strategic legal *policy* directed towards stabilising order conflicts whilst recognising the increasing legal influence of Union norms under the supremacy doctrine. While the doctrine remains the governing parameter of the relationship between Union and Member State orders, the tasks faced by Union and domestic courts in accommodating 'supreme' Union demands while giving due regard to domestic constitutional requirements are not straightforward. Indeed, Schilling has noted that:

> this avoidance of differences is an astonishing feat as the Member State courts continue, at least presumably, to decide on the ultimate basis of their respective constitutions, while the Court of Justice decides on the ultimate basis of the European Treaties. This situation might easily have led to differences in the jurisprudence of the different courts, which could have destroyed the Community. However, it has successfully been dealt with on the one hand by the Member States accepting the superiority of Community law at least as long as that law keeps within certain very wide limits and on the other hand by the Court of Justice respecting those limits as a matter of legal fact. This avoidance of differences may be called a flexible cooperation of these courts. As there is no co-ordinating legal system, in the last analysis such co-operation is based on judicial politics only and cannot be required in law.[50]

50 Schilling, 'The Court of Justice's Revolution' at 462. For Eleftheriadis, any legal justification of the location of *Kompetenz Kompetenz* is impossible and 'begs' the constitutional question. Eleftheriadis links the justification of the supremacy doctrine and hence the extent of Union

While the Court of Justice has consistently affirmed the unqualified superiority of Union over domestic law, Member States' courts have been faced with the arguably more demanding task of reconciling domestic constitutional requirements with the doctrine of Union law supremacy. For both Union and domestic courts, however, the foundational values on which their respective legal orders are based have become, in a limited sense, 'fluid'. Presenting legal outcomes that recognise this fluidity requires Union and domestic courts to engineer an acceptable degree of compatibility between the values underlying their respective legal orders, while recognising their mutual incorporation. This returns us to Schilling's argument that:

> One and the same operator may derive powers from more than one legal system all of which systems therefore must be considered as 'his own' legal systems ... there are no possible legal grounds for the operator's choice among 'his own' legal systems. As however extra-legal decisions of this kind must be anathema to the operator's legal mind, he will try to transform them into, or at least make them appear as, legal decisions.[51]

If we substitute the word 'values' for 'powers' in this quote, it is clear that a sufficient compatibility of the values underlying Union and domestic orders must be present in order for the judge to be faced with a viable choice. While courts will frame their judgments in terms expressive of the values underlying the jurisdiction in which judgment is made they will also draw on those underlying the opposing order. Every expression of Union and domestic legal demands (with a Union connection) involves judicial interrogation of the evaluative foundations of the institutional order within which judgment is given, as well as of the opposing order. The merging of political and legal concerns through diverse responses to claims of invalidity (in light of opposing order demands) in the legal rhetoric of domestic and Union courts illustrates a constitutional fluidity that continues to be successfully maintained and developed.

Conclusions

The Member States originally embraced the Union project in the belief that the Treaty obligations would not disturb their internal constitutional arrangements except to an extent strictly agreed upon.[52] This has proved not to be

Kompetenz Kompetenz not simply to the possibilities inherent in the judicial function, which I have affirmed, but to a 'normative justification of the Union order that encompasses a 'political theory of the Community [Union]'. P Eleftheriadis, 'Begging the Constitutional Question' (1998) 36 *Journal of Common Market Studies* 255 at 269.

51 Schilling, 'The Court of Justice's Revolution' at 448.

52 In *Van Gend en Loos,* three of the then six Member States intervened. All three challenged the ability of the Union provision to take direct effect while two of the three contested the Court's

the case, and presumptions of compatibility between orders has been tested by the evolving largesse of the Union project as a new political architecture throughout the Member States. Both Union and Member State courts, when assessing the relationship between their respective legal orders, recognise the supremacy doctrine as the underlying rationale of all legal outcomes with a Union law element. Given the perennial challenge to domestic legal authority this entails, the success of the Union jurisdiction depends on the Court's ability to set out Union legal demands in a manner that is acceptable to domestic judicial institutions.

The jurisdictional and hence constitutional issues posed by the relationship between the Union and domestic legal orders cannot be resolved by reference to the positive legal demands of either domestic constitutions or the Treaties. As highlighted by Schilling, Union and domestic courts may legitimately take different positions on the same legal question. Resolution of conflicting claims requires a discourse between Union and domestic courts, an exchange of legal rhetoric, to maintain acceptable presumptions of compatibility. As it is the Court of Justice (and not domestic courts) that drives the development of the Union project, it is the persuasive quality of its judgments, and to a lesser extent those of domestic constitutional courts, that is crucial to maintaining a stable co-existence of orders. As Everling has noted,

> Reliance on the power of persuasion is particularly important in a system such as the Community in which the means for enforcing judgments are limited and in which compliance with them ultimately depends on the recognition by all concerned that the common interest requires respect for the Community legal order.[53]

The powers of persuasion of the Court of Justice have combined doctrinal inflexibility in relation to the supremacy of Union over domestic law with substantive concessions to domestic constitutional requirements through their adoption as Union general principles. The successs of the Court in upholding and developing the Union jurisdiction through this approach is illustrated by parallel developments in the judgments of domestic constitutional courts. Here, an original 'radical' rhetorical stance affirming the supremacy of the domestic constitution over Union law has moved [54] towards a more open, flexible perspective, broadly supportive of the supremacy doctrine.[55] Judicial rhetorical expertise by both Union and Member State courts

jurisdiction. See M Mendez, *The Legal Effects of EU Agreements* (Oxford University Press, Oxford 2013) at 95.

53 Everling, 'The Court of Justice as a Decision Making Authority' at 1308.

54 *Solange I*.

55 Compare in the Belgian setting, the judgments in *European School v Hermans-Jacobs and Heuvelmans-Van Iersel* (Case No. 12/94) Belgian Court of Arbitration (3 February 1994) and *Orfinger v Belgian State (Minister for Civil Service)* (Case No. 62.922) Belgian Conseil d'Etat (Sixth Chamber) (5 November 1996).

has, in sum, addressed and matched the ongoing process of integration and corresponding increases in the Union's legal jurisdiction. At the same time, constitutional crises, which would be the result of Union and domestic courts simultaneously claiming and seeking to enforce an exclusive jurisdiction, have been avoided.

7 European Union Law as international law

Introduction

International law principles enable a rationalisation of the values to which the Union order aspires as a collective political and legal commitment amongst the Member States. The doctrine of Union law supremacy, which parallels that of international law supremacy, emphasises the overriding character of Union legal demands as a set of values and objectives over those of purely domestic origin. A common view that the Union legal order is *sui generis* or municipal in character fails to explain the directing character of the values underlying the Union project including its legal order.

In this chapter I explore and defend the view that the Union legal order is essentially based on international law principles. A central contention in this regard is that the supremacy of Union law obligations within the Member States is based on the principle of the supremacy of international law obligations over those originating in domestic arenas. The 'intensive' rationalisation of this principle by the Court of Justice within its case law manages the intrusive domestic legal effects of the values and ideals found in the Union Treaties and illustrates the evolutionary character of the Union project.

I shall explore two strands of inquiry. The first interrogates the proposition that the activities of the Court of Justice form an expression of the doctrine of the supremacy of international over domestic legal rules. This doctrine has traditionally been subject to a number of qualifications peculiar to individual States, relating, for example, to the ability of a later domestic legislative provision to set aside earlier conflicting rules of international law.[1] In the Union setting however, qualifications associated with the doctrine have gradually diminished within Member States. These developments have been paralleled by an increase in the reach and influence of the supremacy doctrine where Union as opposed to 'ordinary' international law demands are concerned. The 'strength in depth' of the doctrine of Union law supremacy is evident

1 The *lex posteriori derogat lex priori* principle, whose application (and rejection by the Court of Justice) in the context of a Union law demand occurred in Case 106/77 *Italian Finance Administration v Simmenthal* [1978] ECR 629.

in relation to the variety of Union legal effects that have emerged within the Court's judgments, the broadening of conditions relating to the 'justiciability' of Union legal rules and finally concerning the location of jurisdictional authority to decide upon the scope of the doctrine which arguably now lies de jure and de facto with the Court of Justice.

A second strand of inquiry concerns a counter-intuitive feature of the international law character of Union legal ordering. Notwithstanding the Court's apparently complex and expansive development of the supremacy doctrine giving effect to the legal demands of the Treaties, the Court of Justice has in fact adopted a restrictive approach to their articulation. The reason for this is that the values or objectives of the Union are open-ended. They are therefore subject to a medium- or long-term process of realisation that takes place within a shifting and often charged political environment. As a result, the Court has consistently qualified and 'managed' the legal potential of the objectives set out in the Treaties to ensure the continued viability of Union legal demands within the Member States and hence that of the entire Union project.[2]

The chapter is structured as follows. I shall consider first arguments for and against the *sui generis* or international law character of the Union order, defending the latter position. Next, I shall attempt to show that Union law, while rooted in the principles and practices associated with international law, represents a significant evolution of these principles. This is evident both in relation to the removal of qualifications previously applicable to international law effects in the domestic setting as well as in the location of the jurisdictional authority to determine these effects. Finally, I shall consider how and why, notwithstanding these developments, the Court of Justice, and hence domestic courts when applying Union legal demands, have in fact adopted a markedly restrained approach towards their articulation given the profound political implications of a 'fully integrated' Europe mandated under the Treaties as a matter of international law.

The character of the Union legal order, *sui generis* or international

In this section I consider arguments for and against the *sui generis* or international law character of the Union legal order respectively. I shall defend the proposition that the Union represents an evolved form of international law as opposed to a *sui generis* form of legal order.

The Union as sui generis *legal order*

The prevailing view concerning the nature of the European Union legal order is that it is *sui generis* in character given the institutional characteristics

2 For example, by limiting the circumstances in which direct effect may arise.

it shares with both international and municipal orders.[3] According to this view, it is said that the extensive regulatory scope, legislative and adjudicatory independence and rule of law character of the Union order all indicate its unique character, which represents a departure from ordinary principles of international law. It is generally agreed that the *origins* of the European Union (originally the European Communities) are to be found in public international law.[4] However, the international law basis of the Union as a dynamic, evolutionary body of 'governmental' institutional practices has been called into question by both the Court of Justice and academic commentators. In its *Van Gend en Loos* judgment the Court refers to the Union as a *new* type of international legal order[5] with similar positions taken by Member State courts.[6] Academics have also sought to distinguish Union from international law, focusing upon the alleged constitutionalisation of Union legal demands. As Weiler notes, '[m]ost commentators focus on the legal doctrines of supremacy of European law, the direct effect of European law, implied powers and pre-emption, and on the evolution of the protection of fundamental human rights as hallmarks of this "constitutionalisation."'[7]

Weiler questions whether the distinction between international and constitutional legal ordering is a relevant one, suggesting that

> Assuming the distinction between an international and a constitutional order makes any sense at all … we would prefer to focus on the following features that distinguish the European legal order from public international law: the different hermeneutics of the European order, its

3 See, for example, J H H Weiler and U R Haltern, 'The Autonomy of the Community Legal Order – Through the Looking Glass' (1996) 37 *Harvard International Law Journal* 411, hereafter Weiler and Haltern, 'The Autonomy of the Community Legal Order – Through the Looking Glass'.

4 'The origins, powers and objectives of the three Communities are all to be found in international treaties.' J F McMahon, 'The Court of the European Communities: Judicial Interpretation and International Organisation' (1961) 37 *British Yearbook of International Law* 320 at 329. Weiler and Haltern have noted that '[t]here is no doubt that the European legal order started its life as an international organisation in the traditional sense, even if it had some unique features from its inception'. Weiler and Haltern, 'The Autonomy of the Community Legal Order – Through the Looking Glass' at 419.

5 The Court stated in its *Van Gend en Loos* judgment that '[t]he Community constitutes a new legal order of international law for the benefit of which the states have limited their sovereign rights, albeit within limited fields, and the subjects of which comprise not only Member States but also their nationals'. Case 26/62 *Van Gend en Loos v Nederlandse Administratie der Belastingen* [1963] ECR 1.

6 For domestic cases that have affirmed the *sui generis* character of the Union legal order, see Weiler and Haltern, 'The Autonomy of the Community Legal Order – Through the Looking Glass' at 421.

7 Ibid. at 420 citing G F Mancini, 'The Making of a Constitution for Europe' (1989) 26 *Common Market Law Review* 595 and E Stein, 'Lawyers, Judges and the Making of a Transnational Constitution' (1981) 75 *American Journal of International Law* 1.

> system of compliance, which renders European law in effect a transnational form of 'higher law' supported by enforceable judicial review, as well as the removal of traditional forms of state responsibility from the system.[8]

A further consideration militating against the international law character of the Union order is its 'governmental' institutional framework and associated conferred powers. In this regard, the Treaties provide for a supranational institutional framework empowered to both legislate and provide legally binding adjudication[9] in relation to the various economic and social objectives they contain. The institutional practices of the Union moreover directly impact on individuals' rights and obligations within the domestic arena. Accordingly, Mark Jones notes that:

> there are two relevant, fundamental distinctions between the objectives of Community Law and those of more traditional international law. First, the legal position of individuals is modified not just by the Treaties themselves, but also by the exercise of *governmental powers* conferred upon the Community institutions by the Treaties. Second, the Treaties and the powers they confer are concerned with modifying the legal position of individuals over an extremely wide range of economic and social activities.[10]

Weiler also highlights the Union's institutional structure as being characterised not by 'general principles of public international law, but by a specified interstate governmental structure defined by a constitutional charter (the Treaties) and constitutional principles'.[11] Do then these features of the Union legal order noted by Weiler and Jones undermine the claim that the jurisdiction conferred under the Treaties can be understood in terms of international law principles? In short, do the directly applicable and supreme character of Union laws, its governmental institutional framework, wide ranging jurisdiction and claimed rule of law basis underline its *sui generis* or even municipal law character? I shall contend that these features do not in fact alter the Union order's essentially international law character.

8 Ibid.

9 Articles 267 and 258 TFEU.

10 M L Jones, 'The Legal Nature of the European Community: A Jurisprudential Analysis Using H L A Hart's Model of Law and a Legal System' (1984) 17 *Cornell International Law Journal* 1 at 28 (emphasis in original), hereafter Jones, 'The Legal Nature of the European Community: A Jurisprudential Analysis Using H. L. A. Hart's Model of Law and a Legal System'.

11 J H H Weiler, 'The Transformation of Europe' (1991) 100 *Yale Law Journal* 2403 at 2407, hereafter Weiler, 'The Transformation of Europe'.

The Union as international legal order

My claim is that the Union order is properly understood in terms of international law principles[12] notwithstanding its developed institutional structure and extensive jurisdictional scope. The intrusive nature of the Union legal order within Member State jurisdictions does not require any departure from established international law principles. The supremacy of Member States' legal obligations arising as a matter of international law can fully explain the domestic legal effects of Union laws and hence the relationship between Union and domestic legal orders. To make out these claims requires that I counter the arguments raised above concerning the supremacy and direct applicability of Union laws, on the one hand, and the sophisticated institutional framework underlying Union governance on the other. Each of these points is dealt with in turn below.

First, the *sui generis* character of the Union legal order is attributed to the supremacy and direct effect doctrines, which relate in turn to the overriding character of Union over domestic legal demands and the ability of individuals to rely upon or invoke Union legal demands before domestic courts. Do these features actually represent a departure from established international law principles? For Spiermann, while the cases involving the 'direct effect' of international law obligations in the early part of the twentieth century are regarded as 'exotica',

> There is however no doubt that under international law, a national court, being an organ of the State, is obliged to reach decisions that are in accordance with the international obligations of the State. This is so even when the holder of the corresponding right does not take part in the proceeding before the national court, though this will often be the case since in modern international law interests in the subject matter governed by a rule normally breed rights (to lay claims and bring actions) on the basis of the rule, also for individuals. [13]

The fact that domestic courts are bound in effect to uphold Union laws and that these laws are capable of modifying the legal rights or obligations of individuals before domestic courts does not of itself represent a principled departure from international law principles. It may be countered that while the 'defining' legal doctrines, of Union law supremacy and direct effect, are entirely familiar to international law, their expansive character within the

12 My arguments in Chapters 1–3 concerning the relevance of the Union legal order to the field of analytic jurisprudence can therefore be seen as part of a broader proposition that international legal orders should properly be accounted for by any adequate analytic account of law.

13 O Spiermann, 'The Other Side of the Story: An Unpopular Essay on the Making of the European Community Legal Order' (1999) 10 *European Journal of International Law* 763 at 770 (footnote omitted), hereafter Spiermann, 'The Other Side of the Story: An Unpopular Essay on the Making of the European Community Legal Order'.

Union setting does in fact represent a significant advance in jurisdictional authority associated with international law regimes. This is correct, however the expansive character of the Union jurisdiction does not of itself compromise the Union's international law pedigree unless we can find a principled justification of the distinction between municipal and international jurisdictions based upon the extent of jurisdictional authority alone. Given that there is no inherent limitation on either the scope or subject matter of international law agreements, such a justification for maintaining a principled distinction between the Union order and international law is likely to fail.

Does then the Union's governmental institutional character suggest the *sui generis* character of its legal order? In terms of the ability of domestic institutions to control or manage Union institutional demands, these demands are far-reaching by comparison with those arising under international law Treaties generally. In addition, it is correct to say that the scope and claimed rule of law basis of these demands does represent a serious challenge to the jurisdictional claims of domestic orders. Finally, the ability to authoritatively interpret the substantive meanings of the Treaties being vested in a supranational judicial institution, the Court of Justice, is arguably a departure from the historically accepted prerogative of domestic executive or judicial branches of signatory States to do so.[14] These features once again do not in my view undermine the Union's international law pedigree for the following reasons.

Any claim as to the distinctiveness of the Union order as a result of its governmental institutional structure including legislative, executive[15] and adjudicatory branches does not mean that its international law character is somehow altered. This would require acceptance of the proposition that, at a certain degree of institutional complexity, an international legal order loses its character as such. This proposition however confuses the core characteristics of international legal order with those of legal orders generally. The distinguishing features of international legal orders are a focus on the achievement of specific objectives or a commitment to the realisation of more broadly drawn social welfare outcomes within a limited jurisdictional sphere, or a combination of both possibilities, by a number of co-operating States by way of Treaty agreements.

14 For example, in relation to practices of US courts, Morgenstern has noted that 'a treaty, as part of the law of the land can be interpreted by the courts, but great weight will be given to the view of the executive'. F Morgenstern, 'Judicial Practice and the Supremacy of International Law' (1950) 27 *British Yearbook of International Law* 42 at 79. The view that within the domestic setting it is the executive as opposed to the judicial branch that may provide authoritative rulings on Treaty requirements has however been called into question by the European Court of Human Rights judgment in *Chevrol v France*, 2003-III Eur. Ct. H.R. 159 which held that the determination of rights arising under public international law must, in order to comply with fundamental procedural guarantees contained in Article 6 of the European Convention on Human Rights, be made by the judicial as opposed to executive branches of States.

15 The executive activities of the Union are shared by the Commission, which is the dominant institution in this regard, and the Council of Ministers.

Legal orders as a generic category are evidenced by the existence of an institutional governmental framework operating in legislative, executive and judicial capacities and governed by values associated with the rule of law. To the extent that an institutional order possesses these features, it will be regarded as a 'developed' legal order. The fact that an international legal order which by definition pursues specified and jurisdictionally contained objectives does so by means of an institutional framework which shares features with developed, rule of law legal orders does not mean that it has departed from its international law basis. The Union order involves institutional practices collectively directed to the achievement of the objectives contained in the Union Treaties. These are the establishment of the common market and the gradual harmonisation of the social and economic policies of the Member States under the overall rubric of closer European integration. The fact that these objectives are supported by complex institutional structures governed by rule of law principles certainly gives an impression of a municipal-type order. However, this can be seen as evidence of the extent to which the Member States have been willing to obligate themselves *as a matter of international law* to their realisation.

Next, it is fully in accordance with international law principles that a supranational institution in the Court of Justice and not domestic constitutional courts should possess authority to adjudicate on the substance, status and scope of Union law obligations. Member States may not agree with the results where this extends Union legal demands beyond what they see as the competences conferred by the Treaties. However, there is no doubt that as a matter of international law, this is precisely the institutional role conferred on the Court by the Treaties. As Weiler notes, 'the European Court, in adopting its position on judicial *Kompetenz Kompetenz*, was not following any constitutional foundation but rather an orthodox international law rationale'.[16] Moreover, domestic courts have on the whole recognised the final authority of the Court of Justice to rule on the legal demands arising under the Treaties, thereby accepting the supreme character of the body of Union obligations and rights in accordance with the principle of international law supremacy.[17]

Finally, the fact that the Union possesses legislative competence in relation to the matters set out in the Treaties does not support an argument that the Union is closer to a municipal or *sui generis* order than one of international

16 Weiler and Haltern, 'The Autonomy of the Community Legal Order – Through the Looking Glass' 411 at 415.

17 In Hartian terms, the recognition of the various international law features of the Union order – Union law supremacy and direct effects as well as the authority of the Court of Justice as the final arbiter of the scope, meaning and legal effects of Union legal norms – has emerged as a Rule of Recognition within Member State legal orders. See Jones, 'The Legal Nature of the European Community: A Jurisprudential Analysis Using H.L.A. Hart's Model of Law and a Legal System'. Interpretations of the effects of Union laws by the Court of Justice will apply as binding legal authority across all the Member States, see the Advocate General's opinion in Joined Cases C-10/97 to C-22/97 *Ministero delle Finanze v I.N.C.O.G.E'90* [1998] ECR I-6307.

law simpliciter. The fact that the Union may enact directly applicable laws that (as such) take automatic effect within the Member States undoubtedly represents a significant advance upon the ability of international law norms to take domestic legal effects. In this regard, the Treaties transfer legislative authority to the institutions created under the Treaties themselves in order to achieve the aims they contain. We may accordingly assume that the Member States are empowered as a matter of international law to confer this authority. It is counter-intuitive to suppose that the resulting obligations arising as a matter of Union legislation, and equivalent in status to the Treaty Articles as far as domestic orders are concerned, are not themselves norms of international law.[18] The legislative competences of the Union rather evidence a supranational competence to create legal obligations that possess the character of international law. That is, they are supreme over all aspects of domestic legal ordering and operate in the service of the ideals or objectives found in the Treaties.

To sum up, the allegedly municipal features of the Union legal order identified by Weiler and Jones inter alia do not represent a principled departure from the international law character of the Union. Any principled distinction between international and municipal law does not rely on the presence or otherwise of developed institutional structures. Nor does it depend on whether institutions created under international agreements possess sovereign powers transferred from domestic jurisdictions beyond some (un)defined level. Nor finally does the distinction depend on the scope or status of legal effects promulgated and adjudicated upon by supranational institutions.

The key elements of an international legal order are that all legal demands arising thereunder prevail over all domestic regulation and are directed to the achievement of defined objectives set out in Treaty agreements among a collectivity of States, including the possibility of the independent institutional promotion of these objectives through the exercise of conferred powers. At this point, the question remains whether the expansive character of the Union's legal jurisdiction adds something to our understanding of the operation of international law and specifically of the role of supranational courts charged with determining the legal effects of a highly intrusive international law jurisdiction.

18 In this respect, Weiler's contention in relation to the direct effects of Union laws that these

> reversed the normal presumption of public international law [that] … if the state fails to bestow the rights, the individual cannot invoke the international obligation, unless internal constitutional or statutory law, to which public international law is indifferent, provides for such a remedy

is contradictory. If internal law were entirely independent of international law then it could not possibly allow the invocation of international law obligations before domestic courts unless these are said to operate as two wholly independent and distinct jurisdictions. This is plainly not the case. Indeed it is the very incorporation of Union law obligations within domestic orders that underlies the viability of the Union's legal jurisdiction.

(Weiler, 'The Transformation of Europe' 2403 at 2413–2414)

The expansive character of the Union's international law jurisdiction

The Court of Justice possesses competence under the Treaties and hence as a matter of international law to ensure that 'in the interpretation and application of the Treaties the law is observed'.[19] The Court therefore determines the status and scope of the legal obligations that flow from the application of Union laws and hence the legal effects deriving from the doctrine of Union law supremacy. The Court's institutional role conferred under the Treaties represents a significant transfer of jurisdictional authority, previously associated with domestic courts, to determine the legal effects of international law norms. This jurisdictional transfer has been 'reflected back' to domestic courts, with the Court counter-intuitively increasing the authority of domestic courts by enabling them to act as de facto 'Union courts' thereby exercising a constitutional power of review over all norms of domestic origin in light of all Union law requirements.[20]

In seeking to promote the substantive aims and objectives found in the Treaties, and in according these a supreme status over domestic law, the Court self-evidently acts as an international tribunal. In this regard, the character of the Treaties themselves has allowed the development of a nuanced and hence viable portrayal of the supremacy doctrine by the Court of Justice. The Treaties contain a combination of aspirational objectives relating to European integration and precise or 'hard' legal rights and obligations designed to put these aspirations into effect. This has allowed the affirmation of a regulatory framework within the Member States supporting the Union's underlying integrationist values while permitting these values to possess a direct legal influence as interpretive authority over all legal regulation connected with the Treaty objectives. This brings us to consideration of the legal effects taken by Union legal rules.

Justiciability factors: the legal effects of Union norms

The legal effects taken by Union norms within the Member States depend on a number of factors, some of which, for example concerning issues of justiciability, also apply in the determination of the legal effects of laws of domestic origin. These factors may be summarised as follows. The first is whether a legal standard concerns subject matter that is *suitable* for judicial determination, a test of institutional suitability. This includes questions of the legislator's intent, the Member States where the Union Treaties are concerned, the suitability of the subject matter for judicial as opposed to executive or legislative determination and broader issues relating to the role of the judiciary in a

19 Article 19 TEU.

20 *R v Secretary of State for Transport ex parte Factortame* [1989] 2 CMLR 353.

rule of law system of governance.[21] Second, whether a measure provides sufficient linguistic certainty (in identifying legal rights or obligations), the test of linguistic suitability. Third, whether further implementing measures are needed in order to put a measure into effect, the test of (un)conditionality.[22] In each of these areas, a single, definitive test is impossible to identify. What may be observed is that justiciability requirements may vary according to the *type* of legal effects taken (by Union laws). As a result, the Court's portrayal of the justiciability of Union norms and their consequent legal effects has been central to its development of the supremacy doctrine.[23]

In this regard, the Court has maximised the impact of Union law over domestic orders by developing a variety of possible legal effects attributable to binding Union laws. These include direct effect in the 'narrow'[24] sense of freestanding, individually enforceable rights, legality review effects and finally indirect or interpretive effects. Cumulatively these legal possibilities

21 A Bickel, *The Least Dangerous Branch: The Supreme Court at the Bar of Politics* (The Bobbs-Merrill Company, Inc., Indianapolis, New York, 1962).

22 These factors are equally applicable in the domestic setting regarding the suitability of domestic norms for judicial application. Carlos Vazquez has noted therefore that '[t]hese questions are not unique to treaties. The lack of "judicially discoverable and manageable standards" is often cited as bearing on whether statutory or constitutional provisions are judicially enforceable.' C Vazquez, 'The Four Doctrines of Self-Executing Treaties' (1995) 89 *American Journal of International Law* 695 at 714 (footnote omitted), hereafter Vazquez, 'The Four Doctrines of Self-Executing Treaties'. In this regard, Vazquez, in considering factors that US courts have looked to in deciding whether Treaty provisions are 'self-executing' and hence give rise to enforceable individual rights, has noted that 'courts have examined under the "self-execution" rubric various concepts that are not unique to treaties. These include matters such as whether the claim is justiciable, whether the litigant has standing, and whether the litigant has a right of action'. Ibid. at 711.

23 In his analysis of the self-executing/non-self-executing distinction set out in US court judgments relating to the internal applicability of Treaty norms, Vazquez has noted that:

> the self-execution 'doctrine' addresses at least four distinct types of reasons why a treaty might be judicially unenforceable. First, a treaty might be judicially unenforceable because the parties … made it judicially unenforceable. This is primarily a matter of intent. Second, a treaty might be unenforceable because the obligation it imposes is of a type that, under our system of separated powers, cannot be enforced directly by the courts. This branch of the doctrine calls for a judgment concerning the allocation of treaty-enforcement power as between the courts and the legislature. Third, a treaty might be judicially unenforceable because the treaty makers lack the constitutional power to accomplish by treaty what they purported to accomplish. This branch of the doctrine calls for a judgement about the allocation of legislative power between the treaty makers and the lawmakers. Finally, a treaty provision might be judicially unenforceable because it does not establish a private right of action and there is no other legal basis for the remedy being sought by the party relying on the treaty.
>
> (Ibid. at 722–723)

24 A broad understanding of direct effectiveness refers to the invocability of Union norms in a domestic context to include additionally legal effects that fall short of the direct conferral of rights. On the difference between broad and narrow definitions of direct effect, see P Craig and G de Burca, *The Evolution of EU Law* (3rd edn, Oxford University Press, Oxford, 2003) 178ff.

have been allied to an evolutionary and complex expression of the supremacy doctrine by the Court and hence the fullest possible expression of the underlying values of the Treaties by Union and domestic courts. In relation to 'direct effect',[25] the most intrusive of Union law effects, the Court stated in *Becker* that Union provisions must be 'sufficiently precise and unconditional' to give rise to enforceable individual rights.[26] For the legality review effects of Union norms to arise, these conditions will generally not need to be met[27] providing that an 'identifiable conflict' between Union and domestic provision(s) is present.[28] Finally, in relation to the interpretive effects of Union laws, we find that criteria of linguistic certainty do not play any part in determining whether these effects arise.[29] This enables the broad concerns of European integration, set out in the opening Treaty Articles, to create legal effects.

Justiciability factors: linguistic certainty, political questions and the intent of the Member States

When domestic courts determine the legal effects of Treaty norms, their linguistic clarity will often be linked to the question of whether the substantive topic raised is one suitable for determination by courts as opposed to other institutional branches. For example, Vazquez has suggested that in relation to the treatment of Treaty rules by US courts, 'precatory', 'hortatory' or aspirational provisions will not be self-executing as they evidence a commitment to achieve certain objectives in the political arena as opposed to an intention to confer legally enforceable rights:

> 'Precatory' treaty provisions are deemed judicially unenforceable not because of the parties' (or anyone's) intent, but because what the parties agreed to do is considered in our system of separated powers, a 'political' task not for the courts to perform.[30]

25 In the 'narrow' sense of the recognition of freestanding Union rights, enforceable by individuals before domestic courts.

26 Case 8/81 *Becker v Finanzamt Munster-Innenstadt* [1982] ECR 53 at paragraph 25 of the judgment.

27 See, inter alia, Case C-129/94 *Criminal Proceedings against Ruiz Bernaldez* [1996] ECR I-1829. For a contrary conclusion, see the Court's judgment in *CIA*, which suggested that in order for the legality review (exclusionary) effects of a directive to arise in a horizontal situation, the conditions for direct effect must be met. Case C-194/94 *CIA Security International SA v Signalson SA* [1996] ECR I-2201.

28 See K Lenaerts and T Corthaut, 'Of Birds and Hedges: The Role of Primacy in Invoking Norms of EU Law' (2006) 31 *European Law Review* 287.

29 Case 6/72 *Europemballage and Continental Can v Commission* [1973] ECR 215, particularly paragraphs 24 and 25 in which the Court held that the Treaty competition rules prohibiting abuse of a dominant position in the market had to be interpreted in light of the overall objectives of the Treaty contained in the opening Articles which affirmed the promotion of the common market amongst the Member States.

30 Vazquez, 'The Four Doctrines of Self-Executing Treaties' at 712.

For the Court of Justice, determination whether a norm reveals a 'political' question requires a broad judgment taking in an array of institutional considerations concerning its role in relation to other Union institutions as well as Member States. Moreover, for the Court, so far as the legal effects of the aspirational provisions of the Union Treaties are concerned, the distinction between vaguely worded aspirations and those that are 'sufficiently precise', relates as noted above, to the *type* of legal effect produced as opposed to being determinative of the question of *whether* legal effects may arise. The proposition that the political objectives of the Union are capable of creating legal effects is supported by the first Articles of the Treaties. These objectives are worded in mandatory terms. Article 3(3) TEU, for example, states that:

> The Union *shall* establish an internal market. It *shall* work for the sustainable development of Europe based on balanced economic growth and price stability, a highly competitive social market economy, aiming at full employment and social progress, and a high level of protection and improvement of the quality of the environment. It *shall* promote scientific and technological advance. It *shall* combat social exclusion and discrimination, and *shall* promote social justice and protection, equality between women and men; solidarity between generations and protection of the rights of the child. It *shall* promote economic, social and territorial cohesion, and solidarity among Member States. It *shall* respect its rich cultural and linguistic diversity and *shall* ensure that Europe's cultural heritage is safeguarded and enhanced.[31]

This wording evidences an intention on the part of the Member States that the overall objectives of the Union – in addition to the precise regulatory demands arising under Treaties and associated secondary legislation – should be able to create legal effects notwithstanding that these objectives undeniably fall under the heading of 'political questions'. Moreover, from the perspective of the Court of Justice, the political objectives found in the Treaties are precisely those matters to which the 'hard' or precise legal provisions of the Treaties are directed to achieve. *All* legal regulation arising under the Treaties is directed in some way to the achievement of the social, economic and political ideals of European integration. For the Court of Justice, as well as domestic courts, the institutional considerations relevant to whether a Union law is justiciable require a reformulation of the political tasks doctrine noted by Vazquez, based on received notions of the separation of powers between the courts and other domestic governmental branches.

Union law effects within the domestic setting then entail a modified understanding of the separation of powers doctrine, one that seeks the constitutionalisation of the body of Union laws through the activities of domestic courts. Such practices redefine the domestic judicial role in relation to the other

31 Article 3 TEU (emphases added).

governmental branches and are in contrast to the manner in which domestic courts have determined the internal legal effects of international Treaties outside the Union context. Here, domestic courts seized with questions of international law will focus exclusively on the separation of powers doctrine embodied within the constitutional settlement of the State concerned without considering how international law measures may themselves qualify or alter that settlement.[32] Finally, in relation to questions of intent, the Court of Justice does not consider the intentions of the Member States in assessing the legal effects of the Union provisions it is called on to interpret and apply. Instead it will assess the language of a provision in light of the overall purposes of the Treaties. In this regard, a 'general' interpretive assumption is that all individual Union measures are intended by the Member States collectively to fit within the overall scheme of the Union legal order, based on the achievement of the Treaty objectives.

In sum, Vasquez's argument that '[w]here the line is drawn between "precatory" [and hence judicially unenforceable] and "obligatory" [and hence judicially enforceable] treaty provisions is a matter of domestic constitutional law',[33] is revised in the Union setting. This revision concerns on the one hand the ability of the Court to authoritatively determine the meaning of Union Treaty provisions and secondary Union laws, and on the other its active constitutionalisation of Union norms within the domestic arena.[34] The evolution of the doctrine of international law supremacy by the Court of Justice in

32 For these reasons, Amstutz, speaking of the Court's practices in relation to the interpretive effects taken by Directives, notes that

> The thoroughly courageous decision to intervene at the level of the rules governing legal reasoning (where the link between text setting and text interpretation is made) and – *propter unitatem juris* – extend the law-making powers of the national judiciaries beyond the *contra legem* boundary drawn by long-established legal theory (and thus into the legislative sphere defined mirror wise by the same legal tradition) is . . . a socially adequate (albeit also highly risky) alternative strategy.
>
> (M Amstutz, 'Marleasing and the Emergence of Interlegality in Legal Reasoning' (2005) 11 *European Law Journal* 766 at 777–778, hereafter Amstutz, 'Marleasing and the Emergence of Interlegality in Legal Reasoning'.)

33 Vazquez, 'The Four Doctrines of Self-Executing Treaties' at 713.

34 In this regard, Jones has noted that:

> the Court consistently has resisted arguments by the national governments that, in accordance with the practice of international law, the question of penetration [of Union laws within the domestic setting] is to be determined by national constitutional law. The practices of Member States vary considerably and, therefore, any solution based on the provisions of traditional national constitutional law will not ensure the full and uniform application of Community Law in all the Member States.
>
> (Jones, 'The Legal Nature of the European Community: A Jurisprudential Analysis Using H.L.A.Hart's Model of Law and a Legal System' at 45 (footnotes omitted))

See also Chapter 6 of this work.

upholding the supremacy of Union over domestic legal requirements does not represent a decisive break from the Union's international law basis but rather expresses its principled development.

In conclusion, all the Member States, whether monist or dualist in their approaches to international law have incorporated, according to the terms of their respective constitutions, the Union legal order as a directly applicable system of supreme legal rules. The fact of incorporation is clearly not conclusive of the legal effects taken by Union norms, a fact illustrated by the gradual evolution of the doctrine of Union law supremacy by the Court of Justice and corresponding acceptance within the Member States. The evolution of Union law effects within the Member States highlights the potential inherent in the Union jurisdiction. In practice, this potential has been incrementally expressed, reflecting an attitude of restraint by the Court of Justice towards the legal demands arising under the Treaties. Reasons for this restraint are explored in the following section.

The restrictive expression of Union law demands by the Court of Justice

The ability of the Court of Justice to promote the Treaty aims depends on the extent to which its conclusions regarding the supremacy of Union over domestic law are accepted by domestic courts. In this regard, Union law supremacy represents a 'value' whose promotion and articulation by the Court of Justice and recognition by domestic courts is crucial to realisation of the Union project.[35] Paralleling the Court's challenge to the role of domestic courts under (pre)-existing separation-of-powers arrangements, the Court's presentation of the supremacy of Union law represents an invitation or challenge to domestic judicial practices regarding their treatment of international legal norms. This does not mean that the international law character of Union legal obligations is somehow qualified. However, the need to ensure uniform Union law effects while developing the Treaty aims has required the careful 'management' of the (supremacy) doctrine by the Court.

Given the character of the legal obligations set out in the Treaties, backed by an independent and sophisticated institutional framework, a significant untapped potential exists in relation to the domestic effects of Union laws as a matter of international law. The legal obligations placed on the Member States under the Treaties are in fact far more extensive than the portrayal of these obligations by the Court of Justice. The Court has offered a moderate and limited expression of Union legal demands. In relation to both the pace and extent of European integration, the Court has vouchsafed the continued development of the Union by remaining responsive to a political imperative that concerns the acceptability of Union legal demands within the Member States.[36]

35 Famously in its *Van Gend en Loos* and *Costa* judgments.

36 As explored in Chapters 3–6 of this work.

The Court of Justice has been faced not only with ensuring that 'in the interpretation and application of the Treaties the law is observed'[37] but also with the need to maintain the viability and indeed survival of the Union's intrusive international law jurisdiction. Recognising that the full import of the Treaties' legal demands would be unacceptable to the Member States and hence practically unenforceable, the Court has therefore developed the doctrine of Union law supremacy by reference to what it deems institutionally possible. While this has entailed an expansive engagement by domestic courts by comparison with other legal demands of international law origin, the Court's articulation of the Treaty demands has at the same time been consistently restrained. It has advanced the doctrine of Union law supremacy in incremental steps, consistently maintaining a limited view of the legal obligations found in the Treaties.

The Court of Justice's allegedly dynamic and extensive approach to Treaty interpretation then obscures the fact that the legal possibilities represented by the Treaties as a matter of international law are in fact diminished by political, legal and jurisdictional concerns restraining their full expression. The Court's case judgments reveal a 'thin' interpretive approach to the principle of international law supremacy where the legal effects of the Treaties are concerned. The articulation of Union law demands by the Court therefore represents, as noted above, a managed challenge to the jurisdictional expectations of domestic courts. In addition, as pointed out by Spiermann, given that the Member States have signed up to a project of international co-operation in the Union Treaties that has clear potential to challenge incumbent notions of State sovereignty, the Court has highlighted the relevance of State sovereignty in developing the Treaties' legal effects, an approach he traces to the Court's judgments in *Costa* and *Wilhelm*:[38]

> as in *Costa v ENEL*, in *Wilhelm*, state sovereignty was treated as a key ingredient of treaty interpretation, essentially because the Court by then had recognised such a strong position of national law in regulating market structures that the Treaty was binding only within the context of national law, thus making precedence an appropriate synonym of *pacta sunt servanda*.[39]

The recognition of domestic legal regulation and hence the *potential* for conflict between Union and domestic law by an international tribunal is, as pointed out by Spiermann, unusual from an international law

37 Article 19 TFEU.

38 Case 14/68 *Walt Wilhelm and Others v Bundeskartellamt* [1969] ECR I. For consideration of this judgment, see J Bengoetxea, *The Legal Reasoning of the European Court of Justice* (Clarendon Press, Oxford, 1993) at 265–266.

39 Spiermann, 'The Other Side of the Story: An Unpopular Essay on the Making of the European Community Legal Order' 763 at 785. For similar arguments, see P Allott, 'Preliminary Rulings – Another Infant Disease' (2000) 25 (5) *European Law Review* 538 and P Pescatore, 'The Doctrine of Direct Effect: An Infant Disease of Community Law' (1983) 8 *European Law Review* 155.

> perspective: '[f]rom the point of view of international law, there can be no conflict between a treaty rule and a national law rule, for the rules do not belong to the same system'.[40] The Court has affirmed, in Spiermann's view, a national lawyer's perspective on the relationship between international (Union) and domestic law, a perspective that prioritises what he terms the international law of co-existence.[41] This approach emphasises (the role of) domestic sovereignty in defining a State's international law obligations and ignores the possibility of an unconditional joint limitation of sovereignty, a possibility which is an established feature of what Spiermann terms the international law of co-operation.[42] By focussing on the international law of co-existence, and neglecting possibilities found within the international law of co-operation, the Court's portrayal of the Union doctrines of supremacy and direct effect indeed evidence a 'new' kind of legal order.[43]

The Treaty obligations have been presented by the Court, not as an unconditional limitation on and transfer of domestic sovereignty that automatically take precedence over domestic law, but instead as effects that occur within the context of (competing) domestic legal demands. It is this engagement with domestic legal concerns by the Court of Justice that is remarkable from an international law perspective in Spiermann's view. The Treaties have never been used as a platform to challenge failures by the Member States to meet the obligations arising as a matter of international law to *positively* promote the aims that they contain.[44] The Court's approach has rather secured

40 Ibid. at 773 citing Article 27 of the Vienna Convention on the Law of Treaties according to which: '[m]unicipal law may not be invoked as a justification for failure to perform international obligations'. Vienna Convention on the Law of Treaties (adopted 23 May 1969, entered into force 27 January 1980) 1155 UNTS 331.

41 'The ahistorical idea of international law embraced by the Court of Justice in *Van Gend en Loos* and *Costa* was the international law of coexistence.' Ibid. at 779.

42 '[A]s an international lawyer will know, when compared to other parts of the international law of cooperation, there is nothing new about direct effect and nothing innovative about precedence'. Ibid. at787.

43 Spiermann notes in relation to the doctrine of Union law direct effects that

> By neglecting the international law of co-operation, the Court ended up with a narrow idea of international law, which explains how the Court could assume that international law is unfamiliar with the idea of direct effect and the involvement of the individual.
>
> (Ibid. at 779)

44 In this regard Spiermann contends that the Court has tended to adopt a narrow interpretive approach to the economic freedoms, focusing on discriminatory practices as opposed to barriers to trade that may not be discriminatory (although in recent years that Court has increasingly allowed challenges to substantive impediments to trade that are not directly discriminatory, maintaining however the requirement that they must operate in an indirectly discriminatory manner towards goods/workers/services from *other* States so maintaining a necessary cross-border element):

the co-operation of domestic courts in expressing these demands. This has promoted the acceptance of Union requirements by domestic institutional actors generally and served to manage conflicts between Union and domestic governmental activities as well as internal constitutional conflicts that may arise from an 'over empowerment' of domestic courts.[45]

Conclusions

In this chapter, I have argued that two essentially competing currents have informed the Court's articulation of Union law demands as a court of international jurisdiction charged with promoting the values of the Union. The first concerns the legal commitments present as a matter of international law within the Union Treaty agreements. These agreements represent a binding commitment to profoundly restructure Member States' governance around the ideals of an integrated European Union. The second concerns the fact that the full realisation of the objectives contained in the Treaties cannot realistically be achieved through the immediate assertion of legal demands. This is because even a limited expression of the overall Treaty objectives entails an acceptance of supranational legal authority with profound constitutional consequences for the Member States.

The Court of Justice has therefore developed the principle of Union law supremacy and hence the values of European integration through a consistently creative expression of its jurisdiction. Domestic courts have been persuaded to cede a 'corresponding' jurisdiction, to decide the limits and qualification of the supremacy of Union law, to the Court. This has paradoxically provided domestic courts with a derivative Union jurisdiction that embraces the Court's reading of the supremacy doctrine, empowering domestic judicial actors to a degree that arguably redefines the separation of powers amongst domestic governmental branches in favour of the judiciary.[46]

Understanding the Union order as one of international law highlights the

> The content of a ban on nationality discrimination is purely negative, saying that the state is not allowed to treat aliens in any way worse than its own national. The EEC Treaty thereby opened a door. But in order to generate a real opportunity for aliens to go through that door, it was arguably necessary, or at least conducive to the objective of making a common market to supplement the negative ban on discrimination with various positive principles; or to put it more crudely, to offer the aliens a pat on the back when they appeared on the doorstep.
> (Ibid. at 781–782)

45 Either internally within Member States or in the relationship between the Union and the Member States. See R Rawlings, 'Legal Politics: The United Kingdom and Ratification of the Treaty on European Union (Part One)' [1994] *Public Law* 214; A M Burley and W Mattli, 'Europe before the Court: A Political Theory of Legal Integration' (1993) 47 *International Organization* 41 at 45; K J Alter, 'Who Are the "Masters of the Treaty"?: European Governments and the European Court of Justice' (1998) 52 *International Organization* 121; D Nicol, *EC Membership and the Judicialisation of British Politics* (Oxford University Press, Oxford 2001).

46 Amstutz, 'Marleasing and the Emergence of Interlegality in Legal Reasoning'.

ideal possibilities found in the Treaties as guiding values of Union institutional practices. The Treaties provide a perennial invitation to the Member States and Union institutions to pursue the ideal of an integrated Europe and to enhance and develop their commitment to a European constitutional ordering that this ideal implies. The almost unlimited potential of the Union project to effect, as a matter of the international law, an institutional restructuring of the Member States has meant that the Court has necessarily developed the ideals of European integration in a qualified and limited fashion.

8 Concluding chapter

Introduction

The focus of this work has been the constituted and constitutional features of the legal order of the European Union viewed through an analytic lens, as well as the institutional role of the Court of Justice expressive of the values underlying the Union project. I have critically evaluated received theoretical jurisprudential accounts in light of the values underlying the Treaties as well in relation to the unique institutional context in which the Court of Justice operates. I have also, and by comparison, considered the institutional role of domestic courts in expressing the values underlying statal legal governance. Finally, I have attempted to evaluate the unique institutional challenges posed by the juxtaposition of Union and Member State orders, each making competing claims of legal sovereignty.

I identified three possible areas of inquiry and debate in relation to the role of values within legal ordering. To recap, these relate to the methods of inquiry into law's necessary or conceptual features,[1] the substantive content of the values underlying legal order and, finally, how institutional practices, of law creation and application,[2] are influenced, determined or constituted by foundational values concerns.[3] The focus of my arguments has been on

1 The debate between positivist and non-positivist methodological approaches highlights disputed claims in this area. For defence of the value of 'social scientific' or 'explanatory/descriptive' approaches to inquiry into legal order affirmed by positivist writers see J Coleman, *The Practice of Principle* (Oxford University Press, Oxford 2001) at 179ff. For defence of the non-positivist position that moral values must be involved in any judgement regarding law's function and hence law itself see S Perry, 'The Varieties of Legal Positivism' (1996) 9 *Canadian Journal of Law and Jurisprudence* 361.

2 In this regard, Kelsen has stated that '[m]ost legal acts are acts of both law creation and law application'. H Kelsen, *Introduction to the Problems of Legal Theory* (Clarendon Press, Oxford 1992) at 70.

3 These three senses of the relationship between law and values tend to be conflated within academic writing, illustrated by the following quote from MacCormick:

> The understanding of a practical category like law is value laden, for reasons that have yet to be thoroughly explored. To construct or rationally construct an account of some branch

the second and third of these areas, the substance and role of the values underlying legal order generally and with reference to the European Union order,[4] and the ways in which underlying value concerns shape judicial practices, those of the Court of Justice where the Union is concerned.

I addressed these areas as follows. In Chapters 2 and 3 I considered different theoretical perspectives concerning the role of values underlying legal order, assessing in each case their ability to account for the Union legal order. I

> of law in some jurisdiction, one must of course expound the value elements essential to that body of law and one must indicate what are the possibilities for developing new arguments that would further develop these values ... Given this rich range of materials, a rational reconstruction yields a critical account of the governing rules in the light of the principles and values which underpin them.
>
> (N MacCormick, *Institutions of Law* (Oxford University Press, Oxford 2007) at 291–292)

The three senses of the relationship between law and values suggested are all present within this quote: first, in relation to the methods of inquiry into law, '[t]he understanding of a practical category like law is value laden', ibid. Second, in relation to the substantive values that form part of an account of law, '[o]ne must of course expound the value elements essential to that body of law'. Ibid. Finally, concerning the role of values within legal practices, '[a] rational reconstruction yields a critical account of the governing rules in the light of the principles and values which underpin them'. Ibid. Although in this final remark, MacCormick refers to a 'rational reconstruction' undertaken by theorists, judges undertake a similar task when articulating legal demands, a point highlighted by Perry who argues that it is the perspective of legal practitioners and legal theorists as participants and virtual participants in legal practices that must be accounted for when formulating a theoretical account of law. S Perry, 'The Varieties of Legal Positivism' (1996) 9 *Canadian Journal of Law and Jurisprudence* at 369ff.

4 In this regard, MacCormick has noted that

> Once premises and mode of argument are settled, it is relatively easy to produce an argument that satisfactorily justifies the conclusions reached. But the problem then becomes one about the reasonable choice of premises and method, so there must be inquiry into pre-understandings.
>
> (N MacCormick, *Rhetoric and the Rule of Law, a Theory of Legal Reasoning* (Oxford University Press, Oxford 2005) at 19, citing J Esser, *Vorverstandnis und Methodenwahl in der Rechtsfindung* (Main Suhrkamp, Frankfurt 1970) at 3–20, hereafter MacCormick, *Rhetoric and the Rule of Law*)

Aarnio has suggested that these 'pre-understandings' may simply have to be assessed as the 'form of life' they constitute. A Aarnio, *The Rational as Reasonable: A Treatise on Legal Justification* (Kluwer Academic, Dordrecht 1987) at 213–218. However, any 'form of life', is a culturally relative construct, highlighting the contingent character of any pre-understanding. Similar difficulties arise in relation to the discourse theoretical claims of Habermas according to which the rightness of legal decisions is linked to the presence of universal, ideal discourse conditions in which they occur. Cooke expresses this difficulty as follows:

> Habermas' strategy is open to the objection that it can justify the principle of universality as the rule for establishing moral validity only by appealing to presuppositions of argumentation that are not in fact universal but specific to the socio-cultural contexts of Western modernity.
>
> (M Cooke, 'Law's Claim to Correctness' in G Pavlakos (ed.), *Law Rights and Discourse: The Legal Philosophy of Robert Alexy* (Hart Publishing, Oxford 2007) at 240–241)

affirmed the suitability of an institutionalist model[5] for understanding the dynamic operation of values within legal order generally as well as within the Union setting. In Chapters 4 and 5 and 6, I contrasted the judicial practices of the Court of Justice expressive of the foundational Treaty value of European integration, with those of domestic courts in relation to the domestic constitution. I suggested that the value of integration operates as a weak evolutionary dynamic over all Union judicial practices, the 'degree' of integration in any given judgment varying as a result of a complex array of political, legal and institutional considerations.

These considerations relate to the aims and objectives of the Union as set out in the Treaties, the respective roles of the Court and other Union and domestic governmental institutions, as well as relevant domestic political and legal circumstances within the Member States at the time of judgment. The Court, I argued, employs rhetorical methods of legal reasoning to internalise and express these institutional concerns within its judgments. In Chapter 7, I applied perspectives of international law to the law of the European Union, suggesting that the Union constitutes a developed form of international legal order while demonstrating that international and domestic legal orders can be brought under the same theoretical paradigm. I also suggested that the developmental aspirations of the Union reflect an innate tendency of legal order to move towards greater jurisdictional inclusivity and hence governmental authority.

This concluding chapter is set out as follows. In the first section I restate and draw together my arguments, developed by reference to the law of the European Union, clarifying the implications of earlier arguments where appropriate. In the second section I consider possible criticisms of these arguments. These critical arguments question my assumption that values are capable of forming the basis of legal order and if so whether the Treaty objectives comprise value concerns as opposed to 'mere' factual objectives. Finally I consider the broader critical point that the model of legal order defended does not in fact advance theoretical understanding in any interesting sense, given my conclusions are simply a necessary implication of existing accounts. In the final section, I consider whether the Union, as a developing legal and political entity, locked in a symbiotic constitutional relationship with the Member States, can ever give rise to an enduring European political identity or polity.

A flexible model of legal order

Introduction

I have affirmed law's formal, institutional character in the service of values of political morality or other 'valued' aspirational objectives. Accordingly,

5 As well as aspects of inclusive positivist accounts.

specific economic, social or political objectives may, subject to compatibility with rule of law demands, form the underlying rationale of legal order. This approach develops MacCormick's view that all legal demands are based upon values representing underlying aims or functions, a point he explains as follows:

> The values pursued through and upheld by legal rules are properly considered to be standing aims of and for the law. It must then count in favour of a ruling in law that it promotes or supports a certain value and this can be expressed in a sort of goal reasoning. But since judicial reasoning proceeds under the constraint of universability, the matter is also one of setting norms of rightness, thus yielding rightness reasons.[6]

Although concerns of political morality, including the protection of fundamental rights, remain 'standing aims' of the Union, its core value is the construction of an integrated Europe as a development of existing constitutional arrangements. This parasitic character highlights that the underlying values of the Union necessarily implicate engagement with and reconstruction of existing legal or political frameworks within the Member States. This suggests a broader point, namely that conceptual accounts of legal order should account for the wider institutional and jurisdictional context in which they operate.

The reasoning of the Court of Justice

I have emphasised two key functions underlying the judgments of the Court of Justice. These are (first) to articulate the demands of the Treaties in an institutionally viable manner and (second) to guarantee and promote the project of European integration. To meet these imperatives, the Court of Justice has consistently developed the Union's rule of law jurisdiction in the general principles as well as the substantive reach of the Treaty objectives, notably in relation to the single market.

In Chapters 3–6, I considered how the Court's legal rhetoric upholds the 'foundational' legal values of the Union order, the Treaty aims and general principles, while engaging with the complex political and legal juxtaposition of Union and Member State orders. The relative importance and character of the various institutional concerns the Court must address contrasts markedly, as I have argued, with those present in domestic settings. At the same time, interesting parallels exist between the complex 'balancing of interests' present in the Court's legal rhetoric, and the practices of domestic constitutional courts in seeking to give effect to the values set out in the constitution. Here, Douglas' comments in relation to the US Supreme Court are instructive:

6 MacCormick, *Rhetoric and the Rule of Law* at 120.

> the Court's own discursive response to its problematic role as constitutional expositor has come to define less a clearly and consistently elaborated logic or theory of legitimation, and more a tight and richly woven rhetoric of reading in which the instabilities within the Court's own hermeneutic project are ceaselessly concealed and revealed, displaced and declaimed.[7]

The Court of Justice, as 'constitutional expositor' of the Treaties is engaged in the 'hermeneutic project' of advancing European integration through the legal demands imposed by the Treaties. Douglas' statement is suggestive of the legal and political instabilities of the Union project,[8] with the 'declaiming' of instabilities, reflecting the Court's institutional roles of promoting the Treaty objectives whilst assuring co-operation on the part of domestic institutions.[9]

I have suggested that the Treaty objectives and Union general principles operate as a self-referential constitution whose underlying values are linked to the objectives the Treaties themselves contain. This constitutional insularity is qualified by a secondary linkage to the value concerns of political morality present within Member States' societies.[10] The practices of the Court of Justice when expressing the demands of the Union constitution therefore contrast with those of domestic constitutional courts,[11] who express a direct

7 L Douglas, 'Constitutional Discourse and its Discontents: An Essay on the Rhetoric of Judicial Review' in A Sarat and T R Kearns (eds), *The Rhetoric of Law* (University of Michigan Press, Arbor 1994) at 227.

8 Absent strong executive mechanisms of enforcement and in the face of often conflicting views held by the Member States.

9 The hermeneutic project of the Supreme Court in expressing the legal demands arising under the constitution by contrast is more focused on separation of powers concerns. That is, to what extent should the Court positively affirm the rights arising under the constitution or defer to the practices of other governmental branches. See for seminal treatment of these issues J H Ely, *Democracy and Distrust* (Harvard University Press, Cambridge, Massachusetts 1980) and A Bickel, *The Least Dangerous Branch: The Supreme Court at the Bar of Politics* (The Bobbs-Merrill Company, Inc., New York 1962).

10 Although in individual cases the Court may offer enhanced fundamental rights protections by comparison with those available under domestic law. See, for example, the *Coote* judgment considered in Chapter 5. Case C-185/97 *Coote v Granada Hospitality Ltd* [1998] ECR I-5199.

11 There are Kelsenian overtones to the suggestion that determined and limited objectives such as those found in the Union Treaties can act both as superior legal principles and the underlying evaluative basis of legal order. It would be incorrect however to say that the Union order comprises an entirely closed, self-referential system of (legal) norms, whose ultimate legality is assumed. The Union order is 'open' to external, background concerns of political morality, for example through recognition of domestic constitutions as a source of general principles (of Union) law. This openness relates to the credibility or legitimacy of the Union's transnational aspirations as set out in the Treaties, to other *institutional* actors, particularly the Member States, as opposed to the Union citizenry at large. Kelsen himself would have denied that the use of evaluative judgements in the determination of legal outcomes could ever be legal in character. Instead, any one of a number of 'logically' possible meanings of the applicable norm would have equal legal validity. See S L Paulson, 'Kelsen on Legal Interpretation' (1990) 10 *Legal Studies* 136; H Kelsen, 'On the Theory of Interpretation' (1990) 10 *Legal Studies* 127.

link between the domestic constitution and the social and political self-understanding of a community.

I developed this contrast in Chapter 5, suggesting that within States, the constitution represents a comprehensive charter for rule of law governance[12] whereas the overriding concern of the Treaties is an ideal of collective social, economic and political ordering amongst the Member States, the ideal of European integration. The 'standing aims', in MacCormick's terms, of the Union are goal-specific, based on an attributed jurisdiction designed for their achievement.[13] By contrast with domestic constitutions' direct concern with the rule of law quality of domestic governance, Union legal regulation is concerned with enhancing the rule of law quality of Member States' governance in an indirect sense. The affirmation of rule of law protections by the Court of Justice in the general principles clearly does not represent an inclusive governmental charter, serving instead the objective of closer Union by presenting a credible constitutional framework to Member States.[14]

In this regard, the similar hierarchical legal effects taken by Union and domestic constitutional norms belie an important distinction.[15] This relates

12 For Marxist, realist or feminist legal theorists, the values underlying legal regulation are of course anything but 'ideal' bur rather serve to promote and uphold existing, unequal power relations.

13 The constitutional status of the Treaty Articles is underlined by the fact that the Court of Justice may not question their legal validity and therefore judicial discretion as to their legal effects reaches only as far as permitted by techniques of interpretation. This reflects a similar incapacity of domestic courts to undertake the legality review of domestic constitutional norms. However, from the perspective of the Union, under the supremacy doctrine, all domestic norms including those of the constitution can be overridden by Union legal demands. Case 11/70 *Internationale Haandelsgesellschaft mbH v Einfuhr- und Vorratsstelle fur Getreide und Futtermittel* [1970] ECR 1125 (*Solange I*). Amendment of the Treaties may occur through the institutional arrangements found within the Treaties themselves. Article 48 TEU provides that the European Council may convene a convention for submitting recommendations to an intergovernmental conference, or where appropriate simply convene an intergovernmental conference directly for the purpose of 'determining by common accord the amendments to be made to the Treaties'. These 'enter into force after being ratified by all the Member States in accordance with their respective constitutional requirements'. Treaty amendments may also be driven by case law developments. For example, Tridimas has noted that '[i]n relation to the general principles, the Court has followed a pro-active approach. The case-law has showed the way, with subsequent Treaty amendments endorsing in many cases judicial developments.' T Tridimas, *The General Principles of EU Law* at 13 citing Case 294/83 *Partie Ecologiste 'Les Verts' v European Parliament* [1986] ECR 1339. See also Case C-70/88 *Parliament v Council (Chernobyl)* [1990] ECR I-2041 and Case C-262/88 *Barber v Guardian Royal Exchange Assurance Group* [1990] ECR I-1889. While domestic constitutional courts have affirmed their ability in principle to perform a legality review function in relation to the Treaties in the event of severe and persistent breaches of domestic constitutional requirements as considered in Chapter 6, this possibility would not be viewed as a legal determination from the Union's perspective.

14 This argument is an extension of the well-known thesis by Coppel and O'Neil that the Court has used Union fundamental rights protections to further the integration process. J Coppel and A O'Neil, 'The European Court of Justice: Taking Rights Seriously?' (1992) 12 *Legal Studies* 227. See also the *Coote* judgment considered in Chapter 5.

15 As legality review standards and interpretive influences.

to the connections between hierarchical status and substantive content evident in relation to the Treaty Articles and domestic constitutional standards respectively. The supremacy of domestic constitutional norms is based on the fact that they express 'inclusive' fundamental or universal ideals of social and political morality. The Treaties, on the other hand, while affirming rule of law concerns in the general principles, are predominantly concerned with the type of social or economic regulation that would form the subject matter of legislative intervention simpliciter within the Member States.

Direct normative justification, of Union law demands by reference to the Treaty objectives, is therefore not available in the manner associated with domestic constitutions, a point underlined by the Treaty Articles' jurisdictional limitation in the scope of application of the general principles. This suggests an affirmation by the Union of a highly contestable link between its limited jurisdictional scope and normative superiority that is absent in domestic settings.

Clearly the legal authority exercised by the Court of Justice would be untenable if it failed to affirm values of political morality, regardless of the Union's jurisdictional reach or focus. This does not however resolve the following difficulty faced by the Union as a legal order that aims for ever more inclusive governance of the Member States. Rule of law values operating within a limited jurisdiction may in effect be 'honoured in their breach'. The solution cannot lie in the application of legal *principle* for this very reason, that the extent of the Union's jurisdiction is both inherently limited and uncertain. In my view, the justification of Union legal demands is based on two factors. First, the political support of Member State governments in light of the perceived beneficial effects of Union membership on social and economic conditions within Member States.[16] Second, on the Court's ability to offer a persuasive account of the Treaty demands by exhibiting sensitivity to the wider institutional context in which the Union order operates.[17] The importance of legal rhetoric as a vehicle for sustaining controversial Union legal demands is one aspect of the flexible notion of legal order I have sought to develop throughout this work.

Developments in the way we think about law in an increasingly globalised legal environment suggest that theoretical approaches should reflect these changes by assessing the significance of the wider legal and political context in which (any given) legal order is situated. These contextual/theoretical factors are accentuated in the Union setting which is not only operating

16 Whether a certain degree of social goods is required in order to be able to speak of rule of law governance, or whether the function of rule of law governance is to positively promote social goods are disputed questions. Suffice for present purposes that the direct link between domestic constitutions and Member States' underlying value concerns are not reproduced in the Union setting.

17 The proposition that there is a conceptual or necessary relationship between legal order and the existence of an inclusive jurisdiction, affirming the foundational values of a given polity, was considered and rejected in Chapter 2.

within a wider European culture in which rule of law values are prized, but is actually a product of the legal orders of the Member States. I have attempted to show that once these wider contextual factors in conjunction with the dynamic influence of underlying functions are fully understood as part of a theoretical paradigm of law, it is possible to gain an adequate jurisprudential understanding of the Union legal order.

The dynamic role of values in legal order

Finally, I have suggested that in any adequate conceptualisation of legal order, underlying axiological conceptions of the 'good' (values) play a dynamic role in the articulation of legal outcomes. This necessary feature of legal order derives from the nature of human society, governed in light of evaluative ideals. In the context of the Union legal order, which is based on uncertain and unstable aspirations relating to the achievement of a political project, the dynamic influence of the values underlying these objectives will be maximised in their institutional expression. Concern that the operation of constitutional values will undermine legal uncertainty to an unacceptable degree is met if the legal effects of the values relating to this project are limited to 'weak' interpretive influences as opposed to the conferral of enforceable rights or legality review capabilities. The function of the principle of legal certainty reaches a limit with the interpretive influences of the values on which legal order is based, whose expression is necessary to allow the law to effectively regulate social existence.

In this regard, the principle of legal uncertainty occupies a role equally, if not more, important than that of legal certainty in relation to law's ability to regulate social relations in the service of valued objectives or functions. Reasoned justification of the application of value concerns requires a degree of uncertainty in relation to new circumstances the courts are asked to adjudicate. Conversely, if the principle of legal certainty, one of a number of principles that collectively contribute to effective legal regulation, was not qualified by the opposing principle, this would effectively preclude the effective prosecution of constitutional values or principles whose role as a feature of the positive law would disappear. In sum, limiting the legal effects of constitutional values to their interpretive influences (and legality review effects in some instances) permits the legal promotion of the functional concerns of the constitution while preventing an unwarranted intrusion of functional concerns over the clarity of legal demands.

Critical arguments

Introduction

In this section I address three possible criticisms of the arguments defended in this work. The first is that values as such cannot form the basis of constitutional legal order. Here I consider Alexy's responses to different aspects of this claim in *A Theory of Constitutional Rights*,[18] as well as the relevance of his arguments to the Union legal order. Second, I address the claim that the model of legal order proposed does not add to existing jurisprudential perspectives regarding the role of values within legal order, merely qualifying these in a theoretically uninteresting sense. Finally, I consider the claim that even if we accept the evaluative basis of legal order, the Union Treaty objectives do not as such constitute values but rather factual objectives which cannot perform the constitutional role attributed.

Critical argument: arguments against the possibility of a value based constitution

In *A Theory of Constitutional Rights* Alexy defends the possibility of a constitutional order of values against 'philosophical, methodological and doctrinal' objections.[19] In what follows, I summarise Alexy's appraisal of and responses to these objections, assessing his conclusions in light of the model of legal order I have applied to the Union setting.

Philosophical objections

These concern the epistemological difficulties associated with identifying 'objective' value qualities and the resulting inadequacy of any theory of legal justification based upon values. Alexy addresses this argument in light of the German Federal Constitutional Court's view of the German constitution as an 'objective order of values':[20]

> The strong, easily criticisable assumptions of the real existence and evidential nature of values are in no way necessarily part of the concept of value ... it is more appropriate to interpret the value-based theses of the Court, according to a weaker and less objectionable account of values. Such an account could include the assumption that values are criteria of evaluation which, like norms generally, are either valid or invalid. Their validity, along with the evaluations they make possible, is not the object of some sort of evidence, but a matter of justification.[21]

Alexy here claims that the validity of evaluative demands of values depends, in common with normative claims generally, on reasoned justification in

18 R Alexy, *A Theory of Constitutional Rights* (Oxford University Press, Oxford 2002), hereafter, Alexy, *A Theory of Constitutional Rights*.

19 Ibid. at 93ff.

20 A phrase used in the German Federal Constitutional Court's *Lüth* judgment. 1 BvR 400/51 BVerfGE 7, 198 I. Senate (1 BvR 400/51) *Lüth*, Federal Republic of Germany, Federal Constitutional Court at 98 and cited in Alexy, *A Theory of Constitutional Rights* at 92.

21 Ibid. at 95 (footnote omitted).

relation to some conception of the good and not on an elusive ontological property of values themselves. In the State setting, these conceptions, in the form of constitutional standards, are generally rule of law concerns, including the protection of fundamental rights, as well as matters of cultural significance to a given society.[22]

By contrast, in the Union setting, values relating to European integration, whilst clearly including fundamental rights/rule of law concerns, express a political project that cannot be reduced to these statal 'goods' alone. The values underlying the Treaties may be said to lack 'inherent' qualities of goodness in the way of, for example, fundamental rights protection. As essentially political objectives which are contestable in principle and (relatively) detached from the cultural mores of individual Member States, the validity of the values underlying the Union legal order arguably depends in a more vital sense upon processes of reasoned justification. In this regard, the 'valued' character of the Treaty objectives and their validity as constitutional legal norms arguably rests not only upon rational justification but also upon their persuasive character, given potential qualifying effects over domestic constitutional arrangements. The rhetorical or persuasive force of the Court's justificatory narrative is crucial to the take up of Union legal demands by domestic institutional actors. As a 'conception of the good' within a politically contested space, the Union project is highly dependent upon the rational, *and successful*, justification of this conception as a vision for the future of Europe.

Methodological objections

In *A Theory of Constitutional Rights*, Alexy notes that '[m]ethodological arguments against the theory of values tend to be directed against two ideas, against the idea of an order of values in the sense of a ranked order of values, and against the idea of balancing values'.[23] While Alexy accepts the epistemological impossibility of establishing what he terms a 'hard' objective order of values, this does not in his view preclude the possibility of balancing different value concerns in a soft form of ordering:

> But the impossibility of such a 'hard' ordering says nothing about the possibility of 'soft' orderings and certainly nothing about the technique of balancing interests. Soft orderings can be created in two ways: (1) through prima facie preferences in favour of particular values or principles or (2) through a network of concrete preference decisions.[24]

Alexy's idea of a soft ordering of values captures well the Court of Justice's approach to the Union constitution, the Treaty Articles and general principles,

22 For example the right to life of the unborn child contained in the Irish constitution.

23 Ibid. at 96.

24 Ibid. at 99.

in the face of potentially conflicting domestic constitutional demands. The complex hierarchical relations of Union and domestic requirements under the supremacy doctrine are based upon 'prima facie preferences' relating to achievement of the Treaty objectives set out in the Preambles and introductory Articles. These preferences relating collectively to European integration are balanced and qualified by 'concrete preference decisions' within the Court's judgments, setting out the relative importance of Union and domestic constitutional concerns in any given case.[25]

Doctrinal arguments

Under the heading of 'doctrinal' arguments against a constitutional order of values, Alexy highlights two points: '[t]he first is that a theory of principles does not take the binding nature of the Constitution seriously. The second is that it leads to interpretative arbitrariness and constitutional instability'.[26] These arguments have been largely addressed in the previous section and concern the *need* for legal order as a value based activity to possess some degree of uncertainty. The related need for an adequate degree of legal certainty is met by confining the legal effects of underlying values to their interpretive influences.[27]

25 Albeit that these will always be stated as a ranking of Union norms alone, as considered in Chapter 6. Union constitutional conflicts may arise not only between fundamental rights objectives but also between fundamental rights and the Treaty objectives, notably the operation of the single market. C-112/00 *Schmidberger Internationale Transporte und Planzüge v Au*stria [2003] ECR I-5659; *Omega Speilhallen-und Automatenauftellungs v Oberburgerermeisterin der Bundestadt Bonn* judgment of 14 October 2004.

26 Alexy, *A Theory of Constitutional Rights* at 110. Alexy contends in response to this argument that his mixed rule/principle model of legal order does not lead to any greater uncertainty than a model of pure rules due to the destabilising effects that would flow from a system of constitutional norms based on pure rules. Moreover he notes that a value based model of constitutional rights allows for their further development, to account for evolving social conditions: 'the character of constitutional rights as principles implies the permanent possibility of more extensive protection'. Ibid.

27 Habermas has defended a similar objection as follows:

> Insofar as a constitutional court adopts the doctrine of an objective order of values, and bases its decision making on a kind of moral realism or moral conventionalism, the danger of irrational rulings increases, because functionalist arguments then gain the upper hand over normative system.
>
> (J Habermas, *Between Facts and Norms* (Polity Press, Cambridge 1997) at 259, hereafter Habermas, *Between Facts and Norms*)

Habermas bases his argument on the existence of a distinction between values on the one hand and principles on the other as follows: '[b]ecause norms and principles, in virtue of their deontological character, can claim to be universally binding and not just specially preferred, they possess a greater justificatory force than values'. Ibid. This distinction relies however upon assumptions linking the deontological, as opposed to axiological character of a norm to its justificatory force. It is counter-intuitive to suppose that it is the deontological character of a

Critical argument: factual objectives as values?

The second criticism addresses my contention that specific social economic or political objectives may form foundational values of legal order. The difficulty with this proposition, so this criticism runs, is that these objectives are closer to factual outcomes than evaluative ideals. For example, the Union single market is aimed at unifying and liberalising market conditions across the Member States and not achieving some idealised state of political Union. Accordingly, the Treaty objectives are not, employing Alexy's classification, 'criteria' but rather 'objects' of evaluation. That is, they may be subject *to* evaluative judgements but do not form premises *for* evaluative judgment.[28] Alternatively, those aspects of the Union project such as the ideal of integration which undoubtedly have an evaluative character do not form any part of the *legal* order of the Union order whose underlying value basis simply mirrors the concerns of Member States' constitutions.[29] Finally,

proposition that provides its justificatory force or that the authority of an axiological proposition can be denied on that basis alone. Rather the justification and hence justificatory force of values *or* principles is based on rational argumentation in light of some notion of the common good. In this regard Alexy affirms the essential similarity of values and principles:

> The difference between principles and values is reduced to just one point. What under a system of values is prima facie the best, is under a system of principles what prima facie ought to be; and what under a system of values is definitely the best, is under a system of principles what definitely ought to be. Principles and values are only distinguished by their respective deontological and axiological characters. Law is concerned with what ought to be. This counts in favour of the model of principles. But on the other hand it is not difficult to move from the idea that a certain solution is the best, constitutionally speaking, to the idea that it is required by the constitution. The moment one accepts that such transitions are possible, it is entirely acceptable for legal reasoning to proceed from a model of values instead of a model of principles.
>
> (Alexy, *A Theory of Constitutional Rights* at 92)

On the operation of values and principles in the Union setting see, M L F Esteban, 'Constitutional Values and Principles in the Community Legal Order' (1995) 2 *Maastricht Journal of European and Comparative Law* 129 at 132.

28 Alexy explains these phrases, using the examples of 'car', 'state of legal regulation' and safety:

> Neither the car nor the state of legal regulation can be said to be a value. As objects of evaluation they have a value, and indeed a different value depending on the criterion one adopts. It is not the objects but the *criteria of evaluation* which can be called 'values'. This corresponds both to systemic considerations and to normal usage. So it is overblown, but not wrong, to say that one car satisfies the values of safety to a higher degree than another, what one cannot say is that one car *is* a higher value than another.
>
> (Alexy, *A Theory of Constitutional Rights* at 90, emphasis in original)

29 The Union's stated purposes within the Treaties are arguably suggestive of evaluative and descriptive elements, captured in Bengoetxea's statement that:

> the purposes of the Treaties, and especially of the EEC Treaty, are clearly expressed. In other words, 'les Traités sont petris de teleologie' they set the aims to be achieved – the

Alexy himself accepts that '[a]ll sorts of things can be the object of evaluation, among other things, natural objects, artefacts, ideas, experiences, actions, and *states of affairs*',[30] a conclusion that suggests the states of affairs envisaged by the Treaties constitute objects as opposed to criteria of evaluation. I would reject these arguments for the following reasons.[31]

A state or process of integration as the overriding concern of the Union is a politico-legal phenomenon and therefore, following MacCormick, an 'institutional' as opposed to 'brute' fact.[32] That is, all Union legal demands represent an interpretation of 'brute' facts concerning the existence and operation of the Union institutions in light of a set of regulative ideals directed to a state or process of integration. As a programme of political, legal, social and economic reform, the Treaty objectives represent functional concerns underlying all Union institutional practices created for their realisation. This functional character of the Treaties in service of the value of integration is, as noted above, highlighted by the fact the Union represents, for the time being, a partially realised project of European integration, contested and uncertain in the manner and pace of its development. Finally, the Treaty objectives are undoubtedly of sufficient generality to allow their 'satisfaction' to varying degrees and therefore form criteria as opposed to objects of evaluation.

Critical argument: a new theoretical perspective?

A third possible criticism of the arguments I have made in this work is the following. If values relating to specific political, economic or social objectives can operate as the foundational or constitutional basis of legal order, as is the nub of my theoretical claim, does this add anything to existing conceptual accounts of law? No new claims are being made regarding the key issue for analytic jurisprudence, the relationship of values of political morality to law. The argument that other objectives may operate alongside rule of law values as foundational concerns of legal order simply restates existing jurisprudential accounts albeit in (slightly) amended form. This criticism fails for two reasons, which refer to the operational and contextual features of the Union as an order based upon the realisation of identified economic, political and social ideals.

achievement of a common market – the ultimate objective of the founding fathers contained in the Preamble – political union – and the means to bring about those aims – the establishment of autonomous and independent institutions.

(J Bengoetxea, *The Legal Reasoning of the European Court of Justice* (Clarendon Press, Oxford 1993) at 252 referring to P Pescatore, 'Interpretation of Community Law and the Doctrine of Acte Clair' in M Bathhurst *et al.* (eds), *Legal Problems of an Enlarged European Community* (Stevens and Sons, London 1972)

30 Alexy, *A Theory of Constitutional Rights* at 89.

31 Habermas, *Between Facts and Norms* at 255.

32 On institutional and brute facts, see N MacCormick and O Weinberger, *An Institutional Theory of Law* (D Reidel Publishing Company, Dordrecht 1986) at 101ff.

The first concerns the impact of Union constitutional values, representing the ultimate objectives of the Union, over the judicial articulation of Union legal demands. These objectives condition every legal outcome in a way that closely parallels the hierarchical legal effects taken by domestic constitutional principles over domestic legislation. The existence of a non-inclusive (limited) jurisdiction constitutionally based on achieving specific economic, political and social objectives and possessing similar operative features to domestic constitutional norms as fully inclusive governmental frameworks challenges and invites reconsideration of existing analytic accounts.

The second reason concerns the sense in which the foundational values of the Treaties operate to qualify in a subtle, ongoing process, the domestic constitutional settlements of the Member States. As explored in Chapter 6, Union legal demands articulated by the Court of Justice have transformed, and continue to transform, both the substantive reach and institutional allocation of governmental powers under existing domestic constitutional arrangements. This process cannot be adequately understood without a reimagining of legal order to account for a flexible ability to mirror and address a wider range of constitutionally significant institutional concerns than was hitherto thought possible. Here the rhetorical shaping of legal argument by the Court of Justice takes on a theoretical significance as the seat of constitutional transformation.

A European political identity

In this final section of the book, I wish to consider briefly a suggested future research question related to the understanding of legal order defended throughout this work. This concerns the possible development of a common European political identity or polity based on the activities of the Court of Justice expressing the legal framework of the European Union. Here I offer a preliminary defence of the proposition that public institutional recognition of Union legal rights, obligations and values within the Member States may incrementally generate a form of European polity. If correct, this suggests an ability of legal order generally, to create 'thick' forms of political allegiance absent the historical or cultural linkages around which such allegiances are typically constructed.[33] I defend this possibility – of polity creation through operation of law – in the Union setting against the following two arguments:

33 Kumm, writing before the demise of the Constitutional Treaty, has stated that:

> If the European Union is to master successfully the tasks assigned to it in the Constitutional Treaty and, using a non-consensual procedure, decide on policies that concern the security of its citizens or have significant distributive effects, then a sufficiently thick common identity is believed to be necessary both to legitimate and to ensure the functioning of the polity in the long term. There is little doubt that such an identity is currently missing.
>
> (M Kumm 'The Idea of Thick Constitutional Patriotism and its Implications for the Role and Structure of European Legal History' (2005) 6 *German Law Journal* 319 at 319, hereafter Kumm, 'The Idea of Thick Constitutional Patriotism')

Argument 1: a common European polity not possible given the Union's limited governmental jurisdiction

According to this argument, only a jurisdictionally inclusive system of governance is competent to address the social needs of a given community and hence to express a common political identity. Given the Union lacks such an inclusive jurisdiction, it is unable to form the basis of a 'thick' European political association. While the Treaties undoubtedly aspire to similar rule of law ideals to those found in domestic constitutions,[34] these aspirations, as previously discussed, are operationally confined by the powers conferred under the Treaties. Any future assumption or transfer of the 'inclusive' rule of law jurisdiction associated with domestic constitutions to the Union,[35] does not moreover form any part of the self-understanding of either Union or Member States at the present time.[36]

Argument 2: a lack of sufficient homogeneity between the peoples of the Member States to give rise to a European polity

A second argument denying the possibility of a European polity emerges from the German Federal Constitutional Court's (FCC) well-known *Maastricht* ruling.[37] The judgment concerned a challenge to the legality of transfer of powers to the Union under the Maastricht Treaty by reference to requirements in the German constitution relating to the democratic character of the German State. The Federal Court, while affirming the legality of the Treaty's adoption, maintained that Member States must retain a significant level of governmental responsibility over their

34 Kumm suggests in this regard that a 'thin' form of constitutional patriotism, namely affiliation to a set of ideals in the abstract, will not suffice to generate a sufficiently thick common European identity, both as a result of the universality (within Member States) of the liberal democratic tradition on which they are based, as well as the fact that these ideals of themselves are not sufficiently 'thick'. As he notes, '[h]ow can abstract moral principles – rather than collectively shed blood, sweat and tears – be the kit for a political community? Ibid. at 320. This does somewhat beg the question of what it is that transforms the 'blood sweat and tears' of individuals as a collective social activity into the basis of a common political identity.

35 For example, by the transferral of an unlimited fundamental rights jurisdiction to the Court of Justice.

36 Given Union laws already operate as both directly applicable and supreme sources of legal authority within the Member States, such an extension of Union authority would arguably signal the demise of Member States' constitutional rights to self-determination. In fact, with the Lisbon Treaty committing the Union to accession to the European Convention on Human Rights, ultimate authority in human rights matters affecting the Union will at some point be removed to the European Court of Human Rights (Article 6(2) TEU). Paradoxically, were the Court of Human Rights to issue rulings in future challenging the Union's ability to exclude human rights considerations on jurisdictional grounds (given this might itself breach fundamental rights requirements), this could trigger moves towards *greater* inclusiveness in the Union's fundamental rights jurisdiction.

37 Cases 2 BvR 2134/92, 2159/92 *Re Maastricht Treaty*, Federal Republic of Germany, Federal Constitutional Court, October

citizenry in order to guarantee legal expression of their social, political and spiritual homogeneity, stating:

> If the peoples of the individual States (as is true at present) convey democratic legitimation via the national parliaments, then limits are imposed, by the principle of democracy, on an extension of the functions and powers of the European Communities. State power in each of the States emanates from the people of that State. The States require sufficient areas of significant responsibility of their own, areas in which the people of the State concerned may develop and express itself within a process of forming political will which it legitimates and controls, in order to give legal expression to those matters which concern that people on a relatively homogen[e]ous basis spiritually, socially, and politically.[38]

The FCC is arguably correct that the lack of spiritual, social or political homogeneity amongst the collective Member States' citizenry, by comparison with that found within individual Member States, militates against the development of a Union polity on this basis alone. However, whether the converse is true – that the Union may not legitimately lay claim to a degree of governmental responsibility capable of generating a common political identity on some other basis – may be disputed. This requires exploration of the possibilities of polity formation through operation of legal institutions.

A Union polity as a product of law

The two claims outlined above, that a common political identity may not emerge from the operation of a non-inclusive legal jurisdiction or derive from an association that does not possess the requisite degree of social, political or spiritual homogeneity, can be criticised. The first claim takes an overly narrow view of the scope of governmental authority, ignoring the possibilities of polity formation associated with limited governmental frameworks. These possibilities are allied to my claims in Chapter 2 that the existence of directly applicable public regulation is the defining characteristic of legal ordering, regardless

38 Ibid. at Section C, Part I, paragraph 2(b)(2) citing H. Heller, 'Politische Demokratie und soziale Homogenitat' in H Heller (ed.), *Gesammelte Schriften Vol. 2* (A.W. Sijthoff, Leiden 1971) 421at 427ff. Weiler and Habermas have highlighted the dangers of this position given its implicit support for nationalist tendencies. J H H Weiler, 'Does Europe Need a Constitution? Reflections on Demos, Telos and the German Maastricht Decision' (1995) 1 *European Law Journal* 219; J Habermas, 'Why Europe Needs a Constitution' (2001) 11 *New Left Review* 5. Self-evidently the emergence of a European polity on the 'homogeneous' basis envisaged by the Federal Constitutional Court implies stronger cultural, ethnic or historical associations amongst the various peoples of the Member States than currently exists given the Union was formed from existing States.

of whether that regulation represents part of an inclusive jurisdiction. Given legal order as a directly and publicly applicable system of regulation is itself a defining attribute of a common political identity, there is no reason why a sufficiency of legal jurisdiction may not give rise to 'thick' political allegiances. These allegiances may relate to a limited, 'independent' body of legal rights, obligations and values and exist alongside existing political affiliations.

The second claim insists that the linkage required between legitimate governmental authority and the associated polity is based on (in my view, unnecessary) notions of homogeneity. This claim is deficient in two respects. First, in failing to recognise the possibility of a common political identity arising in the context of limited governmental jurisdictions as outlined above and second by unnecessarily restricting the possibilities for legitimation of such political associations. The German Federal Constitutional Court's *Maastricht* ruling mistakenly links the conferral of legitimacy upon fully inclusive frameworks of governance, which may indeed require the degree of 'ethnic' homogeneity referred to, with the possibility and legitimation of jurisdictionally limited governmental frameworks and associated political identity, whose legitimacy may derive from other sources. These include the wider institutional context within which a legal framework operates, domestic constitutional frameworks where the Union order is concerned. Domestic legal and political environments afford an implicit legitimation of an emerging European political association, albeit one dependent upon an ongoing, negotiated political and legal consensus, as opposed to direct democratic processes of legitimation as found within individual Member States.

In short, the de facto obedience by State actors, to whom citizens owe settled constitutional allegiances, and 'co-opted' private actors to directly applicable forms of Union legal authority suggests an alternative route to polity formation to that affirmed in *Maastricht*. A common European political identity, corresponding with ongoing and increasing recognition of Union demands in the public and private legal spheres may coalesce around a collective awareness of a body of Union legal values, rights and obligations. The employment of a legal culture as a means to promote political identity is sustained, promoted and developed by Union institutions, notably the Court of Justice employing a persuasive legal rhetoric.

This is a variation upon Habermas' notion of a 'constitutional patriotism' entailing common public allegiance[39] to a body of civic values sustained by a sphere of public discourse. For Habermas, the role of law is essentially procedural, maintaining the conditions of openness and inclusivity required for rational public debate.[40] In the Union context, these conditions already

39 See generally, J Habermas, *The Inclusion of the Other* (Polity Press, Cambridge 1998), hereafter Habermas, *The Inclusion of the Other*.

40 'Discourse theory does not make the success of deliberative politics depend on a collectively acting citizenry but on the institutionalisation of corresponding procedures.' Ibid. at 248. See also R Alexy, 'A Discourse-Theoretical Conception of Practical Reason' (1992) 5 *Ratio Juris* 231.

largely exist in the constitutional frameworks of the Member States and the role of law and judicial institutions is more direct in *generating* allegiance to a body of European constitutional values.

These differences between polity formation in the domestic and Union contexts are illustrated by contrasting domestic constitutional settlements, whose interpretation expresses existing cultural or historical associations,[41] with the Union as an 'impersonal' political aspiration. Přibáň states this point as follows: '[t]he Union's political integration and identity-building, based on the politics of depoliticization, has primarily been a legalistic project'.[42] However, while Přibáň argues that the legalisation of political issues by the Union is a weakness respecting the development of a European identity given the lack of necessary engagement by the citizenry required for identity formation around a set of core values, my contention is that the emergence of a common European identity premised on the ability of the Court of Justice to present Union legal demands as a credible and attractive package of rights and principles, institutionally recognised within the Member States, is a realistic possibility.[43]

Conclusions

The Union experience suggests that given a minimal (sufficient) degree of cultural or historical association, a potential exists, through the operation of law and legal institutions for incremental polity development. This possibility is clearly relevant where the promotion of new constitutional allegiances is seen as beneficial for social or economic reasons. Here polity formation does not derive from the basic need for human society to organise into communities of political governance for survival[44] but instead on the ability of legal order to re-imagine beneficial constitutional forms. This requires an incremental, flexible and negotiated adjustment of existing settlements, a process

41 'The political integration of citizens ensures loyalty to the common political culture. The latter is rooted in an interpretation of constitutional principles from the perspective of the nation's historical experience.' Habermas, *The Inclusion of the Other* at 225.

42 J Přibáň, 'The Juridification of European Identity, its Limitations and the Search of EU Democratic Politics' (2009) 16 *Constellations* 44.

43 Benvenisti's comment in relation to the institutional potential of international law is also relevant here:

> The vision of international law as a legal system creates a space within which decision makers can reach conclusions about specific outcomes using the rhetoric of law, rather than the rhetoric of what is just or efficient. Judges, bureaucrats, politicians and private claimants engage in deliberations about *legal* principles and the legitimate conclusions these principles stipulate.
>
> (E Benvenisti, 'The Conception of International Law as a Legal System' (2008) 83 *Tel Aviv University Law Faculty Papers*)

44 J Locke, *The Second Treatise of Government* (first published 1689, Dover Publications, New York 2002).

which, as I have argued, lies within the ability of legal institutions – the Court of Justice where the Union is concerned – to achieve.

Concluding remarks

I have offered an understanding of the Union legal order based on a co-operative of European States which have collectively ceded limited yet significant governmental powers to a supranational organisation for the achievement of objectives identified as politically beneficial. The tension between the Union as a transnational rule of law legal order dedicated to the achievement of social, economic and political ideals, on the one hand, and as a conferred and hence limited legal jurisdiction, on the other, lends an enduring fascination.

While the Member States remain committed, in the terms of the Treaties, to 'ever closer Union',[45] the Court of Justice must articulate a positive, evolutionary dynamic that embodies and expresses the beginnings of a new constitutional settlement. The necessary association of an evolving Union with a revolutionary restructuring of Member States' existing constitutional settlements demands a rhetorical expertise on the part of the Court of Justice in managing the legal parameters of this process. This clearly involves political judgments concerning the art of the possible[46] by the Court of Justice when 'mobilising the interpretive criteria' of the Treaties, in the service of European integration.[47]

45 Article 1 TEU.

46 'Politics is the art of the possible' is a remark attributed to Otto von Bismark, the pre-eminent nineteenth century German politician.

47 The phrase 'mobilisation of interpretive criteria' is a rephrasing of a working definition of law by Moraitis and Murphy who, in critiquing the language of an undergraduate essay note that 'the student may see the law not as the mobilisation of interpretable criteria, but rather as authoritative rules in themselves'. P Moraitis and H Murphy, 'Language, Law and Identity: A Language and Learning Response to the Challenges of Widening Participation to Law Students' (2013) 47 *The Law Teacher* 159 at 174. This phrase captures nicely the sense in which I have sought to understand the practices of the Court of Justice.

Bibliography

Court of Justice Judgments

Case 1/58 *Stork v High Authority* [1959] ECR 17

Case 26/62 *Van Gend en Loos v Nederlandse Administratie der Belastingen* [1963] ECR 1

Case 6/64 *Costa v ENEL* [1964] ECR 585

Case 57/65 *Lutticke v Hauptzollamt Saarlouis* [1966] ECR 205

Case 14/68 *Walt Wilhelm and Others v Bundeskartellamt* [1969] ECR I

Case 29/69 *Stauder v City of Ulm* [1969] ECR 419

Case 9/70 *Grad v Finanzamt Traunstein* [1970] ECR 825

Case 11/70 *Internationale Haandelsgesellschaft mbH v Einfuhr- und Vorratsstelle fur Getreide und Futtermittel* [1970] ECR 1125 (*Solange I*)

Case 41/71 *Van Duyn v Home Office* [1974] ECR 1337

Case 93/71 *Leonesio v Italian Ministry for Agriculture and Forestry* [1972] ECR 287

Case 6/72 *Europemballage and Continental Can v Commission* [1973] ECR 215

Case 4/73 *Nold v Commission* [1974] ECR 491

Case 167/ 73 *Commission v French Republic* [1974] ECR 359

Case 24/75 *Petroni v ONPTS* [1975] ECR 1149

Case 36/75 *Rutili v Minister for the Interior* [1975] ECR 1219

Case 43/75 *Defrenne v SABENA (Defrenne II)* [1976] ECR 455

Case 35/76 *Simmenthal v Italian Minister for Finance* [1976] ECR 1871

Case 106/77 *Italian Finance Administration v Simmenthal* [1978] ECR 629

Case 120/78 *Rewe-Zentrale AG v Bundesmonopolverwaltung fur Branntwein* [1979] ECR 649

Case 44/79 *Hauer v Land Rheinland* [1979] ECR 3727

Case 8/81 *Becker v Finanzamt Munster-Innenstadt* [1982] ECR 53

Case 53/81 *Levin v Staatssecretaris van Justitie* [1982] ECR 1035

Case 283/81 *CILFIT (Srl) & Lanificio di Gavardo SpA v Ministry of Health* [1982] ECR 3415

Case 14/83 *Von Colson & Kamann v Land Nordrhein-Westfalen* [1984] ECR 1891

Case 294/83 *Partie Ecologiste 'Les Verts' v European Parliament* [1986] ECR 1339

Case 222/84 *Johnston v Chief Constable of the Royal Ulster Constabulary* [1986] ECR 1651

Case 80/86 *Criminal Proceedings against Kolpinghuis Nijmegen* [1987] ECR 3969

Case 126/86 *Fernando Roberto Gimenez Zaera v Instituto Nacional de la Seguridad Social y Tesoreria General de la Seguridad Social* [1987] ECR-3697

Case 157/86 *Murphy v Bord Telecom Eireann* [1988] ECR 673

Case C-70/88 *Parliament v Council (Chernobyl)* [1990] ECR I-2041
Case C-177/88 *Dekker* [1990] ECR I-6155
Case C-262/88 *Barber v Guardian Royal Exchange Assurance Group* [1990] ECR I-1889
Case C-106/89 *Marleasing* [1990] ECR I-4135
Case C-213/89 *Factortame* [1990] ECR I-2433
Case C-260/89 *ERT* [1991] ECR I-2925
Case C-159/90 *Society for the Protection of the Unborn Child v Grogan and Others* [1991] ECR I-4685
Case C-370/90 *Singh* [1992] ECR I-4265
Opinion 1/91 on the draft agreement to create a European Economic Area [1991] ECR I-06079
Case C-271/91 *Marshall v Southampton and South West Hampshire Area Health Authority* [1993] ECR I-4367
Case C-334/92 *Wagner Miret v Fondo de Garantia Salarial* [1993] ECR I-6911
Case C-55/94 *Gebhard (Reinhard) v Consiglio dell'Ordine degli Avvocati e Procuratori di Milano* [1995] ECR I-4165
Case C-129/94 *Criminal Proceedings against Rafael Ruiz Bernaldez* [1996] ECR I-1829
Case C-192/94 *El Corte Ingles v Lazquez Rivero* [1996] ECR I-1281
Case C-194/94 *CIA Security International SA v Signalson SA* [1996] ECR I-2201
Case C-72/95 *Kraaijeveld and others v Gedeputeerde Staten van Zuid-Holland* [1996] ECR I-5403
Case C-180/95 *Draehmpaehl v Urania Immobilienservice* [1997] ECR I-2195
Case C-299/95 *Kremzov v Republik Osterreich* [1997] ECR I-2629
Case C-57/96 *Meints v Minister van Landbouw, Natuurbeheer en Visserij* [1997] ECR I-6689
Case C-85/96 *María Martínez Sala v Freistaat Bayern* [1998] ECR I-2691
Case C-249/ 96 *Lisa Jacqueline Grant v South West Trains Ltd* [1998] ECR I-621
Joined Cases C-10/97 to C-22/97 *Ministero delle Finanze v I.N.C.O.G.E'90* [1998] ECR I-6307
Case C-185/97 *Coote v Granada Hospitality Ltd* [1998] ECR I-5199
Case C-337/97 *C.P.M. Meeusen v Hoofdirectie van de Informatie Beheer Groep* [1999] ECR I-3289
Case C-456/98 *Centrosteel Srl v Adipol GmbH* [2000] ECR I-6007
Case C-413/99 *Baumbast v Secretary of State for the Home Department* [2002] ECR I-7091
Case C-459/99 *MRAX* [2002] ECR I-6591
Case C-50/00 *Union de Pequenos Agricultores v Council* [2002] ECR I-6677
Case C-60/00 *Carpenter v Secretary of State for the Home Department* [2002] ECR I-6279
Case C-62/00 *Marks & Spencer v Commissioners of Customs & Excise* [2002] ECR I-4135
Case C-112/00 *Schmidberger Internationale Transporte und Planzüge v Austria* [2003] ECR I-5659
Joined Cases C-97/01 to C-403/01 *Bernhard Pfeiffer v Deutsches Rotes Kreuz* [2004] ECR I-8835
Case C-109/01 *Secretary of State for the Home Department v Akrich* [2003] ECR I-9607
Case C-36/02 *Omega Speilhallen-und Automatenauftellungs v Oberburgerermeisterin der Bundestadt Bonn*, judgment of 14 October 2004

Case C-200/02 *Chen v Secretary of State for the Home Department* [2004] ECR I-3119
Case C-105/03 *Pupino* [2005] ECR I-5285
Case C-157/03 *Commission v Spain* [2005] ECR I-2911
Case C-144/04 *Mangold v Helm* [2005] ECR I-9981
Case C-1/05 *Yunying Jia v Migrationsverket* [2007] ECR I-1
Case C-287/05 *D.P.W. Hendrix v Raad van Bestuur van het Uitvoeringsinstituut Werknemersverzekeringen* [2007] ECR I-6909
Case C-291/05 *Eind* [2004] ECR I-10719
Case C-402/05 P *Kadi and Al Barakaat International Foundation v Council and Commission* [2008] I-06351
Case C-67/06 *Tadao Maruko v Versorgungsanstalt der deutschen Buhnen* [2008] ECR I-1757
Case C-127/08 *Metock* [2008] ECR I-6241

European Court of Human Rights Judgments

Chevrol v France 2003-III Eur. Ct. H.R. 159
Hirst v The United Kingdom (No. 2) [2005] ECHR 681

Cases from other Jurisdictions

UK

R v Secretary of State for Transport ex parte Factortame [1989] 2 CMLR 353
Thoburn v Sunderland City Council [2002] EWHC 195
Ghaidan v Godin-Mendoza [2004] UKHL 30
A (FC) and Others (FC) (Appellants) v Secretary of State for the Home Department (Respondent) [2004] UKHL 56
Jackson and Others v Her Majesty's Attorney General [2005] UKHL 56
A v Secretary of State for the Home Department (No. 2) [2005] UKHL 71
The Commissioners for Her Majesty's Revenue and Customs v IDT Card Services Ireland Ltd [2006] EWCA Civ 29

Germany

1 BvR 400/51 BVerfGE 7, 198 I. Senate (1 BvR 400/51) *Lüth*, Federal Republic of Germany, Federal Constitutional Court
2 BvR 197/83 *Wunsche Handelsgesellschaft (Solange II)*, Federal Republic of Germany, Federal Constitutional Court
2 BvR 687/85 *Kloppenburg*, Federal Republic of Germany, Federal Constitutional Court
2 BvR 2134/92, 2159/92 *Re Maastricht Treaty*, Federal Republic of Germany, Federal Constitutional Court, October
2 BvL 1/97 *Banana Organisation Constitutionality Case*, Federal Republic of Germany, Federal Constitutional Court
1 BvR 370, 595/07 *Data Protection*, Republic of Germany, Federal Constitutional Court
1 BvR 1602, 1606, 1626/07 *Spiegel*, Federal Republic of Germany, Federal Constitutional Court

2 BvE 2/08, 2 BvE 5/08, 2 BvR 1010/08, 2 BvR 1022/08, 2 BvR 1259/08, 2 BvR 182/09 *Lisbon Treaty Judgment*, Federal Republic of Germany, Federal Constitutional Court

Denmark

Case No. 272/1994 *Carlsen and Others v Rasmussen*, Danish Supreme Court (Admissibility)

Belgium

European School v Hermans-Jacobs and Heuvelmans-Van Iersel (Case No. 12/94) Belgian Court of Arbitration (3 February 1994)

Orfinger v Belgian State (Minister for Civil Service) (Case No. 62.922) Belgian Conseil d'Etat (Sixth Chamber) (5 November 1996)

France

Administration des Douanes v Societe cafes Jacques and Weigel et Compagnie, Court of Cassation (Combined Chamber) 24 May 1975

Israel

H.C. 953/87, *Poraz v Mayor of Tel-Aviv-Yafo*, 42 (2) P.D. 309

Italy

Spa Granital v Amministrazione Delle Finanze Dello Stato, Italian Constitutional Court 8 June 1984

Legislation

European Union Legislation

Council Regulation 1612/68/EEC of 15 October 1968 on freedom of movement for workers within the Community [1968] OJ L257/2

Council Regulation 1408/71/EEC of 14 June 1971 on the application of social security schemes to employed persons and their families moving within the Community [1971] OJ L49/2

Council Directive 75/117/EEC of 10 February 1975 on the approximation of the laws of the Member States relating to the application of the principle of equal pay for men and women [1975] OJ L45/19

Council Directive 76/207/EEC of 9 February 1976 on the implementation of the principle of equal treatment for men and woman, as regards access to employment, vocational training and promotion and working conditions [1976] OJ L39/40

Council Directive 2000/78/EC of 27 November 2000 establishing a general framework for equal treatment in employment and occupation [2000] OJ L303/16

Directive 2002/73/EC of the European Parliament and of the Council of 23 September 2002 amending Council Directive 76/207/EEC on the implementation of the principle of equal treatment for men and women as regards access to employment, vocational training and promotion, and working conditions [2002] OJ L269/15

Regulation 883/2004/EC of the European Parliament and of the Council of 29 April 2004 on the coordination of social security systems [2004] OJ L166/1

Directive 2006/54/EC of the European Parliament and of the Council of 5 July 2006 on the implementation of the principle of equal opportunities and equal treatment of men and woman in matters of employment and occupation [2006] OJ L204/23

Member State Legislation

European Communities Act 1972 (UK)

Sex Discrimination Act 1975 (UK)

International Treaties

International Covenant on Economic, Social and Cultural Rights (adopted 16 December 1966, entered into force 3 January 1976) 993 UNTS 3 (ICESCR)

Vienna Convention on the Law of Treaties (adopted 23 May 1969, entered into force 27 January 1980) 1155 UNTS 331

Convention between Great Britain, Japan, Russia and the United States Requesting Measures for the Preservation and Protection of Fur Seals in the North Pacific Ocean (signed 7 December 1911) 214 CTS 80

Articles

R Alexy, 'A Discourse-Theoretical Conception of Practical Reason' (1992) 5 *Ratio Juris* 231

R Alexy, 'On the Concept and Nature of Law' (2008) 21 *Ratio Juris* 281

P Allott, 'The European Community Is Not the True European Community' (1990–1991) 100 *Yale Law Journal* 2485

P Allott, 'The Crisis of European Constitutionalism: Reflections on the Revolution in Europe' (1997) 34 *Common Market Law Review* 439

P Allott, 'Preliminary Rulings – Another Infant Disease' (2000) 25 *European Law Review* 538

K J Alter, 'Who Are the "Masters of the Treaty"?: European Governments and the European Court of Justice' (1998) 52 *International Organization* 121

M Amstutz, 'Marleasing and the Emergence of Interlegality in Legal Reasoning' (2005) 11 *European Law Journal* 766

G E M Anscombe, 'On Brute Facts' (1958) 18 *Analysis* 59

A Arnull, 'The European Court and Judicial Objectivity: A Reply to Professor Hartley' (1996) 112 *The Law Quarterly Review* 411

M Avbelj, 'Supremacy or Primacy of EU Law – (Why) Does It Matter?' (2011) 17 *European Law Journal* 744

C Ball, 'The Making of a Transnational Capitalist Society: The Court of Justice, Social Policy, and Individual Rights under the European Community's Legal Order' (1996) 37 *Harvard International Law Journal* 307

S Bandes, 'The Negative Constitution: A Critique' (1989–1990) 88 *Michigan Law Review* 2271

Z K Bañkowski, 'Institutional Legal Positivism' (1989) 3 *Rechtstheorie* 289

Z K Bañkowski and E Christodoulidis, 'The European Union as an Essentially Contested Project' (1998) 4 *European Law Journal* 341

E Benvenisti, 'The Conception of International Law as a Legal System' (2008) 83 *Tel Aviv University Law Faculty Papers*

G Betlem, 'The Doctrine of Consistent Interpretation – Managing Legal Uncertainty' (2002) 22 *Oxford Journal of Legal Studies* 397

B Bieber and I Salome, 'Hierarchy of Norms in European Law' (1996) 33 *Common Market Law Review* 909

B Bix, 'Conceptual Questions and Jurisprudence' (1995) 1 *Legal Theory* 465

B Bix, 'Patrolling the Boundaries: Inclusive Legal Positivism and the Nature of Jurisprudential Debate' (1999) 12 *Canadian Journal of Law and Jurisprudence* 17

A M Burley and W Mattli, 'Europe before the Court: A Political Theory of Legal Integration' (1993) 47 *International Organization* 41

N Burrows, C Carter and A Scott, *Subsidiarity and the Draft Treaty*, Discussion Paper, Brussels, 27 April 2004

M Cappelletti, 'Is the Court of Justice "Running Wild?"' (1987) 12 *European Law Review* 3

L Charpentier, 'The European Court of Justice and the Rhetoric of Affirmative Action' (1998) *European University Institute, Working Paper* RSC No. 98/30

A Chaskalson, 'Roundtable – From Wickedness to Equality: The Moral Transformation of South African Law' (2003) 1 *International Journal of Constitutional Law* 590

J Coleman, 'Negative and Positive Positivism' (1982) 11 *Journal of Legal Studies* 139

J Coleman, 'Beyond the Separability Thesis: Moral Semantics and the Methodology of Jurisprudence' (2007) 27 *Oxford Journal of Legal Studies* 581

J Coleman, 'Beyond Inclusive Positivism' (2009) 22 *Ratio Juris* 359

D Cooke, 'The Talking Cure in Habermas' Republic' (2001) 12 *New Left Review* 135

J Coppel and A O'Neil, 'The European Court of Justice: Taking Rights Seriously?' (1992) 12 *Legal Studies* 227

D P Currie, 'Positive and Negative Constitutional Rights' (1986) 53 *University of Chicago Law Review* 864

S Currie, 'Accelerated Justice or a Step Too Far? Residence Rights of Non-EU Family Members and the Courts Ruling in Metock' (2009) 34 *European Law Review* 310

A Dashwood, 'The Relationship between the Member States and the European Union/European Community (2004) 41 *Common Market Law Review* 355

H de Waele, 'The Role of the European Court of Justice in the Integration Process: A Contemporary and Normative Assessment' (2010) 6 *Hanse Law Review* 3

E Drumeva, 'Primacy of the EU Law to National (Constitutional) Law' accessed at www.mkab.hu/index.php?id=twenty_years_of_the_constitutional_court on 26 December 2010

R Dworkin, 'Objectivity and Truth, You'd Better Believe It' (1996) 25 *Philosophy and Public Affairs* 87

P Eleftheriadis, 'Begging the Constitutional Question' (1998) 36 *Journal of Common Market Studies* 255

M L F Esteban, 'Constitutional Values and Principles in the Community Legal Order' (1995) 2 *Maastricht Journal of European and Comparative Law* 129

U Everling, 'The Court of Justice as a Decision Making Authority' (1983–1984) 82 *Michigan Law Review* 1294

U Everling, 'The *Maastricht* Judgment of the German Federal Constitutional Court and its Significance for the Development of the European Union' (1994) 14 *Yearbook of European Law* 1

M J Gerhardt, 'The Ripple Effects of *Slaughter-House*: A Critique of a Negative Rights View of the Constitution' (1990) 43 *Vanderbilt Law Review* 409

D Grimm, 'The European Court of Justice and National Courts: The German Constitutional Perspective after the Maastricht Decision' (1996–1997) 3 *Columbia Journal of European Law* 229

J Habermas, 'The European Nation-State and the Pressures of Globalisation' (1999) 9 *New Left Review* 235

J Habermas, 'Why Europe Needs a Constitution' (2001) 11 *New Left Review* 5

T C Hartley, 'The European Court, Judicial Objectivity and the Constitution of the European Union (1996) 112 *The Law Quarterly Review* 95

G. Hornung, 'Ein neues Grundrecht' [2008] *Computer und Recht* 299

M Huomo-Kettunen, 'Constitutional Structures in the European Legal Space' (2013) 6 *European Journal of Legal Studies* 47

C Joerges, 'What Is Left of the European Economic Constitution? A Melancholic Eulogy' (2005) 30 *European Law Review* 461

M L Jones, 'The Legal Nature of the European Community: A Jurisprudential Analysis Using H.L.A. Hart's Model of Law and a Legal System' (1984) 17 *Cornell International Law Journal* 1

H Kelsen, 'On the Theory of Interpretation' (1990) 10 *Legal Studies* 127

M G G Ketvel, 'The Jurisdiction of the European Court of Justice in Respect of the Common Foreign and Security Policy' (2006) 55 *International and Comparative Law Quarterly* 77

M Kumm, 'To Be a European Citizen? The Absence of Constitutional Patriotism and the Constitutional Treaty' (2004–2005) 11 *Columbia Journal of European Law* 481

M Kumm 'The Idea of Thick Constitutional Patriotism and its Implications for the Role and Structure of European Legal History' (2005) 6 *German Law Journal* 319

T Kyriakou, 'The Impact of the EU Charter of Fundamental Rights on the EU System of Protection of Rights: Much Ado About Nothing?' (2001) 5 *Web Journal of Current Legal Issues*

B Leiter, 'Beyond the Hart/Dworkin Debate' (2003) 48 *American Journal of Jurisprudence* 17

K Lenaerts, 'Constitutionalism and the Many Faces of Federalism' (1990) 38 *American Journal of Community Law* 205

K Lenaerts, 'Interlocking Legal Orders in the European Union and Comparative Law' (2003) 52 *International and Comparative Law Quarterly* 873

K Lenaerts and M Desomer, 'Towards a Hierarchy of Legal Acts in the European Union? Simplification of Legal Instruments and Procedures' (2005) 11 *European Law Journal* 744

K Lenaerts and T Corthaut, 'Of Birds and Hedges: The Role of Primacy in Invoking Norms of EU Law' (2006) 31 *European Law Review* 287

N MacCormick, 'Risking Constitutional Collision in Europe' (1998) 18 *Oxford Journal of Legal Studies* 517

J F McMahon, 'The Court of the European Communities: Judicial Interpretation and International Organisation' (1961) 37 *British Yearbook of International Law* 320

M P Maduro, 'Interpreting European Law: Judicial Adjudication in a Context of Constitutional Pluralism' (2007) 1 *European Journal of Legal Studies* 1

G F Mancini, 'The Making of a Constitution for Europe' (1989) 26 *Common Market Law Review* 595

G Martinico and O Pollicino, 'Between Constitutional Tolerance and Judicial Activism: The Specificity of European Judicial Law' (2008) 10 *European Journal of Law Reform* 97

E-J Mestmäcker, 'On the Legitimacy of European Law' (1994) 58 (4) *Rabels Zeitschrift für ausländisches und internationales Privatrecht* 615

P Moraitis and H Murphy, 'Language, Law and Identity: A Language and Learning Response to the Challenges of Widening Participation to Law Students' (2013) 47 *The Law Teacher* 159

F Morgenstern, 'Judicial Practice and the Supremacy of International Law' (1950) 27 *British Yearbook of International Law* 42

D C Mueller 'Federalism and the European Union: A Constitutional Perspective' (1997) 90 *Public Choice* 255

H J Papier, former president of the Federal Constitutional Court of Germany 'Problems of Enforcing Constitutional Court Decisions' accessed at www.concourt.am/old/almanac2003/papers/3.doc on 3 January 2008

S L Paulson, 'Kelsen on Legal Interpretation' (1990) 10 *Legal Studies* 136

A Peczenik and J Wroblewski, 'Fuzziness and Transformation: Towards Explaining Legal Reasoning' (1985) 51 *Theoria* 24

S Perry, 'The Varieties of Legal Positivism' (1996) 9 *Canadian Journal of Law and Jurisprudence* 361

S Perry, 'Beyond the Distinction between Positivism and Non-Positivism' (2009) 22 *Ratio Juris* 311

P Pescatore, 'The Doctrine of Direct Effect: An Infant Disease of Community Law' (1983) 8 *European Law Review* 155

A Peters, 'Supremacy Lost: International Law Meets Domestic Constitutional Law' (2009) 3 *Vienna Online Journal of International Law* 170

J Přibáň, 'The Juridification of European Identity, its Limitations and the Search of EU Democratic Politics' (2009) 16 *Constellations* 44

H Rasmussen, 'Between Self-Restraint and Activism: A Judicial Policy for the European Court' (1988) 13 *European Law Review* 28

R Rawlings, 'Legal Politics: The United Kingdom and Ratification of the Treaty on European Union (Part One)' [1994] *Public Law* 214

P V F Regueiro, 'Invocability of Substitution and Invocability of Exclusion: Bringing Legal Realism to the Current Developments of the Case-Law of "Horizontal" Direct Effect of Directives', *Jean Monnet Working Paper* No. 7/02

T Schilling, 'The Autonomy of the Community Legal Order: An Analysis of Possible Legal Foundations' (1996) 37 *Harvard International Law Journal* 389

T Schilling, 'The Court of Justice's Revolution: Its Effects and the Conditions for its Consummation: What Europe Can Learn from Fiji' (2002) 27 *European Law Review* 445

B Schlink, 'Roundtable – Hercules in German?' (2003) 1 *International Journal of Constitutional Law* 610

C T Smith and T Fetzer, 'The Uncertain Limits of the European Court of Justice's Authority: Economic Freedom Versus Human Dignity' (2004) 10 *Columbia Journal of European Law* 445

E Spaventa, 'Opening Pandora's Box: Some Reflections on the Constitutional Effects of the Decision in *Pupino*' (2007) 3 *European Constitutional Law Review* 5

O Spiermann, 'The Other Side of the Story: An Unpopular Essay on the Making of the European Community Legal Order' (1999) 10 *European Journal of International Law* 763

S K Spiliotopoulos, 'The Amended Equal Treatment Directive (2002/73): An Expression of Constitutional Principles/Fundamental Rights' (2005) 12 *Maastricht Journal of European and Comparative Law* 327

E Stein, 'Lawyers, Judges and the Making of a Transnational Constitution' (1981) 75 *American Journal of International Law* 1

The Right Honourable Lord Bingham of Cornhill KG FKC Commemoration Oration 31 October, 2007 18.00, Great Hall, Strand Campus

T Tridimas, 'The Court of Justice and Judicial Activism' (1996) 21 *European Law Review* 199

R H S Tur, 'Defeasibilism' (2001) 21 *Oxford Journal of Legal Studies* 355

C Vazquez, 'The Four Doctrines of Self-Executing Treaties' (1995) 89 *American Journal of International Law* 695

V Villa, 'Legal Theory and Value Judgments' (1997) 16 *Law and Philosophy* 447

N Walker, 'The Idea of Constitutional Pluralism' (2002) 65 *Modern Law Review* 317

J H H Weiler, 'The Transformation of Europe' (1991) 100 *Yale Law Journal* 2403

J H H Weiler, 'Does Europe Need a Constitution? Reflections on Demos, Telos and the German Maastricht Decision' (1995) 1 *European Law Journal* 219

J H H Weiler and N Lockhart, '"Taking Rights Seriously" Seriously: The European Court of Justice and its Fundamental Rights Jurisprudence,' (1995) 32 *Common Market Law Review* 51 (Part I) and 579 (Part II)

J H H Weiler and U R Haltern, 'The Autonomy of the Community Legal Order – Through the Looking Glass' (1996) 37 *Harvard International Law Journal* 411

E J Weinrib, 'Law as a Kantian Idea of Reason' (1987) 87 *Columbia Law Review* 472

A Williams, 'Taking Values Seriously: Towards a Philosophy of EU Law' (2009) 29 *Oxford Journal of Legal Studies* 549

J A Winter, 'Direct Applicability and Direct Effect: Two Distinct and Different Concepts in Community Law' (1972) 9 *Common Market Law Review* 155

Books

A Aarnio, *The Rational as Reasonable: A Treatise on Legal Justification* (Kluwer Academic, Dordrecht 1987)

R Alexy, *A Theory of Legal Argumentation* (Oxford University Press, Oxford 1989)

R Alexy, *A Theory of Constitutional Rights* (Oxford University Press, Oxford 2002)

P Amselek and N MacCormick (eds), *Controversies About Law's Ontology* (Edinburgh University Press, Edinburgh 1991) Ch. 2

F Atria, *On Law and Legal Reasoning* (Hart Publishing,Oxford 2001)

J Austin, *The Province of Jurisprudence Determined* and *The Uses of the Study of Jurisprudence* (Hackett Publishing Company Inc., Indianapolis 1998)

A Barak, *Purposive Interpretation in Law* (Princeton University Press, Princeton 2005)

A Barak, *The Judge in a Democracy* (Princeton University Press, Princeton 2006)

C Barnard, *The Substantive Law of the EU: The Four Freedoms* (Oxford University Press, Oxford 2004)

M Bathurst, K R Simmonds, N March Hunnings and J Welch (eds), *Legal Problems of an Enlarged European Community* (Stevens and Sons, London 1972)

J Bengoetxea, *The Legal Reasoning of the European Court of Justice* (Clarendon Press, Oxford 1993)

U Bernitz and J Nergelius (eds), *General Principles of European Community Law* (Kluwer Law International, The Hague 2000)

A Bickel, *The Least Dangerous Branch: The Supreme Court at the Bar of Politics* (The Bobbs-Merrill Company, Inc., New York 1962)

B Bix (ed.), *Analyzing Law: New Essays in Legal Theory* (Clarendon Press, Oxford 1998)

A V Bogdandy and J Bast (eds), *Principles of European Constitutional Law* (Hart Publishing, Oxford 2005)

J Coleman, *The Practice of Principle* (Oxford University Press, Oxford 2001)

P Craig and G de Burca (eds), *The Evolution of EU Law* (Oxford University Press, Oxford 1999)

P Craig and G de Burca, *EU Law: Text, Cases and Materials* (3rd edn, Oxford University Press, Oxford 2003)

C de Burca and J H H Weiler (eds), *The Worlds of European Constitutionalism* (Cambridge University Press, Cambridge 2012)

R Dehousse, *The European Court of Justice: The Politics of Judicial Integration* (Macmillan Publishing Ltd, London 1998)

J Dickson, *Evaluation and Legal Theory* (Hart Publishing, Oxford 2001)

J Dickson and P Eleftheriadis (eds), *Philosophical Foundations of European Union Law* (Oxford University Press, Oxford 2012)

F Dumon, *The Case-Law of the Court of Justice – A Critical Examination of the Methods of Interpretation* (Europa Institut Luxembourg 1976)

R Dworkin, *Taking Rights Seriously* (Duckworth, London 1978)

R Dworkin, *Law's Empire* (Hart Publishing, Oxford 1986)

R Dworkin, *Justice in Robes* (Harvard University Press, Cambridge, Massachusetts 2006)

J H Ely, *Democracy and Distrust* (Harvard University Press, Cambridge, Massachusetts 1980)

J Esser, *Vorverstandnis und Methodenwahl in der Rechtsfindung* (Main Suhrkamp, Frankfurt 1970)

L Fuller, *The Morality of Law* (Harvard University Press, Cambridge, Massachusetts 1964)

R P George (ed.), *The Autonomy of Law* (Oxford University Press, Oxford 1996)

J Goldsworthy (ed.), *Interpreting Constitutions* (Oxford University Press, Oxford 2006)

J Habermas, *Between Facts and Norms* (Polity Press, Cambridge 1997)

J Habermas, *The Inclusion of the Other* (Polity Press, Cambridge 1998)

H Hart, *The Concept of Law* (2nd edn, Oxford University Press, Oxford 1994)

H Heller (ed.), *Gesammelte Schriften Vol. 2* (A.W. Sijthoff, Leiden 1971)

S Hershovitz (ed.), *Exploring Law's Empire: The Jurisprudence of Ronald Dworkin* (Oxford University Press, Oxford 2006)

F G Jacobs *The Sovereignty of Law: The European Way* (Cambridge, Cambridge University Press 2007)

H Kelsen, *Introduction to the Problems of Legal Theory* (Clarendon Press, Oxford 1992)

H Kelsen, *General Theory of Law and State* (Transaction Publishers, London 2008)

M Klatt (ed.), *Institutionalized Reason: The Jurisprudence of Robert Alexy* (Oxford University Press, Oxford 2012)

H Kutscher, *Judicial and Academic Conference* (Court of Justice of the European Communities, Luxembourg 1976)

W D Lamont, *The Value Judgement* (Philosophical Library Inc., New York 1955)

R Lecourt, *L'Europe des Juges* (Brussels, Bruylant 1976)

J Locke, *The Second Treatise of Government* (first published 1689, Dover Publications, New York 2002).

N MacCormick, *Questioning Sovereignty* (Oxford University Press, Oxford 1999)

N MacCormick, *Rhetoric and the Rule of Law: A Theory of Legal Reasoning* (Oxford University Press, Oxford 2005)

N MacCormick, *Institutions of Law* (Oxford University Press, Oxford 2007)

N MacCormick, *Practical Reason in Law and Morality* (Oxford University Press, Oxford 2008)

N MacCormick and O Weinberger, *An Institutional Theory of Law* (D Reidel Publishing Company, Dordrecht 1986)

M P Maduro, *We the Court* (Hart Publishing, Oxford 1998)

C Mann, *The Function of Judicial Decision in European Economic Integration* (Martinus Nijhoff, The Hague 1972)

A Marmor, *Positive Law and Objective Values* (Clarendon Press, Oxford 2001)

A Marmor, *Interpretation and Legal Theory* (Hart Publishing, Oxford 2005)

M Mendez, *The Legal Effects of EU Agreements* (Oxford University Press, Oxford 2013)

D Nicol, *EC Membership and the Judicialisation of British Politics* (Oxford University Press, Oxford 2001)

N Nugent, *The Government and Politics of the European Community* (Duke University Press, Durham 1991)

A Oppenheimer (ed.), *The Relationship between European Community Law and National Law: The Cases, Vol. 2* (Cambridge University Press, Cambridge 2003)

G Pavlakos (ed.), *Law, Rights and Discourse: The Legal Philosophy of Robert Alexy* (Hart Publishing, Oxford 2007)

C Perelman and R V Elst (eds), *Les Notions à contenu variable en droit* (Bruylant, Brussels 1985)

M Perry, *Morality, Politics, and Law* (Oxford University Press, Oxford 1988)

P Pescatore, 'Les objectifs de la Communauté européenne comme principes d'interprétation dans la jurisprudence de la Cour de Justice' in *Miscellanea W.J. Ganshof van der Meersch, Vol. II* (Centre InterUniversitaire de Droit Public et de l'Université Libre 1972) 325

R Posner, *Economic Analysis of Law* (3rd edn, Little Brown, Boston 1986)

R Posner, *Law and Legal Theory in the UK and the USA* (Clarendon Press, Oxford 1996)

S Prechal, *Directives in EC Law* (2nd edn, Oxford University Press, Oxford 2005)

H Rasmussen, *On Law and Policy in the European Court of Justice: A Comparative Study in Judicial Policymaking* (Martinus Nijhoff Publishers, The Hague 1986)

J Raz, *Ethics in the Public Domain: Essays in the Morality of Law and Politics* (Clarendon Press, Oxford 1994)

J Raz, *The Authority of Law* (2nd edn, Clarendon Press, Oxford 2009)

G H Reiss (ed.), *Kant's Political Writings* (H B Nisbet trans., Cambridge University Press, Cambridge 1971)

B Rosamond, *Theories of European Integration* (Palgrave Macmillan, Basingstoke 2000)

W Sandholtz and A S Sweet (eds), *European Integration and Supranational Governance* (Oxford University Press, Oxford 1998)

A Sarat and T R Kearns (eds), *The Rhetoric of Law* (University of Michigan Press, Ann Arbor 1994)

J R Searle, *Speech Acts* (Cambridge University Press, Cambridge 1969)

N Simmonds, *Law as a Moral Idea* (Oxford University Press, Oxford 2007)

C Sunstein, *Designing Democracy* (Oxford University Press, Oxford 2001)

S Toddington, *Rationality, Social Action and Moral Judgment* (Edinburgh University Press, Edinburgh 1993)

T Tridimas, *The General Principles of EU Law* (2nd edn, Oxford University Press, Oxford 2006)

D Vaughan (ed.), *Law of the European Communities, Vol. 1* (Butterworths, London 1986)

W J Waluchow, *Inclusive Legal Positivism* (Clarendon Press, Oxford 1994)

J H H Weiler and M Wind (eds), *European Constitutionalism Beyond the State* (Cambridge University Press, Cambridge 2003)

A Williams, *The Ethos of Europe* (Cambridge University Press, Cambridge 2010)

Index

www.ingramcontent.com/pod-product-compliance
Lightning Source LLC
LaVergne TN
LVHW021109300926
849160LV00009B/665
* 9 7 8 1 1 3 8 6 8 5 1 1 6 *